Siegel's

CRIMINAL PROCEDURE

Essay and Multiple-Choice Questions and Answers

Fifth Edition

BRIAN N. SIEGEL
J.D., Columbia Law School

LAZAR EMANUEL
J.D., Harvard Law School

Revised by

Christian M. Halliburton
Associate Professor of Law
Seattle University School of Law

Wolters Kluwer
Law & Business

The authors gratefully acknowledge the assistance of the California Committee of Bar Examiners, which provided access to questions on which many of the essay questions in this book are based.

About Wolters Kluwer Law & Business

Wolters Kluwer Law & Business is a leading global provider of intelligent information and digital solutions for legal and business professionals in key specialty areas, and respected educational resources for professors and law students. Wolters Kluwer Law & Business connects legal and business professionals as well as those in the education market with timely, specialized authoritative content and information-enabled solutions to support success through productivity, accuracy and mobility.

Serving customers worldwide, Wolters Kluwer Law & Business products include those under the Aspen Publishers, CCH, Kluwer Law International, Loislaw, Best Case, ftwilliam.com and MediRegs family of products.

CCH products have been a trusted resource since 1913, and are highly regarded resources for legal, securities, antitrust and trade regulation, government contracting, banking, pension, payroll, employment and labor, and healthcare reimbursement and compliance professionals.

Aspen Publishers products provide essential information to attorneys, business professionals and law students. Written by preeminent authorities, the product line offers analytical and practical information in a range of specialty practice areas from securities law and intellectual property to mergers and acquisitions and pension/benefits. Aspen's trusted legal education resources provide professors and students with high-quality, up-to-date and effective resources for successful instruction and study in all areas of the law.

Kluwer Law International products provide the global business community with reliable international legal information in English. Legal practitioners, corporate counsel and business executives around the world rely on Kluwer Law journals, looseleafs, books, and electronic products for comprehensive information in many areas of international legal practice.

Loislaw is a comprehensive online legal research product providing legal content to law firm practitioners of various specializations. Loislaw provides attorneys with the ability to quickly and efficiently find the necessary legal information they need, when and where they need it, by facilitating access to primary law as well as state-specific law, records, forms and treatises.

Best Case Solutions is the leading bankruptcy software product to the bankruptcy industry. It provides software and workflow tools to flawlessly streamline petition preparation and the electronic filing process, while timely incorporating ever-changing court requirements.

ftwilliam.com offers employee benefits professionals the highest quality plan documents (retirement, welfare and non-qualified) and government forms (5500/PBGC, 1099 and IRS) software at highly competitive prices.

MediRegs products provide integrated health care compliance content and software solutions for professionals in healthcare, higher education and life sciences, including professionals in accounting, law and consulting.

Wolters Kluwer Law & Business, a division of Wolters Kluwer, is headquartered in New York. Wolters Kluwer is a market-leading global information services company focused on professionals.

Introduction

Although law school grades are a significant factor in obtaining a summer internship or entry position at a law firm, no formalized preparation for finals is offered at most law schools. For the most part, students are expected to fend for themselves in learning how to take a law school exam. Ironically, law school exams may bear little correspondence to the teaching methods used by professors during the school year. At least in the first year, professors require you to spend most of your time briefing cases. This is probably not great preparation for issue-spotting on exams. In briefing cases, you are made to focus on one or two principles of law at a time; thus, you don't get practice in relating one issue to another or in developing a picture of an entire problem or the entire course. When exams finally come, you're forced to make an abrupt 180-degree turn. Suddenly, you are asked to recognize, define, and discuss a variety of issues buried within a single multi-issue fact pattern. Alternatively, you may be asked to select among a number of possible answers, all of which look inviting but only one of which is right.

The comprehensive course outline you've created so diligently, and with such effort, means little if you are unable to apply its contents on your final exams. There is a vast difference between reading opinions in which the legal principles are clearly stated and applying those same principles to hypothetical essay exams and multiple-choice questions.

The purpose of this book is to help you bridge the gap between memorizing a rule of law and *understanding how to use it* in an exam setting. After an initial overview describing the exam-writing process, you will find a large number of hypotheticals that test your ability to write analytical essays and to pick the right answers to multiple-choice questions. *Read them—all of them!* Then review the suggested answers that follow. You'll find that the key to superior grades lies in applying your knowledge through questions and answers, not through rote memory.

GOOD LUCK!

Table of Contents

Essay Answers

Multiple-Choice Questions

Multiple-Choice Answers

Table and Index

Preparing Effectively for Essay Examinations

To achieve superior scores on essay exams, a law student must (1) learn and understand "blackletter" principles and rules of law for each subject, (2) recognize how those principles of law interact, and how the rules will apply to a given fact pattern, and (3) clearly and succinctly discuss each principle or rule and how it relates to the facts. A common misconception about law school is that you must memorize each word on every page of your casebooks or outlines to do well on exams. The reality is that you can commit an entire casebook to memory and still do poorly on an exam. Our review of hundreds of student answers has shown us that most students can recite the rules in the abstract. The students who do **best** on exams are able to spot salient issues, analyze how the rules they have studied relate to the facts in the questions, and communicate their analysis to the grader. The following pages cover what you need to know to achieve superior scores on your law school essay exams. Your goal is to identify and exploit every available opportunity to show your professor the substantive knowledge and analytical skill you developed in the course.

The "ERC" Process

To study effectively for law school exams you must be able to "ERC" (*E*ssentialize, *R*ecognize, and *C*onceptualize) each legal principle covered in your casebooks and course outlines. *Essentialize* means reducing each legal theory and rule you learn to a concise, straightforward statement of its essential elements. Without knowledge of these elements, it's difficult to see all the issues as they arise.

For example, if you are asked "what is the automobile exception?" it is not sufficient to state that "the automobile exception is when, if a car gets searched, the evidence is admissible." This imprecise and incomplete statement of the doctrine would leave a grader unable to determine whether you understand the rules and relevant case law. A better articulation of the automobile exception might be as follows: "The automobile exception permits an officer who possesses probable cause to believe that an automobile, found in a public place, may contain contraband or other evidence of crime to conduct a search of the entire car (including any containers found therein) without first securing a warrant." This formulation of the automobile exception correctly shows that there are four separate and distinct elements that must be analyzed in order to properly apply the rule: (1) the officer must possess probable cause, (2) the automobile must be in a public place and not private location, (3) it must be determined whether the scope of the search is consistent with the exception, and (4) the automobile exception, when properly invoked, provides a basis on which to excuse an officer's failure to secure a warrant prior to conducting the search or seizure.

Recognizing means perceiving or anticipating which words or ideas within a legal principle are likely to be the source of issues and how those issues are likely to arise within a given hypothetical fact pattern. With respect to the automobile exception, there are four ***potential*** issues. Did the officer possess probable cause? Was the automobile located in public? Was the scope of the search consistent with the justification which triggered it? Does the doctrine support the officer's decision to conduct a search without a warrant?

Conceptualizing means imagining situations in which each of the elements of a rule of law can give rise to factual issues and understanding what the rule is designed to achieve. ***Unless you can imagine or construct an application of each element of a rule and can explain why the rule or test is composed as it is, you don't truly understand the legal principles behind the rule!*** In our opinion, the inability to conjure up hypothetical fact patterns or stories involving particular rules of law foretells a likelihood that you will miss issues involving those rules on an exam. It's ***crucial*** (1) to ***recognize*** that issues result from the interaction of facts with the elements of a rule of law and (2) to develop the ability to ***conceptualize*** rules and ***imagine*** fact patterns using the words or concepts within the rule.

Issue-Spotting

One of the keys to doing well on an essay examination is issue-spotting. In fact, issue-spotting is ***the*** most important skill you will learn in law school. If you recognize a legal issue, you can find the applicable rule of law (if there is one) by researching the issue. But if you fail to see the issues, you will be unable to engage in legal analysis whether on an exam or in practice. It is important to remember that (1) an issue is a question to be decided by the judge or jury and (2) a matter is "at issue" when it can be disputed or argued about at trial. The bottom line is that ***if you don't spot an issue, you can't raise it or discuss it.***

The key to issue-spotting is to learn to approach a problem in the same way an attorney does. Let's assume you've been admitted to practice and a client enters your office with a legal problem involving a dispute. He will recite his facts to you and give you any documents that may be pertinent. He will then want to know if he can sue (or be sued, if your client seeks to avoid liability). To answer your client's questions intelligently, you will have to decide the following: (1) what principles or rules can possibly be asserted by your client; (2) what defense or defenses can possibly be raised to these principles; (3) what issues may arise if these defenses are asserted; (4) what arguments each side can make to persuade the fact finder to resolve the issue in his favor; and (5) finally, what the *likely* outcome of each issue will be. *All the issues that can possibly arise at trial will be relevant to your answers.*

How to Discuss an Issue

Keep in mind that *rules of law are the guides to issues* (i.e., an issue arises where there is a question whether the facts do, or do not, trigger or satisfy a component of a rule); a rule of law *cannot dispose of an issue* unless the rule can reasonably be *applied to facts that raise the issue*. The rules or applicable tests also provide a structure or roadmap for your answer.

A good way to learn how to discuss an issue within the framework of a rule is to consider the following mini-hypothetical and the two student responses that follow it.

Mini-Hypothetical

A and B were pacing back and forth outside a small convenience store shortly after midnight when they caught the attention of Patrol Officer P. Officer P observed the two as they continued to pace, occasionally looking inside the store, and then up and down the street. Officer P continued her surveillance as A and B were approached by C, with whom they briefly conferred and then appeared to exchange something by hand. Her suspicions aroused, Officer P approached A and B (C had left the scene), identified herself as a police officer, and asked them about their activities. When neither A nor B responded in any intelligible way, she spun them both around to face the wall of the store and conducted a pat-down inspection of the outer surface of their clothing. Then, reaching into A's pocket, Officer P found a large Ziploc bag full of many smaller Ziploc bags each containing a small amount of white powder that her training and experience led her to recognize as methamphetamine. She informed both A and B that they were under arrest. After placing both in handcuffs, Officer P returned to a backpack B had been carrying, opened it, and conducted a thorough search of the various pockets and compartments. In an outer zipper pocket Officer P discovered a fully loaded semi-automatic handgun and several extra rounds of ammunition.

Discuss the criminal procedure doctrines that would determine the admissibility of the narcotics and the handgun and A & B's criminal prosecution.

Pertinent Principles of Law:

1. According to the doctrine announced in *Terry v. Ohio*, a law enforcement officer may conduct a brief public "stop," or investigative detention, of an individual where specific and articulable facts known to the officer would reasonably support the officer's suspicion that criminal activity may be afoot. In addition, where the facts known to the officer support her reasonable belief that the person with whom she is dealing may presently be armed and dangerous, the officer may conduct a limited "frisk," or pat-down inspection, starting on the outer surface of the suspect's clothing in order to disarm the suspect or assure her own safety.

2. The Fourth Amendment permits a warrantless search of an individual in conjunction with or "incident to" a lawful custodial arrest. The authority to search an individual incident to arrest extends to the "person" of the arrestee, and the area within his or her immediate control.

First Student Answer

The Drugs

The drugs are probably admissible because they were discovered in the course of a lawful search. Officer P's belief that A and B were involved in criminal activity was reasonable under the circumstances because the pacing back and forth and looking around is clearly suspicious. Also, when C approached and conferred with A and B and appeared to make an exchange, this added to the level of suspicion that Officer P had already developed. Because A and B appeared to be involved in criminal activity (i.e., drug selling) that frequently involves a gun or other weapon, Officer P's decision to frisk A was justifiable, and the drugs there therefore found in the course of a lawful frisk.

The Gun

The gun will be found to be admissible for similar reasons. After arresting B, Officer P searched B's backpack, which was within B's wingspan and thus searchable. Assuming B's arrest was lawful, the decision to conduct such a search incident to arrest is categorically reasonable.

Second Student Answer

The Initial Encounter

While an officer may approach an individual in public for any reason, Officer P's encounter with A and B is likely subject to the rule laid out in *Terry v. Ohio*. The two-part *Terry* rule allows an officer to stop, or briefly detain, an individual in a public place where specific and articulable facts support the officer's reasonable suspicion that further investigation of criminal conduct is warranted. If the officer has generated such reasonable suspicion, *Terry* allows an officer to engage in limited questioning aimed at confirming or dispelling their suspicion. If, in the course of such a *Terry* stop, the officer becomes aware of facts or circumstances that would support her reasonable belief that the individual stopped may be armed and dangerous, the officer may conduct a limited frisk, or pat-down inspection, of the outer surface of the suspects clothing for the limited purpose of identifying and neutralizing any dangerous weapon.

A and B would argue that Officer P lacked a reasonable basis to believe that they might be involved in criminal activity. Their conduct, while unusual, was not plainly illegal nor sufficiently indicative of criminal intentions such that Officer P should not have approached and questioned them. Indeed, neither standing on a public street, nor looking up and down the block, nor greeting and conferring with an acquaintance provide any suggestion of criminal purpose. However, the government will contend that none of these actions can be viewed in isolation, and that they can be properly evaluated only within the specific context in which they took place. When considered in the aggregate rather than individually, these behaviors could lead a reasonable person to conclude that A and B might be actively involved in or planning a crime. It is therefore likely that the state will prevail in its argument that the defendants' behavior, coupled with the suspicious exchange with C, generated reasonable suspicion in the totality of the circumstances that justifies Officer P's decision to intervene.

A and B would also challenge the Officer's decision to frisk them after their brief verbal exchange. The record contains no facts that suggested that A or B might be armed or that Officer P otherwise perceived them to be threatening or dangerous. Nevertheless, a court will evaluate the officer's safety concerns from the standpoint of an objective hypothetical officer confronting the same circumstances and could reasonably conclude that the totality of the circumstances, combined with the nature of Officer P's suspicion regarding A and B's conduct, created a lawful basis for the frisk. In evaluating Officer P's conduct, it will be important to determine whether the scope of the frisk was consistent with the limits of the *Terry* authority, that is, whether Officer P started on the outer surface of the suspects' clothing and only reached into pockets where her reasonable suspicion supported the incrementally increased intrusion.

The Arrest

Even assuming the stop and frisk were permissible and that the discovery of the narcotics was valid, a court must still determine whether Officer P had probable cause to arrest A and B. Probable cause exists where the facts and circumstances would warrant a reasonable person's belief in the suspect's guilt. A's possession of narcotics that appeared to be packaged for sale, together with his close collaboration with B, are sufficiently suggestive of a joint criminal enterprise to support her decision to arrest them both.

The ultimate question is whether Officer P discovered the handgun in B's backpack in the course of a permissible search. Officers are authorized to conduct a warrantless search of an individual when executing an otherwise lawful arrest, including both the person of the arrestee and the area within his or her immediate control. The area within an arrestee's immediate control is generally measured by the suspect's constructive "wingspan," or the accessible area surrounding the point of arrest.

A and B may argue that the backpack was beyond the scope of this search-incident-to-arrest doctrine because it was no longer within the area of their immediate control. A and B had already been handcuffed before Officer P decided to search the backpack, and thus the backpack was effectively within Officer P's control. A and B would therefore contend that any concerns regarding their ability to access a weapon or destroy evidence, which are the primary justifications for the doctrine, had dissipated before the search. The state would contend that the backpack was still within the suspects' constructive wingspan and thus lawfully still subject to search incident to arrest. Because the doctrine is a general justification for a warrantless search of the area within an arrestee's immediate control, it permits such searches regardless of whether the relevant law enforcement needs justify the search in any particular case. Recognizing the general or categorical nature of the search-incident-to-arrest doctrine, a court would likely validate the search and conclude that the handgun is admissible.

Critique

While there is no one "magic formula" for exam writing, there are certainly ways to distinguish a high-quality answer from a poor answer. Let's start by evaluating the First Student Answer, which reflects both structural and analytical flaws, in order to identify some missteps to avoid.

The first paragraph begins with a conclusory assertion that is centered on the narrow question of evidentiary admissibility rather than on the broader threshold question of whether the encounter that produced the evidence followed the constitutionally required course. That focus on the ultimate evidentiary question narrows the discussion and the range of issues that can be addressed before the discussion even begins, and it causes the writer to omit steps in the analysis that must be shown to the reader in order to fully demonstrate your knowledge. In addition, beginning an answer with a conclusion not preceded by any analysis does not properly orient the reader within your discussion framework and does not clearly signal your appreciation of the relevant criminal procedure questions.

The First Student Answer then jumps from its initial conclusory sentence into a discussion of the relevant facts. While these may be the right considerations to address, the answer embeds the few rule statements it contains within its characterization of the facts. The second and third sentences indicated that the facts would likely meet the legal standard without any clear or explicit articulation of what that legal standard is. The first paragraph ends, and the second paragraph begins, by compounding all of the errors above: in one sentence the author predicts an admissibility ruling without identifying a legal issue or providing analysis and then characterizes potentially relevant facts in a way that avoids and obscures the applicable legal rules. These common but avoidable mistakes will impair performance on law school examinations because they do not produce a response that is structured in such a way as to (1) demonstrate command of and (2) encourage attention to each component of the relevant doctrinal analysis.

The Second Student Answer, by contrast, is very deliberate in beginning each discussion by framing the specific legal issue to be addressed. It provides an overview of the application rule or analytical framework and a working definition of the relevant standards or concepts to be applied to the facts before beginning that application. In discussing the relevant facts, the answer explores the potential room for the parties' competing arguments, but it ultimately suggests a likely outcome based on the particular or distinguishing facts contained in the hypothetical. Finally, where the facts are close or a judgment is called for, the second student shows her mastery of the subject matter by connecting her analysis to the purposes or policies served by the underlying rules regulating the criminal justice system. This move clearly demonstrates to the reader that the student understands how procedural rules apply in diverse and evolving factual settings, has a nuanced appreciation for how facts may heighten the relevance of discrete elements of a multi-part test, and is familiar with the analytical tendencies of courts deciding such questions.

Structuring Your Answer

Graders will give high marks to a clearly written, thorough, and well-organized answer. Each issue you discuss should follow a specific and consistent structure that a grader can easily follow.

The Second Student Answer basically utilizes the *I-R-A-A-O format* with respect to each issue. In this format, the *I* stands for *Issue*; the *R* for *Rule of law*; the first *A* for *one side's Argument*; the second *A* for *the other party's rebuttal Argument*; and the *O* for your *Opinion as to how the issue would be resolved*. The *I-R-A-A-O* format emphasizes the importance of (1) discussing **both** sides of an issue and (2) communicating to the grader that, where an issue arises, an attorney can only advise his or her client as to the **probable** decision on that issue.

A somewhat different format for analyzing each issue is the *I-R-A-C format*. Here, the *I* stands for *Issue*; the *R* for *Rule of law*; the *A* for *Application of the facts to the rule of law*; and the *C* for *Conclusion*. *I-R-A-C* is a commonly used approach to the discussion of a particular issue taught at most law schools, and it can be an effective way to organize your answer as long you stay within the time constraints imposed by the question. The *I-R-A-C format* must be applied to each issue in the question; it is not the solution to the entire answer. If there are six issues in a question, for example, you should offer six separate, independent *I-R-A-C* analyses.

We believe that the *I-R-A-C* approach may be more fluid and is generally preferable to the *I-R-A-A-O* formula. However, either can be used to analyze and organize essay exam answers, and you should think about what works best for you and for the question you are answering. Whatever format you choose, however, you should be consistent throughout the exam and remember the following rules:

First, **analyze all of the relevant facts**. Facts have significance in a particular case **only as they come under the applicable rules of law**. The facts presented must be analyzed and examined to see if they do or do not satisfy one element or another of the applicable rules, and the essential facts and rules must be stated and argued in your analysis.

Second, you must communicate to the grader the **precise rule of law** controlling the facts and any test a court would use. In their eagerness to commence their arguments, students sometimes fail to state the applicable rule of law or test first. Remember, the *R* in either format stands for **Rule of law**. Defining the rule of law **before** an analysis of the facts is essential in order to allow the grader to follow your reasoning. It also provides a structure to your answer that you can follow as you write.

Third, it is important to treat **each side of an issue with equal detail**. If a hypothetical describes how an innocent person was injured during a police encounter, your sympathies might understandably fall on the side of the individual. The grader will nevertheless expect you to see and make every possible argument for the government. Similarly, a hypothetical might describe the arrest and interrogation of a suspect who, according to all available information, has clearly engaged in criminal activity. Your instincts may naturally lead you to prefer the admission of evidence consistent with the suspect's guilt and to seek ways to validate the law enforcement officer's conduct. The grader must still see that you appreciate the importance of careful, impartial analysis and that you can recognize the strategic or analytical approaches that could serve the defendant. Don't permit your personal viewpoint to affect your answer—a good lawyer never does. When discussing an issue, always be sure you can recognize the arguments for each side.

Finally, don't forget to **state your opinion or conclusion** on each issue. Keep in mind, however, that your opinion or conclusion is probably the **least** important part of an exam answer. Why? Because your professor knows that no attorney can tell his or her client exactly how a judge or jury will decide a particular issue. By definition, an issue is a legal dispute that can go either way. An attorney, therefore, can offer the client only his or her best opinion about the likelihood of victory or defeat on an issue. Because the decision on any issue lies with the judge or jury, no attorney can ever be absolutely certain of the resolution.

Discuss All Possible Issues

As we've noted, a student should draw **some** type of conclusion or opinion for each issue raised. Whatever your conclusion on a particular issue, it is essential to anticipate and discuss **all of the issues** that would arise if the question were actually tried in court. Remember that your goal is to take every legitimate opportunity to show what you know about a particular criminal procedure doctrine, so follow every line of analysis through to its last possible step.

Let's assume that a *Miranda* hypothetical involves issues involving custody, interrogation, and waiver. If the government prevails on any one of these issues—that is, it can successfully show that defendant was not in custody, was not interrogated, or that he tendered a knowing and intelligent waiver of his rights—any incriminating statements can be admitted over the defendant's objection. However, if you were to terminate your answer after a discussion of the custody element only, you will necessarily receive an inferior grade by "leaving points on the table," or not earning points every time a scoring opportunity exists.

Why should you have to discuss every possible issue if you are relatively certain that the outcome of a particular issue would be dispositive of the entire case? Because at the commencement of litigation, neither party can be **absolutely positive** about which issues he or she will prevail upon at trial. We can state with confidence that every attorney with some degree of experience has won issues he or she thought he or she would lose, and has lost issues on which victory seemed assured. Because one can never be absolutely certain how a factual issue will be resolved by the fact finder, a good attorney (and exam writer) will consider **all** possible issues.

To understand the importance of discussing all of the potential issues, you should reflect on what you will do in the actual practice of law. If you represent the defendant, for example, it is your job to raise every possible defense. If there are five potential defenses, and your pleadings rely on only three of them (because you're sure you will win on all three), and the plaintiff is somehow successful on all three issues, your client may well sue you for malpractice. Your client's contention would be that you should be liable because if you had only raised the two additional issues, you might have prevailed on at least one of them, and therefore liability would have been avoided. It is an attorney's duty to raise **all** legitimate issues. A similar philosophy should be followed when taking essay exams.

What exactly do you say when you've resolved the initial issue in favor of the defendant, and discussion of any additional issues would seem to be moot? The answer is simple. You begin the discussion of the next issue with something like, "Assuming, however, the plaintiff prevailed on the foregoing issue, the next issue would be . . . . " The grader will understand and appreciate what you have done.

The corollary to the importance of raising all potential issues is that you should avoid discussion of obvious nonissues. Raising nonissues is detrimental in three ways: First, you waste a lot of precious time; second, you usually receive absolutely no points for discussing an issue that the grader deems extraneous; and third, it suggests to the grader that you lack the ability to distinguish the significant from the irrelevant. The best guideline for avoiding the discussion of a nonissue is to ask yourself, "Would I, as an attorney, feel comfortable about raising that particular issue or objection in front of a judge?"

Delineate the Transition from One Issue to the Next

It's a good idea to make it easy for the grader to see the issues you've found. One way to accomplish this is to cover no more than one issue per paragraph. Another way is to underline each issue statement. Provided that time permits, we recommend that you use both techniques. The essay answers in this book contain numerous illustrations of these suggestions.

One frequent student error is to write two separate paragraphs in which all of the arguments for one side are made in the initial paragraph, and all of the rebuttal arguments by the other side are made in the next paragraph. This organization is *a bad idea*. It obliges the grader to reconstruct the exam answer in his or her mind several times to determine whether all possible issues have been discussed by both sides. It will also cause you to state the same rule of law more than once. A better-organized answer presents a given argument by one side and follows that immediately in the same paragraph with the other side's rebuttal to that argument.

Understanding the "Call" of a Question

The statement *at the end* of an essay question or of the fact pattern in a multiple-choice question is sometimes referred to as the "call" of the question. It usually asks you to do something specific such as "discuss the issues you think defendant might raise on appeal," or "describe how a court would determine the admissibility of the challenged confession." The call of the question might also ask you to make certain predictions, such as "what would be the best grounds on which to overturn the defendant's conviction," "what other evidentiary issues could be raised during the trial," "how should the court rule on the state's motion," and so forth. The call of the question should be read carefully because it tells you exactly what is expected of you. If a question asks, "How would you analyze the automobile search that occurred in this case," you don't want to spend precious time discussing a subsequent interrogation. You will usually receive absolutely no credit for discussing issues or facts that are not required by the call. On the other hand, if the call of an essay question is simply "discuss" or "what arguments might the parties make," then *all* foreseeable issues must be covered by your answer.

Students are often led astray by an essay question's call. For example, if you are asked "what would be defendant's best argument for suppression" or to "advise your client," you may think you may limit yourself to the defendant's or any one party's viewpoint with respect to the issues. This is *not correct*! You cannot resolve one party's rights against another party without considering the issues that would arise (and the arguments the other side would assert) if litigation occurred. In short, although the call of the question may appear to focus on the rights of one of the parties to the litigation, a superior answer will cover all the issues and arguments that person might *encounter* (not just the arguments he or she would *make*) in attempting to pursue his or her rights against the other side.

The Importance of Analyzing and Outlining the Question Carefully Before Writing

The overriding *time pressure* of an essay exam is probably a major reason why many students fail to analyze a question carefully before writing. Five minutes into the allocated time for a particular question, you may notice that the person next to you is writing furiously. This thought then flashes through your mind: "Oh my goodness, he's putting down more words on the paper than I am, and therefore he's bound to get a better grade." It can be stated *unequivocally* that there is no necessary correlation between the number of words on your exam paper and the grade you'll receive. Students who begin their answer after only five minutes of analysis may have seen only the most obvious issues and missed many, if not most, of the subtle ones. They may also tend to be less well organized.

Opinions differ as to how much time you should spend analyzing and outlining a question before you actually write the answer. We believe that you should spend at least 10 to 15 minutes analyzing, organizing, and outlining a one-hour question before writing your answer. This will usually provide sufficient time to analyze and organize the question thoroughly *and* enough time to write a relatively complete answer. Remember that each word of the question must be scrutinized to determine if it (1) suggests an issue under the operative rules of law or (2) can be used in making an argument for the resolution of an issue. Because you can't receive points for an issue you don't spot, it is usually wise to read a question *twice* before starting your outline.

When to Make an Assumption

The instructions for a question may tell you to *assume* facts that are necessary to the answer. Even when these instructions are *not* given, you may be obliged to make certain assumptions about missing facts in order to write a thorough answer. Assumptions should be made only when you are told or when you, as the attorney for one of the parties described in the question, would be obliged to solicit additional information from your client. On the other hand, assumptions should *never be used to change or alter the question*. Don't ever write something like "if the facts in the question were . . . , instead of . . . , then . . . would result." If you do this, you are wasting time on facts that are extraneous to the problem before you. Professors want you to deal with *their* fact patterns, not your own.

Students sometimes try to "write around" information they think is missing. They assume that their professor has failed to include every piece of data necessary for a thorough answer. This is generally *wrong*. The professor may have omitted some facts deliberately to see if the student *can figure out what to do* under the circumstances. However, in some instances, the professor may have omitted them inadvertently (even law professors are sometimes human).

The way to deal with the omission of essential information is to describe (1) what fact (or facts) appears to be missing and (2) why that information is important. As an example, go back to the hypothetical encounter between A, B, and Officer P discussed above. That fact pattern did not disclose whether there was any indication that A or B might be armed or otherwise dangerous. This fact could be extremely important. If the officer noticed a suspicious bulge or heavy outline in a suspect's pocket, or was confronting threatening behavior or postures, then the frisk will likely fall within the scope of the *Terry* rule. On the other hand, if the totality of circumstances showed cooperative individuals not showing the capacity or likelihood of being armed, then the frisk might well have exceeded Officer P's lawful authority. The last sentence of the Second Student Answer shows that the student author understands these subtleties and made a defensible assumption about the missing or additional facts necessary for resolution of the issue. Notably, the student chose to assume or characterize facts that *allow the answer to proceed to the next viable issue.*

Indeed, unless it is otherwise unreasonable to do so, you should generally construe ambiguity in a hypothetical in a manner that keeps the other issues open – your assumptions should ideally lead to a discussion of all the other possible issues and not force you into dispositive "dead ends.". Don't assume facts that would virtually dispose of the entire hypothetical in a few sentences. Suppose that defendant challenges the admissibility of eyewitness identification testimony offered at his criminal trial as failing to meet the minimum standards of due process. If the compelled confrontation is "necessary" given the needs of law enforcement, it may be admissible even if it might also have been "suggestive." If the facts do not describe the pressing need or exigency in conducting the lineup at issue, it would not be wise to write "Because the police probably only do those things they need to, we'll assume that the lineup procedure used by the police in this case was also necessary, so it satisfied due process." A better way to handle the situation would be to state "Unless the identification was otherwise found to be necessary under the circumstances, the state would have to show that any suggestiveness in the conduct of the identification is sufficiently outweighed by specific indicia of its overall reliability." This way you have communicated to the grader that you recognize the need to assume an essential fact and you've assumed it in a way that enables you to proceed to discuss all other issues.

Case Names

While it is generally advisable to refer to cases by name if you can, a law student is ordinarily **not** expected to recall the name of each and every case discussed during the semester for use on the exam. The professor knows that you have read several hundred cases for each course and that you would have to be a memory expert to have all of the names at your fingertips. If you confront a fact pattern that seems similar to a case you have reviewed (but you cannot recall its name), just write something like, "under similar circumstances the court held that . . . " or "In the thermal imaging case the Court determined that. . . . ." In this manner, you have informed the grader that you are relying on a case that contained a fact pattern similar to the question at issue.

The only exception to this rule is in the case of a landmark decision (e.g., *Katz v. United States*) or those case names that have come to stand for a particular doctrine or test (e.g. a *Terry* stop, or *Miranda* warnings). Landmark or watershed opinions are usually those that alter established law or announce new tests. These cases are usually easy to identify, because you will probably have spent an entire class period discussing each of them, and you will think of them as the source of the rules you have learned. *Gideon v. Wainwright* is a prime example of a landmark case with respect to the right to counsel; *Chimel v. California* is the foundation of the modern search-incident-to-arrest doctrine. Given the importance of these cases, you should be able to recall the case by name, as well as the proposition of law it stands for.

How to Handle Time Pressures

What do you do when there are five minutes left in the exam and you have only written down two-thirds of your answer? One thing **not** to do is write something like, "No time left!" or "Not enough time!" This gets you nothing but the satisfaction of knowing you have communicated your personal frustrations to the grader. Another thing *not* to do is insert in the exam booklet the outline you may have made on a piece of scrap paper. Professors will rarely look at these. One way to improve your use of time is to develop a solid outline for your answer and follow it systematically. You should also note any suggested time allocation indicated on the exam and be careful to go over the time allotted for one question.

Remember, it is not necessarily a bad thing to be pressed for time. The person who finishes five minutes early could possibly missed some important issues. The more proficient you become in knowing what is expected of you on an exam, the greater the difficulty you may experience in staying within the time limits. Second, remember that (at least to some extent) you're graded against your classmates' answers and they're under exactly the same time pressure as you. In short, don't panic if you can't write the "perfect" answer in the allotted time. Nobody does!

Perhaps the best protection against misuse of time is to **complete as many practice exam questions as possible**. These exercises will give you a familiarity with the process of organizing and writing an exam answer, which, in turn, should result in increased efficiency and an enhanced ability to stay within the time boundaries. If you nevertheless find that you have 15 minutes of writing to do and only 5 minutes to do it in, write a paragraph that summarizes the remaining issues you've identified and the arguments you would discuss if time permitted. As long as you've indicated that you're aware of the remaining legal issues, you'll probably receive some credit for them. Your analytical and argumentative skills will already be apparent to the grader by virtue of the issues that you have previously discussed.

Formatting Your Answer

Make sure that the way you write or type your answer presents your analysis in the best possible light. In other words, if you write, do it legibly. If you type, remember to use many paragraphs, one for each issue or component in your answer, instead of just creating a document with all of your ideas merged into a single lengthy block of print. Remember also that your professor may have a hundred or more exams to grade. If your answer is difficult to read, you will rarely be given the benefit of the doubt. On the other hand, a paper that is easy to read creates a very positive mental impact upon the professor.

The Importance of Reviewing Prior Exams

As we've mentioned, it is ***extremely important to review old exams***. The transition from blackletter law to essay exam can be a difficult experience if the process has not been practiced. Although this book provides a large number of essay and multiple-choice questions, ***don't stop here***! Many law schools have recent tests online or on file in the library, by course. If they are available only in the library, we strongly suggest that you make a copy of every old exam you can obtain (especially those given by your professors) at the beginning of each semester. The demand for these documents usually increases dramatically as "finals time" draws closer.

The previous or practice exams for each course should be scrutinized ***throughout the semester***. Try to complete a practice exam at the end of every chapter or section in your casebook. Sometimes the order of exam questions follows the sequence of the materials in your casebook. Thus, the first question on a law school test may involve the initial three chapters of the casebook; the second question may pertain to the fourth and fifth chapters; and so forth. In any event, ***don't wait*** until the semester is nearly over to begin reviewing old exams.

Keep in mind that no one is born with the ability to analyze questions and write superior answers to law school exams. Like any other skill, it is developed and perfected only through application. If you don't take the time to analyze numerous sample examinations or tests from prior years, this evolutionary process just won't occur. Don't just ***think about*** the answers to past exam questions; take the time to ***write the answers down***. It's also wise to look back at an answer a day or two after you've written it. You will invariably see (1) ways to improve your organizational skills and (2) arguments you missed.

As you practice spotting issues on past exams, you will see how rules of law become the sources of issues on finals. As we've already noted, if you don't ***understand*** how rules of law translate into issues, you won't be able to achieve superior grades on your exams. Reviewing sample exams from prior years may also reveal that certain issues tend to be lumped together in the same question. For instance, where a fact pattern involves a custodial arrest, you might also expect to deal with a search incident to that arrest or *Miranda* issues; where the facts involve a police chase, you might also have to sort through issues of custody, use of force, and hot pursuit. You need to be prepared to recognize the interconnectedness of many criminal procedure issues so that you can invoke and apply the correct rules.

Finally, one of the best means of evaluating if you understand a subject (or a particular area within a subject) is to attempt to create a hypothetical exam for that subject. Your exam should contain as many issues as possible. If you can write an issue-packed exam, you probably know that subject well. If you can't, then you probably haven't yet acquired an adequate understanding of how the principles of law in that subject can spawn issues.

As Always, a Caveat

The suggestions and advice offered in this book represent the product of many years of experience in the field of legal education. We are confident that the techniques and concepts described in these pages will help you prepare for, and succeed at, your exams. Nevertheless, particular professors sometimes have a preference for exam-writing techniques that are not stressed in this book. Some instructors expect at least a nominal reference to the ***prima facie*** elements of all pertinent legal theories (even though one or more of those principles are ***not*** placed into issue). Other professors want their students to emphasize public policy considerations in the arguments they make on a particular issue. Because this book is intended for nationwide consumption, these individualized preferences have ***not*** been stressed. The best way to find out whether your professor has a penchant for a particular writing approach is to ask him or her directly, and ask them to provide you with a sample exam and model answer. If a model answer is not available, ask the professor to go over their grading and describe their expectations, or speak to second- or third-year students who received a superior grade in that professor's class.

One final point. Although the rules of law stated in the answers to the questions in this book have been drawn from commonly used sources (casebooks, hornbooks, etc.), it is still conceivable that they may be slightly at odds with those taught by your professor. In the area of criminal procedure, there are differences from jurisdiction to jurisdiction, at least insofar as states have the latitude to depart from the federal standards. In instances in which a conflict exists between our formulation of any legal principle and the one used by your professor, ***follow your professor's view***! Because your grade is determined by your professor, his or her views should always supersede the positions reflected in this book.

Essay
Questions

Question 1

Donald and his brother Ronald were small-time crooks whose business had suffered a downturn. They devised a plan to increase their income by responding to Internet ads offering valuable items for sale and then robbing the sellers at gunpoint. Wearing clever disguises and taking turns as the gunman, all went well until one of their victims resisted their demands to hand over his goods and was shot in the struggle. While recovering from his injuries, the victim was able to give investigators enough information to identify Donald and Ronald as suspects. Donald and Ronald were subsequently arrested outside of a grocery store near their home. At the time of their arrest, a police officer told each, "Anything you say can and will be used against you in court; you have the right to consult with counsel prior to questioning; and if you are unable to afford counsel, a lawyer will be appointed for you." Neither made any statements when they were arrested.

Later, at the police station, Ronald was interrogated by detectives from the Major Crimes Unit over a three-hour period. Before they began questioning, they repeated the warnings recited above. For the first two hours and 45 minutes, he sat silent and refused to answer any questions. However, at that point in the interrogation Ronald suddenly blurted out, "We just wanted the money—we never meant to hurt anybody!" and then began to sob uncontrollably.

Donald and Ronald were charged with robbery, attempted robbery, and assault with a deadly weapon. The two were tried together after the court denied a motion by each for severance. Ronald's statement to the robbery detectives was admitted at trial over the objection of each defendant, and both were convicted as charged.

Did the court err in admitting Ronald's statement

1. against Ronald? Discuss.
2. against Donald? Discuss.

Question 2

Detective Trace received a telephone call from an informant who had given reliable information to Trace on several prior occasions. The informant truthfully told Trace, "Doris is planning to sell stolen silicon chips to Vic and probably will deliver the chips to Vic within the next two weeks. Doris usually rents a room at the Savoy Hotel to use when she makes her sales." Trace immediately prepared an affidavit detailing the informant's past reliability and quoting the informant's statement. On the basis of the affidavit, a magistrate issued a warrant authorizing a search for silicon chips in any Savoy Hotel room rented by Doris in the two weeks following the date of the affidavit.

One week after the warrant was issued, Trace learned from the hotel manager that Doris had rented a room at the Savoy Hotel. Armed with the warrant, Trace went to the hotel intending to search the room in Doris's absence. As he listened at the door to determine whether the room was occupied, however, he overheard Doris offering to sell silicon chips to Vic. He then heard the two arguing, the sounds of a struggle, a crash, and silence. Trace knocked on the door and announced, "Police with a search warrant—open the door." He entered when Doris opened the door. Seeing Vic on the floor unconscious and apparently injured, Trace drew his gun and asked Doris, "What did you do to him?" Doris replied, "I pushed him and he hit his head against a table." Trace summoned an ambulance, but Vic died of head injuries before it arrived.

Doris has been charged with murder and attempting to sell stolen property, both of which are felonies. She moved to exclude testimony by Trace regarding his observations in the hotel room, all silicon chips found in the hotel room, Doris's statement to Vic that Trace had overheard, and Doris's statement to Trace after he entered the room, all on the ground that the evidence had been obtained in violation of Doris's Fourth and Fifth Amendment rights. The trial court denied the motion.

Was the trial court correct in denying the motion? Discuss.

Question 3

Fred, a federal customs inspector, saw Dan speaking to Anon as Dan and Anon walked across the international border into the United States. Fred recognized Anon as someone who had previously been convicted of smuggling narcotics. Over Dan's protests, Fred searched Dan's and Anon's luggage. Fred found a packet of glassine envelopes and some dextrose powder in Dan's suitcase and a large quantity of heroin in the lining of Anon's suitcase.

Fred knew that dextrose powder is used to dilute heroin, and that heroin is sold in envelopes like those carried by Dan. Fred, therefore, ordered that Dan be searched in private by a male physician, who found a small quantity of heroin in a body cavity. Dan was then arrested on a federal charge of importing illegal narcotics.

Fred notified state narcotics agents of the arrest. Olson, a state agent, located Dan's car parked legally on a street in the United States near the border crossing. Olson impounded the car and, during a search of the car on the following day, discovered a large quantity of heroin. Dan was then charged with violation of a state statute prohibiting possession of narcotics for sale.

At a pretrial bail hearing, Dan now argues that he is entitled to have bail fixed or, because he is indigent, to be released on his own recognizance. A state statute permits denial of pretrial bail when a defendant poses too great a risk to society to remain free pending trial.

1. How should the federal court rule on Dan's motion to exclude the envelopes and powder discovered in Dan's suitcase? Discuss.

2. How should the federal court rule on Dan's motion to exclude the heroin found on his person from evidence at the federal trial? Discuss.

3. How should the state court rule on Dan's motion to exclude the heroin found in his car from evidence at the state trial? Discuss.

4. How should the state court rule on Dan's claim that he is entitled to have bail fixed or to be released pending trial on the state charge? Discuss.

Question 4

State Officer Abby, an undercover agent, told her superior, Officer Sue, that Deer, a suspected dealer in stolen property, had (three hours earlier) shown Abby 12 stolen U.S. Army pistols that were stored in Deer's car trunk. Sue immediately prepared an arrest warrant affidavit alleging that "a reliable informant has reported that Deer possesses stolen property." The affidavit was presented to a magistrate, who then issued an arrest warrant. After the warrant was issued, a police bulletin was issued for Deer's arrest.

One hour later, Sue observed Deer on the public walkway outside Deer's home, watering his front lawn with a garden hose. After Sue informed Deer of the outstanding warrant, she arrested Deer, searched him, and found one of the stolen pistols in a pocket of Deer's jacket.

Concurrently with the arrest, Sue read Deer his *Miranda* warnings and then demanded that Deer reveal the location of the remaining weapons. Deer refused to say anything until he spoke with an attorney. Sue then told Deer that Deer was subject to both federal and state prosecutions, but that only the state charge would be prosecuted if he "talked immediately." In response, Deer told Sue that the other 11 pistols were in the trunk of his car parked across the street.

Sue had the car towed to a police parking lot, where the trunk was pried open and the remaining 11 pistols removed. A thorough search of the trunk also turned up a notebook, which listed the serial numbers of all the pistols, including the one Sue had taken from Deer's pocket.

Deer has been charged with receiving stolen property. He has made a motion to exclude from evidence, on federal constitutional grounds, the 12 pistols, Deer's statement to Sue, and the notebook. What results on Deer's motion to exclude? Discuss.

Question 5

The Rural Fire Department extinguished a small hay fire in a barn at 11:00 P.M. At 11:15 P.M., Deputy Carr, a member of the Rural Sheriff's Department, walked through the barn and detected the odor of gasoline.

At 11:30 P.M. on the road right by the barn, Carr set up a checkpoint (roadblock) designed to obtain more information about the fire. Carr and his colleagues stopped every vehicle approaching the checkpoint to ask if the occupants had seen anything suspicious that evening. The typical vehicle was stopped for an average of 30 seconds. Pursuant to that procedure, Carr stopped a truck that Denise was driving. While the truck was stopped, Denise bent down to the floor twice and kept looking at Carr. Carr approached the truck and ordered Denise to get out. Denise complied and closed the vehicle door behind her. Carr then asked Denise if she had seen any vehicles speeding past her or anything else "out of the ordinary." When Denise answered in the negative, Carr told Denise she could leave.

As Denise reopened the truck door, Carr saw a red gasoline can on the floor. He advised Denise to "stay right there, please." Carr then commented, "I guess some people don't know how to set a good fire." Denise retorted, "I didn't burn the barn." Carr then seized the can, told Denise she was a suspect in an arson investigation, and took her to the sheriff's office. At the sheriff's office and after receiving proper *Miranda* warnings, Denise admitted, "Okay, I torched the barn."

Later, authorities learned that Denise owned the barn and a nearby farmhouse, and had leased the house and barn to Tenant (who had fallen behind in rent payments).

Denise was charged with arson. Evidence of these facts was admitted at trial over appropriate objections. Denise was convicted.

As Denise's attorney, what issues should you raise on appeal with respect to the evidence admitted against her, and how should the appellate court rule on each? Discuss.

Question 6

Detective Randall, a knowledgeable and experienced narcotics law enforcement officer with the State Police, received information from a proven and reliable informer that Adam was using heroin from a supply that Adam maintained in his apartment at a particular address. Randall had arrested Adam for possession of heroin on two previous occasions, and the arrests had led to convictions. Randall conducted surveillance of Adam's apartment house from a position in the building's lobby.

When Adam stepped into the lobby, Randall briefly observed Adam's physical appearance and immediately concluded that he was then under the influence of a narcotic. Randall arrested Adam in the lobby and searched his person, finding a key to Adam's apartment. Randall entered the apartment, then found and seized a large quantity of powder he suspected to be heroin. Randall had neither a search nor an arrest warrant.

At the police station, over Adam's violent objection, a forensic technician removed a sample of blood from Adam's finger for the purpose of testing it for narcotics. After running the blood test, the technician also conducted a chemical analysis, which verified that the powder seized at Adam's apartment was in fact heroin. Adam was susquently charged with "possession of heroin" and with being "addicted to the use of a narcotic" in violation of state law.

The state's rules of criminal procedure provide for a preliminary hearing for the sole purpose of testing the sufficiency of the state's evidence for holding an accused to answer charges. Adam, claiming that he was an indigent, moved for, but was denied, the right to be represented by counsel at the hearing. He was held to answer by the magistrate.

Unable to afford to retain private counsel, Adam was represented by appointed counsel at his trial. The forensic technician's reports on both the blood test and the chemical analysis were admitted into evidence, but the technician (whose employment had since been terminated) was not available to testify in person. Adam was convicted on both counts. On appeal to the state's highest court, appointed counsel stated in her brief only that she had made a thorough examination of the record and, in her considered opinion, there were no meritorious contentions that could be raised on appeal.

Assume that Adam has preserved all objections and claims he might have made at trial or on appeal, and that all such objections and claims are now before the U.S. Supreme Court for decision. What would be the likely result of each? Discuss.

Question 7

Dan planned to rob XYZ Bank. He entered through the open doors of the bank during business hours, pointed a loaded revolver at a teller, and demanded money. A bank guard ordered Dan to drop his gun. When Dan hesitated, the guard fired a warning shot in Dan's direction. Acting purely on reflex, Dan fired his revolver at the guard, killing him instantly. He then fled.

Two days later, after Dan had been identified to the police as the probable killer, Norma, a plainclothes police detective, went to Dan's house. Pretending to be a door-to-door salesperson, Norma led Dan into a lengthy conversation concerning the killing. Dan made incriminating statements that, unknown to him, were recorded by a device concealed in Norma's clothing. The following day, the police arrested Dan, who blurted out, "I didn't mean to kill him."

At the police station, Dan was advised for the first time that he had a right to an attorney, that he had a right not to make any statements, and that any statements he might make could be used against him at the trial. Dan made no further statements and retained an attorney. At the trial, Dan exercised his right not to testify. Norma and the arresting officers testified for the state about the statements made by Dan before and at his arrest. In closing arguments, the prosecutor, over objections by Dan's counsel, commented on Dan's failure to testify and urged the jurors to draw an adverse inference of Dan's guilt. Dan was convicted of murder and sentenced to death.

On appeal to the state's highest court, Dan argued that the judgment must be reversed because the evidence by the police officers was improperly admitted against him and because the prosecution's comments at trial were improper.

What are the merits of each of Dan's arguments? Discuss.

Question 8

Jones, a police officer in a small town in state X near an interstate freeway, was told by the police chief that, according to a report she had received, a lone male driving in a car with an out-of-state license plate would be coming through town within a few days, traveling in an easterly direction, and carrying an illegal shipment of heroin. Shortly thereafter, while on a routine patrol, Jones saw a car with an out-of-state license plate traveling east. The car was being driven by a lone male, Don. Jones pulled Don over and asked him for his driver's license. Don's license had expired, so Jones placed Don under arrest for violation of a state X law requiring a valid license for anyone operating a vehicle in the state. The maximum penalty for violation of the law is a $100 fine and ten days in the county jail.

Under state X law, an arresting officer had the discretion to issue a citation for violation of the license statute, but it was normal practice in this town to take a license violator who was from out of town into custody and to require bail to be posted before the person could be released.

Jones removed Don from the vehicle, placed him under arrest, and patted him down. While doing so, Jones felt something small and round; Jones thrust his hand into Don's coat pocket to retrieve the object. The object turned out to be a small clear plastic vial containing ten pills. Jones asked Don if he had a doctor's prescription for the pills, and Don replied that he did not. Jones then asked Don for permission to search the car, and Don replied, "Go ahead, why not?"

During his search of the car, Jones found a plastic bag taped behind the glove compartment; the bag contained a substance that looked and smelled like marijuana. After laboratory analysis, the pills found in Don's possession were determined to be a drug the possession of which is illegal under state X law without a prescription, and the substance in the plastic bag was determined to be marijuana.

Don was charged with (1) illegal possession of marijuana and other dangerous drugs (the pills) and (2) violation of the state X vehicle license statute. Don's attorney filed a motion to suppress the evidence, seeking to exclude Don's statement to Jones, as well as the pills and marijuana, from introduction at trial.

The constitution of state X has a clause identical to the fourth Amendment of the U.S. Constitution.

What rights, if any, under the federal and state constitutions could be asserted for Don in support of the motion to suppress evidence, and how should the state X court rule on the motion? Discuss.

Question 9

Mike and Donna entered the Shorecliff Pharmacy just before closing time to steal money and narcotics. While Mike ransacked the store, Donna took the proprietor, Fred, outside. Donna pointed a gun at Fred to persuade him to reveal the location of valuables, but the gun accidentally discharged, wounding Fred. Donna dropped the gun and fled the scene on foot, but she was arrested the next day. Mike ran outside, saw Fred bleeding profusely, and picked up Donna's gun. As he drove away at high speed, Mike accidentally struck and ran over Fred. Fred's gunshot wound was not serious, but he died from the injuries sustained from being run over by Mike.

A neighbor called the police and reported that he had heard a gunshot. He also reported that he had seen a dark blue car speed away from the pharmacy. Police saw Mike's car speeding two blocks from the pharmacy. The police stopped Mike's car for speeding and to investigate if he was involved in the shooting. When an officer asked Mike where he had been that afternoon, Mike hesitated and looked unusually nervous. The officer ordered Mike out of the car. As Mike got out, the officer noticed a bulge in Mike's pocket. The officer reached into the pocket and pulled out Donna's gun. Mike was immediately arrested.

The next day Mike's car was towed to the station and searched. Under the front seat, police found a Shorecliff Pharmacy envelope filled with drugs taken from the robbery at the pharmacy. When Officer Bill showed the envelope to Mike (who was then in a holding cell), Mike blurted out, "Donna was the one who did the shooting."

When Donna was interrogated, she asked for a lawyer. Before a lawyer arrived, Donna was interrogated further and admitted her part in the events.

Mike and Donna were indicted for the murder of Fred. Separate trials were ordered at the request of each defendant. Mike testified against Donna at her trial.

On appropriate motion, which (if any) of the following items of evidence should be suppressed at Donna's trial?

1. The gun taken from Mike's pocket
2. The Shorecliff Pharmacy envelope and contents taken from Mike's car
3. Mike's statement
4. Donna's admission

Question 10

Officers with the Big City Vice Squad have been conducting a series of stings aimed at black market firearms sales. One such operation has undercover officers meeting a man named Henry, who has offered to sell them an "untraceable" .45 caliber pistol. The undercover agents arrange to meet Henry in the parking lot of a large apartment complex, and their transaction is completed in short order.

The undercover agents give a prearranged signal to another team of officers who are waiting nearby, and the latter close in to make the arrest. Before they can reach the scene, Henry slips away from the undercover agents' car, makes his way up a flight of stairs, and heads down a second-floor hallway. Officers lose sight of Henry as he turns down the hall and then hear the sound of a door closing coming from the direction in which he ran.

The arrest team hustles up the stairs and down the hall, where they are faced with two identical doors on either side of the hall. Following a hunch, Officer Louis knocks on the door on the left and identifies himself as a police officer. As soon as he does, the officers hear someone making "shushing" sounds and a series of quick movements on the other side of the door, and then everything goes quiet. Thereupon the officers make a forcible entry into the apartment, where they find four people—two of whom are obviously adults and two of whom very much appear to be minors—sitting around a table with drinks in hand. Noticing the quartet's bloodshot eyes and flushed faces, Officer Jay grabs a glass from the youngest looking occupant and gives it a sniff. He immediately perceives a strong alcoholic odor and simultaneously sees a bottle marked "Mixer's Gin" under the table. While the rest of the officers make their way from the apartment, Officer Jay stays behind and conducts a pat-down search of all four people. In the process, he locates the subjects' identifications and verifies his suspicion regarding their respective ages. He then arrests the adults, Dee and Jay, for providing alcohol to a minor, and releases the kids into the custody of their parents.

Meanwhile, Officer Louis and the others go back to the door on the right side of the hall. Fearing that the occupants might already be alerted to their presence, the officers make an immediate, unannounced entry into the second apartment and find a man named Otis sitting at his computer. Stacked beside the monitor the officers spot a number of DVD cases with the title "Dog Fight to the Death," followed by a number and date, printed on the spine. One such DVD, showing graphic scenes of animal mutilation before a crowd of cheering spectators, is being displayed on the computer screen. The officers are aware that local statutory law criminalizes the production, possession, or distribution of visual depictions of wanton animal cruelty and believe that the video they observed qualifies as such. Hoping to discover additional DVDs or related evidence, Officer Louis begins opening drawers in the computer desk while other officers place Otis under arrest. In the top-center drawer of the desk, Louis discovers a small plate containing what appears (and later proves) to be cocaine. Otis is ultimately charged with possession of narcotics and the illegal animal cruelty videos. Henry, through all this, managed to escape down a rear balcony and has since eluded capture.

1. Dee and Jay, who share the apartment where they were arrested, are charged with contributing to the delinquency of a minor, and the evidence described above is offered and admitted at their trial. Assuming all relevant objections are made and preserved, what issues might be raised on appeal?

2. Between the time of Otis's arrest and his subsequent trial, the United States Supreme court decides that the statute criminalizing depictions of animal cruelty impermissibly infringes on the freedom of expression protected by the First Amendment and is therefore invalid. The criminal complaint against Otis is amended to reflect the change in underlying law, but the prosecutor insists on going ahead with the remaining narcotics charges. The evidence described above is offered and admitted at his trial. Assuming all potential objections are raised and preserved, what arguments could Otis raise on appeal?

Question 11

During an afternoon at the bar, Dave pulled a gun on Babs, the bartender, and demanded money. Babs took a gun from under the bar and shot at Dave. Dave shot back, killing Babs. John, a customer in the bar, then attacked Dave with a broken bottle, whereupon Dave shot and killed John. Wounded by John's attack, Dave dropped his gun and slumped to the floor. Officer Leslie heard the gunfire and entered the bar with her gun drawn. Seeing the three wounded people, Officer Leslie cried, "What the devil happened here?" Dave replied, "I killed them both in self-defense."

Dave was charged by state X with the first-degree murder of Babs. Under state X law, first-degree murder includes murder committed during an "attempt to perpetrate a robbery." Any other nonpremeditated murder is second-degree murder.

At Dave's trial, the prosecution presented Officer Leslie's testimony that Dave had admitted to the shooting. Dave then testified that he had been in a drunken stupor and was only "joking with Babs," that he never intended to take any money from Babs or to harm her, and that he shot her only in self-defense. Defense counsel offered no supporting testimony because he was told by the prosecutor that there was only one eyewitness to the shooting (Witt), and that Witt had said Dave was sober when he demanded money from Babs.

The only defense objection at trial was to the following jury instruction: "Whether Dave was drunk or intended to frighten Babs into giving him money is irrelevant; the crucial issue, for first-degree murder, is whether Babs reasonably was put in fear of being harmed unless she gave up her money."

Dave was convicted of the first-degree murder of Babs.

After the verdict, Dave's attorney discovered that the eyewitness (Witt) had, in fact, told the prosecutor that while he had not witnessed the shooting, he had seen Dave in the bar and that Dave was quite drunk shortly before the shooting.

1. What issues might be raised by Dave on appeal, and how should they be decided? Discuss.

2. If Dave's conviction is reversed on appeal and he is acquitted of the charge of murdering Babs on retrial, can he thereafter constitutionally be convicted of the first-degree murder of John? Discuss.

Question 12

Ashley entered a small federally chartered bank located in state X and, armed with a revolver, robbed the three tellers. As Ashley was leaving the bank, she shot Fred who was then entering it. Fred was a federal bank examiner who was about to conduct an audit.

The state charged Ashley with three separate counts of armed robbery (a separate count for each teller). At the state's trial on the first charge, Ashley's sole defense was an alibi that she was out of the city at the time of the robbery. The jury, apparently believing the alibi, returned a verdict of not guilty. Ashley was then tried on the second state charge. The evidence was substantially the same as at the first trial. The jury, apparently disbelieving the alibi, returned a verdict of guilty.

Ashley was also indicted by the federal government on three joined counts of armed robbery of a federal bank. After the jury was selected and sworn in for the trial of all three counts, the U.S. attorney asked that the case be adjourned for 48 hours because a key witness was unable to appear. The judge, however, discharged the jury over Ashley's attorney's objection.

The U.S. attorney and Ashley's attorney then agreed that if Ashley pleaded guilty to one of the indictments, the other two charges would be dismissed. This would make it much more likely that Ashley would receive a more lenient sentence than if she were convicted after trial on all three charges. Ashley's attorney fully explained this to Ashley, and she agreed to plead guilty after admitting to her attorney that she had robbed the tellers.

The next morning, Ashley, her lawyer, and the U.S. attorney appeared before the judge. Ashley's attorney announced that Ashley wished to change her plea to guilty to one of the indictments. The judge asked Ashley, "Do you wish to change your plea to guilty?" Ashley replied, "Yes, I wish to plead guilty to the one charge." The judge stated, "The guilty plea will be recorded." The other charges were dismissed, and Ashley was sentenced to federal prison.

There is a federal statute (the "Statute") that provides: "Whoever assaults, with a deadly weapon, any federal officer engaged in the performance of his or her duties is guilty of a felony."

In proper proceedings, Ashley appealed her state conviction and sought to vacate her federal sentence. Both cases are now properly before the U.S. Supreme Court.

1. How will the Court decide

    a. on the state conviction? Discuss.

    b. on the federal sentence? Discuss.

2. If Ashley succeeded in vacating the federal sentence, could she then be successfully prosecuted by federal authorities under the Statute? Discuss.

Question 13

Police Detective Smart set up an officially authorized "fencing" operation, which purported to buy and sell stolen goods under the cover of an import-export business. He quickly filled a warehouse with stolen property that he purchased from thieves.

Dan, who had prior convictions for burglary and larceny, posed as a customer and looked over the operation, intending to burglarize the warehouse. Smart recognized Dan and hoped to arrest him for receiving stolen property. Smart told Dan that he was working for Thug, and that the "merchandise" was stolen property. He said that the two of them could make some money if Dan would break into the warehouse, make it appear that a burglary had occurred, take the merchandise, sell it elsewhere, and divide the receipts between them. Dan agreed.

Late that night, Dan entered the warehouse through a skylight that Smart had left unlocked. After Dan loaded his truck with items from the warehouse, he noticed that uniformed police officers were approaching him. Dan fled, dropping a gun (which he was not legally authorized to carry). Dan was soon captured and taken back to the warehouse, where investigating officers truthfully told him the gun had been identified as belonging to him. Dan then blurted out a confession, was given *Miranda* warnings, and confessed again.

Dan has been charged with possession of stolen property and an illegal firearm.

In an attempt to lessen any sentence he might receive, Dan told officers that he had recently delivered a large quantity of forged stamps to Betty.

A federal officer visited Betty's stamp shop, purchased four stamps from her, and delivered them to experts for examination. Upon receipt of a report that they were forgeries, the officer returned to Betty's shop without a warrant and arrested Betty for the federal felony of knowingly possessing forged stamps. Over Betty's objections, the officer searched the display cabinet in front of her and seized 200 stamps, later found to be forgeries.

After her release on bail, Betty offered a hotel detective $500 to let her into a hotel room occupied by her Aunt Emma to retrieve a suitcase that Aunt Emma was keeping for her. Emma was away on a trip. The detective told Betty to return later and, curious as to why Betty wanted the suitcase so badly, entered the room with a passkey, searched it, and found Betty's suitcase under the bed. The hotel detective opened the suitcase and saw that it contained bonds in Betty's name and a gun. The hotel detective took the suitcase and its contents to his office. The detective then called the police and showed them the suitcase and its contents. Upon her return to the hotel, Betty was arrested under a statute for felonious possession of a weapon.

1. What objections based on the U.S. Constitution should Dan make to the admission of his confessions at his trial?

2. Should Dan prevail on an entrapment defense to the charge of receipt of stolen property?

3. What objections should Betty make to the admission of the stamps at her trial?

4. What objections should Betty make to the admission of the gun?

Question 14

Two plainclothes police officers, Able and Baker, were walking to their cars after attending a mutual friend's birthday party. They saw Cain and Doe, two reputed gamblers, leave Eddy's home. Eddy had been arrested on two previous occasions by Able. These arrests had resulted in convictions for running a "bookmaking operation."

Suspecting that Eddy might be taking bets in his home, Able and Baker walked over to the front of Eddy's house. They noticed several windows, about nine feet above the ground, along the side of the dwelling. There were no curtains or drapes over the windows. They knocked on the door of the home next to Eddy's. When no one answered, they went to the back of that house. They found a ladder, which they then used to climb to the roof of the neighbor's house. They were then able to peer into a side window of Eddy's home. The room they looked into contained several telephones, charts and other electronic equipment often used in bookmaking operations.

Able and Baker decided they had enough information to question Eddy. Before they could get down from the neighbor's roof, they saw Eddy leave his house, shouting to someone who was apparently just inside his front door, "I'm going to get a paper and a cup of coffee, I'll be back soon." Eddy did not see Able and Baker.

After Eddy got into his car and drove away, Able and Baker knocked on the front door of his house. A little girl's voice answered, "Who is it?" Able replied, "It's Miss Able, I know your father, I need to ask him some questions." Cathy, Eddy's 14-year-old daughter, opened the door and said, "My daddy's not home." Able responded, "Well, could we wait for him?" Cathy replied, as she opened the door wide, "Okay, you can sit in the living room." After Able and Baker were seated, Cathy excused herself, saying that she had lots of homework to do.

About one minute after Cathy left, through a door down the hallway (about 20 feet from the living room), the officers heard a telephone ring and someone say, "All right, that's $50 on Mountain Man in the third in Santa Anita. Got it." Able and Baker then went to that room and slowly nudged the door open. Inside, they saw that a bookmaking operation was obviously in progress. They immediately arrested the two people inside the room. They also confiscated the books, records, and charts found in the room.

Suddenly, there was a knock on the door. Able said she would answer the door while Baker instructed the two prisoners to remain silent and stay inside the room. When Able opened the door, she saw Joe, an underworld kingpin. Able asked Joe, "May I help you?" Joe replied, "I want to put $1,500 on Citation in the Sixth at Santa Anita." Able then informed Joe that he was under arrest for attempted illegal gambling.

At Joe's trial, the prosecution introduced into evidence the books and records that had been seized at Eddy's house. These items contained numerous references to Joe. Officer Able also testified as to what Joe had said in response to her inquiry.

Assuming that all appropriate objections were made in a timely manner, what constitutional issues are presented, and what result is likely to occur? Discuss.

Question 15

Debbie, 17, was a student at City High, a public high school in the state of Central. One evening, a water pipe leak caused water to seep onto a row of student lockers. The school principal was summoned to the school by the janitor. The principal immediately opened all the lockers in the row with a master key to determine what damage had been done and to initiate repairs. When he reached Debbie's locker, he moved a water-soaked paper bag that fell apart in his hands, revealing, among other things, three marijuana cigarettes.

When she arrived at school the next day, Debbie was called into the principal's office. The principal told her what he had found, advised her that her possession of marijuana violated a school regulation against bringing contraband onto campus, and immediately expelled her from school. The principal also notified the State Youth Authority, which instituted proceedings in juvenile court to have Debbie declared a delinquent. Delinquency in the state of Central is defined as "violation of any Penal Code provision that is punishable by at least six months imprisonment." Possession of marijuana falls within this definition.

At the hearing in juvenile court, Debbie was represented by counsel of her own choosing. The only evidence presented by the State Youth Authority was testimony of the principal concerning his search, the three cigarettes (which were determined to be marijuana), and a written form previously signed by Debbie that authorized "any member of the faculty or staff of the school I am attending to inspect my locker at any time." A rule adopted by the local school board required each student renting a locker to sign such an authorization at the beginning of the school year.

Debbie testified that the bag and its contents did not belong to her, but to another student who had used Debbie's locker when he lost the key to his own locker.

Following the hearing, Debbie was adjudged a juvenile delinquent on the grounds of possession of marijuana. She was committed to the custody of the State Youth Authority for three months.

Debbie, through her attorney, has now instituted proceedings in the state superior court for her release, claiming that the juvenile court proceedings (i.e., the lack of a jury trial) violated her Fourteenth Amendment rights. Debbie also attacked the admissibility of the marijuana. Assuming that all such claims were properly asserted and preserved in the prior proceeding, how should the superior court rule? Discuss.

Question 16

Cindy was a wealthy stockbroker. Allen was one of her customers. After Allen slapped Cindy in the face during a violent argument over money at Allen's apartment, Cindy stabbed Allen with a metal letter opener. Her clothes spotted with blood from Allen's wound, Cindy ran from the apartment screaming, "What will I ever do? What will the Stock Exchange do with me?" Sylvia, Allen's friend, arrived at the front door of the apartment just as Cindy fled. Sylvia saw the blood on Cindy's clothes and heard her screams.

After Sylvia had entered the apartment and found Allen wounded and unconscious, she called the police. When the police arrived, Sylvia described the woman who had fled the apartment. Allen's dining room table was covered with documents and records dealing with Allen's recent stock transactions. The police concluded that the assailant might well be someone who had participated in these transactions, perhaps Allen's broker.

Finding Cindy's address among the documents on Allen's dining room table and relying on the description provided by Sylvia, the police arrived at Cindy's home within 5 minutes after she arrived home. The police rang the bell, and Cindy opened the door and stood directly in the doorway. Upon seeing Cindy and concluding that she fit the description given by Sylvia, the police arrested Cindy in her doorway. Cindy was immediately taken to Allen's hospital room. Allen, who was on the critical list and was not expected to live through the night, identified Cindy as his assailant. Allen died the next day.

After the hospital visit, Cindy was taken to police headquarters and placed in a lineup. At the demand of the police and over her objection, Cindy was forced to repeat the words, "What will I ever do? What will the Stock Exchange do with me?" At the lineup, Sylvia identified Cindy both by sight and by voice as the woman she had seen and heard leaving Allen's apartment. Later, over Cindy's objection, a police officer confiscated all the clothing she was wearing at the time of her arrest. Subsequent laboratory analysis matched Allen's blood type with the blood on the clothes Cindy was wearing. Cindy was charged with murder and placed in detention.

The police told Paula, another prisoner, that they were going to put her in the same cell with Cindy. They told Paula that they were interested in obtaining incriminating statements from Cindy. The police further advised

Paula not to initiate any conversations or elicit information from Cindy. She was told to listen if Cindy wanted to speak.

Unable to restrain herself, Cindy confided in Paula that she felt "very guilty about stabbing Allen."

Was Cindy's arrest valid? Discuss.

Cindy has moved to prevent the introduction into evidence at her trial of

1. any testimony relating to Allen's identification of her.
2. any testimony relating to Sylvia's visual identification at the lineup.
3. any testimony relating to Sylvia's voice identification at the lineup.
4. Cindy's clothing and the result of the laboratory analysis of the blood found on it.
5. Cindy's statement to Paula while awaiting trial.

How should the court rule on each of the five motions? Discuss.

Question 17

Doug was driving home from a party with his friend, Thompson. They were both very drunk. Thompson began to make insulting remarks about Doug's girlfriend. Doug warned him to stop, but Thompson persisted. Unable to take it any longer, Doug reached into the glove compartment of his car, took out a gun, and shot Thompson. Doug then pulled over to an unlighted part of the roadway and pushed Thompson's body out of the car.

The next morning, Doug left his house carrying the same gun in his pocket. He was stopped at one of the boarding gates of the local public interstate bus terminal when the gun activated a metal detector. Pursuant to governmental regulations about interstate bus travel, the bus company, which was privately owned, instituted the metal detector procedure and staffed it with its own employees.

A security guard of the bus company stopped Doug, reached into Doug's pocket, and found the gun. The morning newspapers had been full of the story of Thompson's death, and the guard knew that the gun Doug was carrying fit the description of the gun used on Thompson. Doug saw an opening and ran. Later that morning, the security guard took the gun to the police and told the police why he had taken it from Doug.

The day after the bus terminal incident, Officer West spotted Doug driving his car with his hazard lights on and with one taillight burned out. Officer West pulled Doug over, intending to ask Doug about his hazard lights. When Officer West came alongside Doug's car, he noticed that Doug appeared to be very nervous. Officer West asked, "Everything all right?" Doug shot back in a sarcastic voice, "Oh yes, I'm just getting out of town because there's way too much acid rain." Perplexed and troubled by this reply, Officer West decided to look into Doug's car and saw bloodstains on the front seat. Taking a closer look at Doug, Officer West realized that he resembled the description of Thompson's assailant. Officer West then arrested Doug. He told Doug that ballistics tests had proved that his gun had fired the bullet that killed Thompson. Doug then blurted out, "I shot him because he provoked me and I was drunk."

Doug has been charged with murder.

What objections based on the U.S. Constitution should Doug make to the admission into evidence of the gun, the bloodstains, and his statement to Officer West? Discuss.

Question 18

Tony was glad his law school exams were finally over. He partied long and hard after his last final, consuming alcoholic beverages, marijuana, cocaine, and five dozen Twinkies. He started to drive home, but was soon pulled over by Officer Meane, who had observed Tony driving his sports car (1) lawfully, but 20 mph under the speed limit; and (2) with a weird smile on his face.

Meane asked Tony to step out of the car and gave Tony a field sobriety test, which Tony flunked. Before arresting Tony, Meane said, "What in the world have you been drinking?" Meane patted Tony on the back good-naturedly and laughed in a friendly way.

Tony replied, also with a laugh, "Twinkies, many Twinkies."

Meane replied, "But you can't *drink* Twinkies. Have you been drinking anything?"

Tony answered, "A six-pack of Genny Cream Ale, and about 20 Jello shooters, give or take 5 or 6."

Meane placed Tony under arrest on a charge of "willful drunken driving." Meane then took out a little notecard from her jacket and read Tony his *Miranda* rights. After listening to them, Tony replied, "I waive my rights."

Meane then proceeded to interrogate Tony. Tony admitted that he had used marijuana and that he knew he should not have been driving while intoxicated. As a gesture of friendship, Tony reached into the breast pocket of his shirt and handed Meane his last marijuana cigarette.

Tony was taken back to the station house and placed in a holding cell. About two hours later, after again receiving proper *Miranda* warnings, he was questioned about the incident by Officer Phil. Tony confessed to being drunk and having marijuana in his possession.

Tony was charged with "willful drunken driving" and "possession of an ounce or less of marijuana." Prior to trial, Tony told the judge that he wanted to represent himself. The judge said, "Absolutely not, young man!" The judge then appointed an excellent public defender to be Tony's attorney.

1. Which of the preceding pieces of evidence will be admissible in the criminal prosecution against Tony? Discuss.

2. Assuming Tony loses at trial, what other issues are available on appeal?

Question 19

Dot was one of 50 women employed by Store. Nine months ago, on a day when Dot was on duty at Store, a man dressed as a delivery clerk stole several radios from Store during the lunch hour. Grace, a customer, told Marsh, the store manager, that at the time of the theft and from a distance of about 30 feet, she had observed a clerk, whom she described as a young woman of average build and wearing a Store smock, speaking to a delivery man. In the presence of Police Officer Brown, Marsh showed Grace a photograph of Dot. Grace stated, "She could be the one." A few minutes later, Marsh asked Dot in Brown's presence if she had been in the store during the lunch hour. Dot answered that she had been, but had seen nothing unusual.

Recently, Officer Brown validly arrested Dot's ex-husband, Hal, on another matter. After being advised of his rights, Hal confessed to the Store theft, stating that Dot had helped him and that the stolen radios were in her apartment. Brown immediately obtained both a search warrant for Dot's apartment and an arrest warrant for Dot, after submitting an affidavit that stated in part:

> I have information from a reliable source who knows Dot that the radios stolen from Store nine months ago are now in the apartment of Dot. . . .

The affidavit also stated that Dot had previously been convicted of grand larceny and has been known to associate with other convicted felons.

Dot was arrested the next afternoon as she was returning home from work. After she was shown the search warrant, Dot asked if she could telephone her sister to come over, so that someone would be in the apartment when Dot's daughter (Ann) returned home from school. Officer Brown agreed, but accompanied Dot as she entered her apartment and walked to the telephone. They had to walk through the living room to enter the kitchen where Dot's telephone is located. While walking through the living room, Officer Brown noticed two rows of small boxes, stacked one on top of the other in a corner. Officer Brown walked over to the boxes and visually inspected the outside of the boxes. He saw that these radios were the ones stolen from Store. Officer Brown seized these items.

Dot and Hal were indicted. Hal pleaded guilty and Dot not guilty. At Dot's trial, Grace identified Dot as the Store clerk she had seen speaking to the delivery man. Dot testified in her own defense and denied being in Store during the lunch hour. The prosecution called Marsh as a rebuttal witness, and he testified that Dot had told him she was in Store during the lunch hour on the day of the theft.

As counsel for Dot, what motions or objections would you have made before or during the trial? How should the court have ruled on each motion or objection? Discuss.

Question 20

Dunn, a 25-year-old adult, worked as a computer programmer at Arcon Enterprises. Dunn had been seeing Sally, who was a 17-year-old minor.

Buck was jealous of Dunn. He wanted to win Sally's affections, but realized he could never do so with Dunn around. Buck knew that Sally was only 17. He decided that the best way to get rid of Dunn was to get him prosecuted for violation of a state law that provides that any adult who has sex with a person under the age of 18 has committed statutory rape. Buck began to follow Dunn and Sally around on their dates. Buck noted that on two occasions, Dunn and Sally entered Dunn's apartment at about 11:00 P.M. and did not come out until 10:00 the next morning. Buck reported his observations to the police, suggesting that they prosecute Dunn for statutory rape.

The next evening, the police began a surveillance of Dunn's apartment. Watching with the aid of high-powered binoculars from a nearby apartment building, they saw Dunn and Sally kissing. Dunn suddenly picked Sally up and carried her into what was presumably his bedroom.

The next day, after Dunn left his office to have lunch, the police were given permission by his employer to search his work area. The officers found a letter (which apparently Dunn had decided not to send) in a trash can that Dunn shared with another employee. The letter was addressed to Sally. It said that he hoped they would have "another hot night next weekend."

The next morning, the police arrested Dunn on the street as he was getting into his car to drive to work. The charge was statutory rape; the police had no arrest warrant. The arresting officers searched the vehicle and found two marijuana cigarettes under the front seat. A charge of possession of an illegal substance was then added to the charge of statutory rape.

What arguments can Dunn make to suppress the marijuana cigarettes, and what arguments is the prosecution likely to make in rebuttal?

Question 21

Defendant, affectionately known as the "Godfather," is suspected of being the leader of an organized criminal gambling and prostitution enterprise involving multiple secret betting locations and brothels. Officers have difficulty locating any of these sites because they are constantly rotated around the sprawling city. In order to gather intelligence on the gang, officers (without a warrant or other authorization) decide to install a GPS device underneath the bumper of the Godfather's car in order to track his movements over time. While this investigation is ongoing, police receive a detailed 911 report from an anonymous caller describing two men (one fitting the Godfather's description) beating and kicking another man on a street corner very near the Godfather's suspected headquarters. Police and paramedics arrive to treat the victim, Sam, but find neither assailant.

Investigators collect enough information from the GPS tracking device to plot the defendant's movements (in minute detail) over a period of two months and use the data to generate a map and schedule of the gambling and prostitution outposts. Officers then exploit that spatial map and schedule to send undercover officers into the businesses, and eventually they gather enough evidence to secure arrest warrants for the Godfather and many of his suspected associates. Arresting officers executing the warrant advise the Godfather of his *Miranda* rights, and he emphatically states that he "does not want to communicate with officers at any point without an attorney present."

Three weeks later, after the Godfather has been timely charged with bookmaking and promoting prostitution and denied bail pending trial, detectives question him at the detention facility about his suspected role in Sam's beating. They provide fresh *Miranda* warnings, and the Godfather immediately makes several incriminating statements in an effort to shift the blame to a third party.

All of the evidence described above, including the anonymous caller's report and the Godfather's jailhouse statements, is offered at his trial for bookmaking, promoting prostitution, and on the newly added charge of aggravated assault for the attack on Sam. Defense counsel files pretrial motions seeking to keep each piece of evidence out of the trial record, but the court denies the motions summarily. You are a law clerk for the court hearing the Godfather's appeal. What issues would you expect to see during the appeal, and how would you suggest that your judge resolve those issues?

Question 22

The small town of Pleasantville had recently experienced a rash of arson attacks directed against public buildings, including the City Hall and local high school. The Pleasantville Police Department was unable to generate any leads in the case, so they decided to turn to the public for help. The Pleasantville police erected a checkpoint on the town's busiest roadway at which they randomly stopped motorists in order to ask the occupants if they had witnessed any unusual or suspicious activity. These brief inquiries were conducted in a cordial and easy-going manner, and generally lasted about 30 seconds.

On the day after the fire at City Hall, Officer Olsen was managing the checkpoint along with her partner Sergeant Smalls when Dan drove up in his late-model sedan. Olsen signaled for Dan to stop at the checkpoint, and made her standard inquiry about the fires. Dan responded that he had not seen anything out of the ordinary, although he had read about the fires in the newspaper. Officer Olsen was satisfied with Dan's answer, and had no reason to suspect his involvement. Nevertheless, Olsen gave a prearranged signal to her partner, and Sergeant Smalls proceeded to walk his specially trained narcotics detection dog around Dan's vehicle while Olsen finished her conversation. While Olsen was making the usual request that Dan contact the police with any new information, Smalls' dog "alerted" at Dan's passenger side door, indicating the presence of narcotics. Dan was then instructed to pull out of traffic and over to the side of the road. Dan complied with this order.

Once pulled over, Olsen continued her conversation with Dan, asking him if there were any drugs or other contraband items in the car. Dan initially said "no," and then added that "if there was something in the car, [he] didn't know anything about it." Olsen then informed Dan that she suspected that he was, in fact, carrying narcotics, and she ordered him out of the car. Olsen then conducted a brief pat-down of Dan's outer clothing and, finding him unarmed, had him sit in the back of her police cruiser while she returned to his car. Olsen then searched the passenger compartment of the vehicle, finding nothing other than a black backpack. Upon opening the backpack, Olsen found some clothing and personal effects, along with a charred glass pipe.

Olsen smelled the pipe and, after detecting what her training told her was the odor of burnt cocaine on the pipe, she concluded that it had been used for smoking "crack." Applicable state law criminalizes the possession of drug paraphernalia, although it provides that suspected violators of the provision be issued a citation rather than arrested. Olsen then retrieved Dan from her cruiser, informed him that he was under arrest for possession of drug paraphernalia, handcuffed him, and put him back in her car. Sergeant Smalls then joined Olsen in a more thorough search of the entire car, which included both the glove compartment and the trunk, where they found a small plastic bag of a substance that later proved to be crack cocaine.

Assume that Pleasantville is located in a state with constitutional criminal procedure provisions identical to the federal Constitution.

In Dan's subsequent prosecution in state court for possession of cocaine and drug paraphernalia, what constitutional issues might he raise?

How would the trial court most likely resolve those issues? Discuss.

Question 23

Uniformed Officers Pounce and John were on routine street patrol near the campus of Central University when two men unloading a nearby car caught their attention. They observed the men remove a large number of identical duffel bags from the trunk of a car and carry the bags into an adjacent home. While this was not unusual in a college town, Officer Pounce noted that the bags seemed very heavy, and to be filled with many square, brick-like objects, and Officer John noticed the men looking around nervously as they worked. The officers decided to approach the men, but the unloading had been completed by the time Pounce and John arrived and one of the subjects was just closing the now-empty trunk. When they saw Officers Pounce and John, the two men immediately took off—the first, Freddie, walked briskly toward the door of the home, while the second, Samson, ran down the street and around the block with the last of the duffel bags over his shoulder.

Acting quickly, Officer Pounce commanded Freddie to "freeze" while Officer John pursued Samson. John caught Samson just two blocks away, placed him under arrest, and walked him back to the house. Meanwhile, Pounce approached Freddie, who had obeyed Pounce's order and remained on the porch, and asked him about the bags. Freddie said he knew nothing about any bags, and that he was just going into his house to get ready for class, but he got visibly more nervous and fidgety when he saw Officer John return with Samson in handcuffs and the duffel in hand.

Upon rejoining the others, Officer John opened the duffel Samson had been carrying and discovered a large quantity of powder later shown to be high potency methamphetamine. The officers radioed a report of their encounter to their superior officer, and arranged for Samson's transportation to the police station. Officer Pounce was additionally instructed to "detain the suspect on the porch until we can arrive with a search warrant for the residence." Officer Pounce complied, and told Freddie that while he was not under arrest, he was not free to leave until the search had been completed.

After Samson's arrest and during his transfer to the station, one of the officers recognized Samson as having previously been arrested for methamphetamine manufacture. Knowing that Samson was an "experienced, hard-core criminal" who would likely invoke the right to silence if given the chance, the police decided to question Samson prior to "reminding" him of his *Miranda* rights. In response to the officer's questions, Samson squarely implicated himself in the production of narcotics. Once at the station, the same officer read Samson the required *Miranda* warnings, and then repeated the litany of questions about drug manufacturing that he posed in the car. Believing he now had nothing to lose, Samson agreed to waive his rights, repeated his earlier confession, and signed a written transcript of what he had told the officers in the car.

Upon execution of the search warrant on the home where Freddie was earlier detained, the police found ten of the duffel bags they saw carried into the house, and each was found to contain several large "bricks" of methamphetamine along with multiple small discrete plastic baggies typical of those sold on the street. The officers also encountered one additional person inside the home—a young woman named Mary, who had been asleep in an upstairs bedroom. The officers handcuffed Mary and kept her laying face down on the bed for the two hours they spent conducting the search.

Freddie, Samson, and Mary are each subsequently charged with felony possession of methamphetamine with intent to distribute. Samson is also charged with methamphetamine manufacture based on his post-arrest statements to the police. Assume that state law parallels the federal Constitution in all relevant respects. What evidentiary challenges might each of the defendants raise, and how would a court likely rule on any requests for suppression?

Question 24

Winken, Blinken, and Nod were reputedly members of a local street gang. Police Detective Friendly received a tip from a confidential informant indicating that Nod had been the shooter in a recent, unsolved killing of a rival gang member. Detective Friendly's confidential informant, who had proved reliable on more than a dozen prior occasions, did not provide any details about the shooting other than to implicate Nod, but he did state that he had heard about the shooting directly from Nod. The confidential informant further stated that Nod could usually be found at the apartment owned jointly by Winken and Blinken on weekday afternoons.

Acting on this tip, Detective Friendly went to Winken and Blinken's apartment on the following Monday at 3:00 P.M. Friendly knocked on the door, was greeted by Winken who answered it, and then explained the purpose of her visit. Winken stated that he and Nod were friends, and that the detective was welcome to come in and talk to him. This exchange was immediately interrupted by Blinken, who stated that he was co-owner of the house and that he didn't "want any cops setting a single foot inside my house without a warrant." "Well, it's fine with me," repeated Winken, and he opened the door further. Based on this invitation, Detective Friendly entered the home and was ushered to a back bedroom where Nod sat reading on a bed.

Detective Friendly introduced herself to Nod, and again explained the purpose of her visit. In the course of their conversation, during which Nod provided a seemingly credible alibi for the night of the killing, Detective Friendly learned Nod's full name and date of birth. Although satisfied with Nod's alibi, the detective nevertheless radioed to his office to request a background check on Nod, and was soon informed by a colleague at the station that there was an outstanding warrant for Nod's arrest on suspicion of armed robbery. Upon receiving this information, Detective Friendly placed Nod under arrest and conducted a search of his person. While that search produced nothing of significance, Detective Friendly did locate an illegal firearm from under the pillow of the bed on which Nod sat. Friendly seized that weapon, and began to walk Nod out of the apartment. As the detective and Nod walked down the hall, Friendly observed a small mirror with piles of white powder resembling cocaine on a bedroom side table. After slyly determining that the bedroom in question belonged to Blinken, Detective Friendly placed him under arrest, too, and arranged to transfer both Blinken and Nod to the local precinct.

Subsequent investigation showed that there was no arrest warrant for Nod, and that a young police recruit had entered the wrong date of birth into the computer that produced the report. Notwithstanding that error, Nod was charged with felony firearm possession, and Blinken with felony narcotics possession.

At Blinken's arraignment, he indicated that he understood the charges against him and requested the appointment of an attorney to represent him. Blinken, through counsel, subsequently filed a motion to suppress the drugs found in his bedroom, but was denied relief by the trial court. Blinken then entered a conditional guilty plea, preserving his right to modify the plea after appealing the denial of the suppression motion.

Nod also requested the appointment of counsel on his behalf, and entered a plea of not guilty. During detention and prior to trial, the prosecuting attorney sought additional evidence against Nod by arranging for the placement of an undercover officer in Nod's jail cell. The prosecutor instructed the undercover officer to "encourage the defendant to share any incriminating information without going so far as to ask about the crimes directly." The ploy succeeded, and the undercover officer collected additional incriminating statements (albeit indirectly) from Nod which implicated him in the gang-related killing. At his eventual trial, Nod took the stand and repeated his alibi defense. The prosecutor then sought to introduce the statements Nod made to the jailhouse informant in order to rebut this alibi defense.

Assume that state and federal law are equivalent on matters of constitutional criminal procedure. What evidentiary issues could Blinken raise on appeal, and how would those likely be decided?

What other evidentiary issues might be raised during Nod's trial?

How should the court rule on the prosecution's proffer of Nod's statements?

Essay
Answers

Answer to Question 1

1. Did the court err in admitting Ronald's statement against him?

Ronald may challenge the admission of his statement to the detectives as an unwarned confession elicited in violation of his Fifth Amendment privilege against self-incrimination. *Miranda* requires that, prior to any custodial interrogation, a suspect be informed of his or her right to remain silent, that statements will be used against him or her, of his or her right to any attorney during questioning, including the right to appointed counsel if necessary. Custody exists where a reasonable person would not feel free to leave, and interrogation occurs when the individual faces direct questioning or its functional equivalent.

Ronald would argue that his formal arrest and detention at the police station satisfies the custody element of *Miranda* and that the officers' direct questioning regarding the robberies constitutes interrogation. Officers were therefore obligated to provide *Miranda* warnings before any questioning could proceed, and any unwarned statements must be suppressed.

Even though the detectives recited warnings prior to beginning the interrogation, Ronald could argue that the warnings themselves were defective. The detectives (repeating the arresting officers' earlier advisement) said that Ronald had a right to counsel **prior to** any questioning. *Miranda's* prophylactic protection requires the presence of counsel **during** questioning whenever a subject so desires, and the warnings must adequately communicate the substance of that right to the suspect for the warnings to be effective.

The government would not dispute that the *Miranda* warnings are a necessary precondition to a valid custodial interrogation. Instead, the government would likely contend that the warnings given here were sufficient. The exact language used in *Miranda* is not of talismanic importance, and some variation in the wording or delivery of the warnings is permissible. *California v. Prysock*. The fundamental requirement is that the warnings as given adequately convey the essence of the protections, and they need not be expressed in any particular form. *Duckworth v. Eagan*.

Based on existing law, a court would likely agree with the government's formulation of the test, so the narrow question in this case is whether the warnings given to Ronald while in custody prior to interrogation adequately communicated to him that he had the right to counsel not just before but also during the detectives' questioning. While it is true that the officers informed Ronald had a right to counsel prior to questioning, they also indicated that he could invoke this right at any time. Standing alone, the right to counsel advice does not match perfectly the *Miranda* phrasing and may not properly communicate the right, but combined with the "invoke at any time" proviso it was sufficient to inform the suspect that his right to counsel was available to him **both** before and during the interrogation. *Florida v. Powell.*

Ronald may also argue that his statement was collected in violation of his right to silence. If a suspect facing custodial interrogation at any time invokes the right to remain silent, all questioning must cease. *Miranda v. Arizona.* Ronald will argue that he categorically invoked his right to silence by being so for almost three hours. He will point out that officers continued to question him throughout his effort to remain silent and that they never secured an explicit or formal waiver of the right he had functionally invoked.

The government will respond that refusing to answer questions is not necessarily an invocation of the right to silence and will likely emphasize the fact that Ronald at no point indicated his desire to terminate the interview. The *Miranda* protections are designed to protect against a suspect's will being overborne and the suspect coerced into waiving his rights. An invocation of the right to silence may signal the suspect's sense of vulnerability to the pressures of custodial interrogation, but actually manifesting the ability to remain silent does not send the same message.

A court will likely admit the statement because Ronald's invocation of the right to silence was not explicit, clear, and unambiguous. It has previously been established that the right to counsel must be invoked in clear and unambiguous terms that would communicate to a reasonable officer the suspect's need. *Davis v. United States.* The Fifth Amendment has been construed to require that invocation of the right to silence meet the same standard. *Berghuis v. Thompkins.* By contrast, waiver of these rights need not be similarly explicit, and can be inferred from the defendant's conduct including the decision to answer police questions. Here, the facts do not indicate that Ronald made any invocation of or other reference to his right to remain silent. Moreover, even though he waited for two hours and 45 minutes, he unquestionably responded to police questioning and this choice may be construed as a knowing and intelligent waiver of his rights. *Id. See also North Carolina v. Butler.*

2. Did the court err in admitting Ronald's statement against Donald?

The facts do not tell us whether Ronald testified in his own defense. If he did and he repeated his statement, then Donald had the ability to confront and cross-examine him on those issues. On the other hand, if Ronald asserted his Fifth Amendment privilege against testifying, Donald could argue that Ronald's statement was inadmissible against him because the statement would violate Donald's Sixth Amendment right to confront witnesses against him (i.e., Bert was denied the opportunity to cross-examine Ace). *See, e.g., Crawford v. Washington.* If Ronald did not testify, Donald is likely to prevail on the issue of confrontation.

Furthermore, before *Crawford*, the Supreme Court held that if two co-defendants are tried simultaneously, the rights of one are violated if the other refuses to testify but his confession is introduced against both. This is true even if the jury is instructed to use the confession only against the defendant who made it. *Bruton v. United States.* The prosecution had the option of trying Ronald and Donald separately or of asking for two separate juries, both of which would hear all the testimony except Ronald's statement, which would be heard by only Ronald's jury if admitted into evidence. The prosecutor's failure to exercise either of these options should result in a new trial for Donald.

Answer to Question 2

Was the warrant validly issued?

Evidence obtained with an invalid search warrant may be inadmissible against the defendant at trial. The validity of a search warrant is one of the elements guaranteed by the Constitution. Therefore, the admissibility of all the evidence Trace obtained in the hotel room rests on the validity of his warrant.

Doris should have contended that the warrant was not validly issued because (1) there was no probable cause (i.e., the warrant rested primarily upon the hearsay statement of the informant, without any corroboration that the information was accurate); (2) a search warrant ordinarily must be executed (i.e., acted upon) within a reasonable time from the date it was issued; and (3) a specific location was not designated (*any* Savoy Hotel room could be searched).

The prosecution should have argued in rebuttal that, under the "totality of the circumstances" test for informants (*Illinois v. Gates*), probable cause did exist in light of the declarant's prior history of furnishing correct information and the specificity of his information (i.e., the exact building and the time frame within which the transaction would occur). Furthermore, 14 days was a reasonable period of time in the light of the informant's data. In any event, the search was actually made within one week of the warrant's issuance. Also, the location was as precise as possible under the circumstances.

The trial court probably was correct in determining that the search warrant was validly issued and in refusing to suppress the items found in the room.

Even if the warrant was *not* validly issued, the court probably was correct in admitting the evidence because (1) there was a reasonable basis for issuing the warrant, and (2) Trace acted reasonably in believing that the warrant was valid. *See, e.g., United States v. Leon.*

Was the evidence obtained as a result of Trace listening admissible?

Doris could contend that Trace's listening at her door constituted a search within the meaning of the Fourth Amendment (applicable to the states via the Fourteenth Amendment). As this alleged search was beyond the scope of the search warrant, its fruits (hearing Doris's offer to sell silicon chips to Vic and the subsequent scuffle) would be inadmissible. However, Trace simply used his unenhanced sense of hearing to listen to what Doris had exposed to any member of the public walking by in the hotel corridor. As such, the prosecution will argue that Trace's listening was not a search at all and thus Doris's voluntary statements, which were not induced by anything Trace did or didn't do, are admissible.

The trial court probably was correct in refusing to suppress Doris's statement.

Assuming Trace's entrance into Doris's hotel room was valid, is Doris's statement admissible?

Statements made to police officers during a custodial interrogation are not admissible in the prosecution's case-in-chief, unless (1) *Miranda* warnings preceded the questioning, and (2) there was a waiver of *Miranda* rights. Doris should have contended that (1) since Trace had drawn his gun, a custodial situation ensued; and (2) Trace's question ("What did you do to him?") was interrogation (i.e., reasonably calculated to elicit an incriminating response). The prosecution should have argued in rebuttal that Trace's statement was a spontaneous, on-the-scene inquiry made to determine Vic's physical condition so that the proper medical attention could be given; in that case, *Miranda* would not apply under the "public safety" or "rescue" exception. *See, e.g., New York v. Quarles; People v. Dean.* However, because Trace's question seems to have been addressed more to eliciting Doris's statements about her own actions rather than to finding out whether Vic needed medical help, that conclusion is at least debatable. The court reasonably could have concluded that the "public safety" or "rescue" exception did not apply and that Doris's statement should have been excluded.

Assume the warrant was not properly issued and that Trace did not have an objective, good faith belief that it was valid. Would Trace's observations and the evidence seized in Doris's hotel room nevertheless be admissible?

Evidence obtained by lawful means **independent** of any illegal taint is admissible. If the argument between Vic and Doris was of such volume that persons walking through the hallway would hear it, Doris would have lost all expectation of privacy in the consequences of her words. The sounds of a violent argument and of an ensuing crash probably would constitute exigent circumstances, justifying a warrantless entry by Trace into Doris's hotel room. It would be reasonable for a police officer to verify whether a violent felony had occurred and to ascertain the cause and the persons involved.

Once inside, Trace had probable cause to arrest Doris because Vic was unconscious and Doris was the only other person in the room. Trace's resulting observations (i.e., those items that were in plain view) within the room would be admissible. Under this theory, Trace probably would not have the right to search anything not in the area within Doris's immediate control without obtaining a warrant. But evidence (i) within Trace's view upon entering the hotel room, (ii) upon Doris's person, and (iii) within Doris's immediate control would be admissible, even if the warrant was invalid.

Summary:
Of the evidence presented against Doris, her offer to sell silicon chips to Vic, her scuffle with Vic (both of which Trace heard through the door), and Trace's observations of Vic's physical condition and of any physical evidence found in the immediate vicinity are all admissible against Doris. The court was correct in denying her suppression motion as to these items. Only Doris's statement to Vic is questionable.

Answer to Question 3

The question assumes that Dan will be tried separately in the federal and state courts.

1. Dan's motion to exclude the evidence found in his suitcase:

Under the Fourth Amendment, a federal governmental agent must, in order to search a person's suitcases, ordinarily obtain a warrant based on probable cause. However, an exception to this rule exists with respect to "border" searches of a person's belongings when he enters this country from abroad. Border searches generally are limited to vehicles, suitcases, and personal searches that are not excessively intrusive. These objects may be searched without probable cause (or even reasonable suspicion). Therefore, the search of the suitcases was valid.

2. Dan's motion to exclude the evidence found on his person:

Dan would next contend in his federal trial that Fred did *not* have sufficient grounds to order a search of Dan's body cavities. However, the need to safeguard the nation's borders means that customs agents may conduct even reasonably intrusive body searches based on less than probable cause. In one case, the Supreme Court held that an incoming traveler's body cavities may be searched as long as the agents have "a particularized and objective basis for suspecting [the traveler] of alimentary canal smuggling." *United States v. Montoya de Hernandez.*

True, all that Fred had seen in Dan's suitcase were two items of heroin-related paraphernalia. But the government probably could argue successfully that Fred had sufficient suspicion to detain and body-search Dan on the following basis: (1) the items found in Dan's suitcase, (2) the items found in Anon's suitcase (Dan probably had no standing to object to the search of Anon's suitcase), (3) Anon's prior criminal record, and (4) Fred's probable experience that persons smuggling heroin frequently use body cavities to conceal as much as they can. Taken together, these facts would appear to meet the "particularized and objective basis" test of *Montoya.*

Nothing in the facts indicates that the search was performed in other than a reasonable manner (i.e., it was carried out by a male physician who presumably made no greater intrusion upon Dan than necessary under the circumstances to determine if he had placed illegal drugs in his body cavity). Nor is there any indication that Dan was detained for longer than necessary before the examination was completed.

The federal court should deny Dan's motion to exclude the heroin found in his person.

3. Dan's motion to exclude the evidence found in his car:

In the state court action, Dan will assert that because the search of his car and seizure of the heroin found within it were conducted without a warrant, evidence of the heroin in the car is not admissible.

When the police have probable cause to believe that a vehicle on a public road contains evidence of a crime, the vehicle may be searched without a warrant. The state could contend that given Dan's earlier federal arrest and the close proximity of the car to the border, there was probable cause to believe that the vehicle contained evidence of criminal activity. However, it is questionable that there was probable cause on these facts alone. The state likely would lose on the issue of probable cause to search, in the absence of other factors.

However, when a car is lawfully in police possession pursuant to an arrest, a warrantless "inventory" search of the vehicle may be made (without probable cause) provided that there is a standard police procedure allowing inventory searches. *See Colorado v. Bertine.* The facts are silent as to whether the state agents here adhered to a standard procedure for impounding the car of a suspect while its owner was in custody. Also, it can be argued that the car was seized illegally because there was no accompanying arrest by state authorities. Fred was arrested by a federal customs agent, not by Olson, the state agent. Much will depend on the preexisting state standard procedures. If the search of the vehicle satisfied the standard-procedure test, then the search likely will be valid even if it was made without the required probable cause.

We have been assuming that the heroin in Dan's car could not be seen from outside the car. If the heroin could be seen—and reasonably identified as heroin—from the sidewalk or street, then the sighting itself would supply probable cause for the search. (This would be an application of the plain view doctrine.)

In summary, it is questionable whether the heroin found in Dan's car should be admitted against him.

4. Is Dan entitled to have bail fixed or to be released pending trial?

Under the Eighth Amendment, "excessive bail" (i.e., an amount exceeding the sum reasonably calculated to assure the defendant's presence at trial) is impermissible. The Supreme Court has never decided whether this provision is binding on the states via the Fourteenth Amendment. Even if the Eighth Amendment were binding on the states, the courts have held that when a suspect poses a danger to society, bail is *not* constitutionally required. Preventive state detention statutes like the one under scrutiny here generally have been upheld on the bail issue, provided the defendant is afforded the right to a hearing and to individualized consideration of his circumstances. *See, e.g., United States v. Salerno.*

The state probably will contend that all heroin distributors (a large quantity of the drug was found in Dan's car) pose a great risk to society. Furthermore, the state likely will allege that Dan presents a flight risk given his recent international travel and the illicit funds often available to drug dealers. In contrast, Dan will argue that because there is no indication that Dan was a habitual trafficker in heroin, a complete denial of pretrial bail would be unwarranted in this instance.

Dan might also claim that the Due Process and Equal Protection Clauses of the Fourteenth Amendment require that he should be released on his own recognizance if he cannot afford even reasonable bail. The clauses probably require that the bail scheme of a state not work an invidious discrimination upon the poor. However, a suspect is not entitled to release simply because he is indigent. (That theory would discriminate against persons who are *not* poor.) Thus, it does not appear that Dan would be entitled to be released upon his own recognizance solely because of his indigence.

On these facts, Dan seems unlikely to be "entitled" to have bail fixed, and the state court will exercise its discretion pursuant to the relevant state statute.

Answer to Question 4

Is the pistol found in Deer's jacket admissible?

Deer can be expected to contend that the pistol found in his jacket is inadmissible because the arrest warrant was invalid. He would argue that the gun was found as a consequence of the illegal arrest. Under *Illinois v. Gates*, a warrant based on an informant's information is measured, on the issue of probable cause, in the same way as warrants based on other sources (e.g., direct observation by a police officer). Deer would argue that even this broad standard was *not* satisfied: Sue's affidavit did not describe (1) the basis for her statement that the informant was reliable (i.e., had the informant given accurate information to the police in the past or had he personally been witness to Deer's conduct?); (2) how the stolen property came into Deer's possession (did Deer "knowingly" have possession?); or (3) what items constituted the stolen property (guns, jewels, etc.).

The prosecution would make several arguments in reply. First, no arrest warrant is necessary when (1) the defendant is not taken into custody within his home, and (2) there is probable cause to believe that the defendant has committed a felony. Because the possession of stolen firearms constitutes a felony, the prosecution would argue that the arrest was proper in that (1) the probable cause element was satisfied by Abby's statement to Sue that she had actually seen the stolen pistols only a few hours earlier, and (2) the arrest occurred **on the sidewalk**, not in Deer's home. Deer could respond that, because he was just outside his residence and performing a function related to the home, he should be considered to have been within his house. The prosecution probably would prevail. And, because the police may search a suspect's outer clothing incident to a valid arrest, the pistol found in Deer's jacket would be admissible. *See Chimel v. California*. Thus, even in the absence of a valid warrant, Deer's arrest was proper.

Second, assuming that Deer prevailed on the invalid-warrant issue, the prosecution could argue that Sue acted reasonably and in good faith in relying on the warrant (even if probable cause did not exist). *See United States v. Leon*. However, Deer probably would respond that the basis for Sue's affidavit (i.e., a "reliable" informant's report that Deer had possession of stolen property) was so obviously conclusory that no reasonable police officer would have relied on it. However, because Abby, a police officer, was Sue's "informant" and because Sue herself had prepared the affidavit, Sue probably was justified in relying on the warrant despite any possible deficiency in its form.

Therefore, under either prosecution argument (i.e., no warrant was necessary under the circumstances, or there was reasonable reliance on the warrant), the gun seized from Deer's jacket pocket is probably admissible.

Are the 11 guns in Deer's trunk admissible?

Even if Deer's arrest was valid, he would contend that the pistols found in his trunk were unlawfully seized because (1) Sue did not have a warrant to search the car; and (2) the location of the pistols was obtained as a consequence of an illegal interrogation (i.e., Sue induced Deer to disclose the location by offering to drop the federal charges, pressure that caused Deer to abandon his request for an attorney and violated his *Miranda* rights).

However, the prosecution could offer several arguments in rebuttal. First, it will argue that the search was incident to a valid arrest. *Thornton v. United States; New York v. Belton.* Although the *Belton* case authorized warrantless searches limited to the passenger compartment, later cases have arguably extended the incident-to-arrest principle to other sections of the car. *See United States v. Ross.* Deer's temporal and spatial distance from the car, however, casts doubt on this theory. Second, and more persuasively, where probable cause exists to believe that contraband or evidence of crime will be found in a vehicle that is temporarily at rest on a public highway (Deer's car was parked *across the street* from his home), the police may make a warrantless search that is co-extensive with the search that might have been authorized by a judicial magistrate. *See Ross.* Based on Abby's statement to Sue that she had actually seen the stolen army pistols in the trunk of Deer's car just four hours earlier, probable cause to search that area would appear to have existed. Thus, the warrantless search of that area was proper. The fact that the trunk was not opened until the day after Deer's car was towed back to the station house is insignificant.

Third, the prosecution might argue that even if the discovery of the guns was the fruit of an illegal interrogation, the illegality should be ignored under the "inevitable discovery" exception. *See Nix v. Williams.* Under this exception, the guns would inevitably have been discovered; a valid search warrant (based on Abby's observation) would ultimately have been issued and executed. Deer will argue, however, that it was not likely that a search warrant for the car would be obtained—four hours had passed since Abby saw the pistols and no warrant had been sought. But the prosecution may win on this point by arguing that it was more important for officers to focus first on arresting Deer (to prevent him from removing any of the pistols) than to seize the guns.

Finally, the prosecution will assert that the requirement of a search warrant did not apply to the search of the trunk because "exigent circumstances" existed. That is, if the guns were not seized immediately after the arrest, they would be disposed of and used to take innocent lives. But, given the fact that (1) there was sufficient time to obtain an arrest warrant, and (2) Deer was in custody, this argument probably would *not* be successful.

In sum, because the prosecution probably would prevail on at least one of its arguments, the guns in Deer's trunk are likely to be admissible.

Is Deer's statement admissible?

Deer will contend that his statement to Sue about the location of the guns was inadmissible as a violation of his *Miranda* rights. Once a suspect says he wants a lawyer, the police cannot question him until they provide one, unless the suspect himself initiates further communication. *See Edwards v. Arizona.* This is a "bright-line" rule that has few, if any, exceptions.

The only possible rebuttal that the prosecution could make is that "exigent circumstances" existed justifying Sue's pressure on Deer: Failure to confiscate the weapons immediately might have resulted in their transfer to persons who would use them to rob and murder. *See, e.g., New York v. Quarles.* However, the "exigent circumstances" exception to *Miranda* generally has been limited to situations in which the danger to the public is immediate, which was not the case here. Deer's statement to Sue as to the location of the 11 guns should probably be suppressed.

Is the notebook admissible?

Whether the notebook is admissible probably will turn upon whether police were entitled to search the car's trunk without a warrant. (See discussion above.) If they were not, the notebook would be inadmissible. If they were, they would be allowed to examine anything that might constitute evidence (or contain evidence) of the crime they were investigating. Since the crime was possession of stolen guns, the police could reasonably have believed that the notebooks might contain evidence relating to the purchase of stolen guns. This possibility justified them in opening the notebook. Once they saw the serial numbers in the notebook, they were justified in impounding the notebook.

Answer to Question 5

Was the walk-through of the barn by Deputy Carr an unreasonable search?

Denise can contend that Carr's walk-through of the barn (presumably for the purpose of detecting evidence pertaining to the source of the fire) was an unreasonable search because it was done without a warrant. Denise would argue that "but for" this action by Carr, she would not have been stopped, and consequently her admission would not have occurred.

The prosecution can assert in rebuttal that (1) Denise has no standing (i.e., a reasonable expectation of privacy in the area searched) because she had leased the barn to Tenant; and (2) exigent circumstances to inspect existed (i.e., unless a walk-through was performed relatively quickly, the smell of gasoline, which is often used to start fires, might dissipate in the night air). Also, an immediate post-fire inspection was justified as an administrative or regulatory search or because of the exigency of the fire itself. *See, e.g., Michigan v. Tyler.* Since the prosecution probably would be successful with respect to at least one of these arguments, Carr's conduct (and the evidence derived from it) was proper.

Did Carr have the right to stop Denise and ask her to get out of her vehicle?

Denise can next contend that Carr had no right to stop her since she was not driving illegally. If Denise had not been stopped by Carr, none of the evidence implicating Denise would have been discovered; the evidence was therefore the "fruit of a poisonous tree."

The prosecution will argue in rebuttal that Carr's initial act in stopping Denise as part of the checkpoint was not an unlawful detention. She was flagged down in connection with an important ongoing criminal investigation—a legitimate and reasonable police procedure—rather than for questioning with respect to her own culpability. Although the timing of Carr's checkpoint may provide some room for Denise's argument, the Supreme Court has approved of this kind of information-gathering checkpoint. *See Illinois v. Lidster.*

Denise can also claim that even if Carr had the right to pull her over, he did not have the right to order her out of her car. She will point out that while a person who is stopped for a traffic violation may be requested to leave her car (*see Pennsylvania v. Mimms*), she herself had been driving in a lawful manner and, thus, could not be ordered to get out of the car. If Denise can convince the court on this point, she probably can exclude the evidence of the gas can and perhaps her confession. The gas can probably would never have come to light if Denise had not been ordered out of the car, and the discovery of the can (and the later confession stemming from that discovery) would be illegal fruit resulting from the unlawful order to exit the car.

But the prosecution has a convincing response to these arguments. Once Carr saw Denise making two furtive movements toward the floor of the driver's seat, Carr had a reasonable suspicion that Denise was armed or was attempting to conceal some element of criminal activity. At that moment, he had the right to investigate further—by having Denise get out of the car—even though the initial stop was to seek help with his investigation rather than because of Denise's wrongdoing.

The prosecution probably would prevail on these issues relating to the stopping of Denise's car and Carr's order that she exit the car.

Did Carr lawfully seize the gasoline can?

Next, Denise can claim that Carr's seizure of her gas can was unlawful in that it occurred without a warrant.

But Denise is unlikely to prevail on this point. Under the **plain view** doctrine, when police observe evidence from a vantage point they have a right to occupy, they may seize items that they have probable cause to believe are indicia of criminal activity. *See, e.g., Horton v. California.* Assuming (as discussed above) that Carr lawfully (1) stopped Denise's vehicle, and (2) ordered her out of it, Carr had probable cause to believe that the gasoline can in Denise's vehicle was connected with the recent fire at the nearby barn (given the gasoline odor he had discovered during this walk-through). On this basis, Carr's seizure of the gasoline can probably was valid.

Is Denise's statement to Carr admissible?

A statement made by a suspect who is in custody in response to interrogation is not admissible unless it is preceded by *Miranda* warnings. Denise can assert that (1) she was in custody (she was ordered to "stay right there"), and (2) Carr's statement was an "interrogation" because it was reasonably likely to elicit an incriminating response by Denise (why else would Carr have made his statement?).

The prosecution will respond that Denise was not in custody. First, roadside questioning after the operator of a vehicle has been stopped for a minor traffic violation does not constitute "custody" for *Miranda* purposes—a reasonable driver who is stopped under these circumstances is not likely to think that she's being restrained. *See, e.g., Berkemer v. McCarty.* Second, Carr's direction included the word "please" (a word seeking cooperation, not a demand). While Denise will continue to argue that a reasonable person in her position would have felt constrained by Carr's statement, the prosecution probably will prevail on this issue. Furthermore, the prosecution will argue that Carr did not "interrogate" Denise for *Miranda* purposes. *See Rhode Island v. Innis.* The prosecution will contend that Carr had no reason to anticipate that Denise would respond in the way she did to a remark that was not directed against her and did not even require a reply.

The prosecution probably will prevail on at least one of its contentions, and Denise's response is probably admissible.

Is Denise's confession at the sheriff's office admissible?

Denise will contend that because her statement to Carr was inadmissible, her subsequent confession at the sheriff's office was also inadmissible. The earlier statement was inculpatory—it indicated that Denise knew that a fire had occurred. This was something she would not be expected to know unless she was involved. Having blurted out her reply to Carr—Denise will argue—she assumed that she had already "let the cat out of the bag" and had to respond to questioning by admitting her guilt. Consequently, confession in the sheriff's office was the tainted fruit of her illegally obtained "I didn't burn the barn" statement.

A similar argument was resolved against the accused in *Oregon v. Elstad.* In that case, the Supreme Court refused to treat a later confession as the fruit of an earlier inadmissible confession. Instead, the Court considered whether the later confession was "voluntary" in light of all the circumstances; if it was, then it is admissible, even though it followed an inadmissible confession. Here, the passage of time, the change in location, the proper *Miranda* warnings, and the absence of police trickery, taken together, suggest that the later confession was voluntary and wasn't an outgrowth of the earlier (assumedly illegally obtained) statement. Therefore, Denise probably will lose on her "cat out of the bag" argument.

Answer to Question 6

Was the surveillance of Adam's apartment house by Randall a "search" within the Fourth Amendment?

Adam will contend that the surveillance constituted a "search" of his home and required a warrant. Because Randall had no warrant, any evidence she obtained would be inadmissible against Adam.

Under the Fourth Amendment (applicable to the states via the Fourteenth Amendment), an individual has no right to object to the search of an area in which he does not have a reasonable expectation of privacy. Adam will contend that the lobby of his apartment house was an extension of his own apartment and that he had a reasonable expectation of privacy while in the apartment house lobby. We may assume that the apartment lobby had no security that prevented access to nonresidents because Randall apparently was able to gain easy access. Adam's argument probably will fail. Even if the lobby was inaccessible to nonresidents, the fact that other residents of the apartment house would have free access to the lobby substantially diminishes Adam's expectation of privacy in the lobby. Thus, the surveillance of Adam in the lobby was lawful.

Was Adam's arrest valid?

Consistent with the Fourth Amendment, an individual may be arrested without a warrant outside his home when the arresting officer has probable cause to believe that the individual is committing or has committed a crime.

But because Adam was arrested for possession of heroin and for being a narcotics addict (rather than for being under the influence of a narcotic), he can argue that probable cause did not exist for the arrest that actually occurred. A person under the influence of a particular drug at a particular time is not necessarily either (a) "in possession of heroin" or (b) "addicted" to the use of a narcotic. While the prosecution can reply that one who is under the influence of a particular drug probably has that substance on his person or is addicted to it (especially in light of the informant's finding that Adam had a huge supply of heroin in his possession in the apartment), Adam probably would prevail on this issue. Briefly observing someone who appears to be under the influence (even an individual who has a prior history of drug-related arrests) probably would *not* constitute adequate probable cause to arrest. On this theory, because all the evidence against Adam was derived from an arrest that would be considered illegal, the evidence is inadmissible.

Because the Court may reject our conclusions, however, we will discuss all of the other issues raised by these facts.

Was the search of Adam's apartment valid?

Pursuant to a *valid* arrest, police officers may search the suspect (whether or not the officers actually fear for their safety or believe that evidence of a crime will be found). *See, e.g., United States v. Robinson.* Assuming Adam's arrest was proper, the resulting discovery of a key to his apartment was also valid.

Adam will contend that the search of his apartment was nevertheless improper. Under the Fourth Amendment, a warrantless search and seizure of an individual's residence is generally unlawful (exceptions to the rule do exist). The only exception that would be plausible on these facts is the "exigent circumstances" exception. The prosecution will argue that exigent circumstances were present (i.e., unless Adam's apartment was searched, he would use his right to make a telephone call after his arrest to advise others to destroy or move the heroin), but this argument probably will fail. The prosecution would have to show a stronger basis for believing that the evidence would be destroyed or removed.

Are the forensic technician's reports admissible against Adam?

Adam will claim that the forcible extraction of his blood in effect compelled him to furnish evidence against himself, in violation of the Fifth Amendment's prohibition against compulsory self-incrimination. However, the Fifth Amendment (applicable to the states via the Fourteenth Amendment) bars only testimonial communications; blood samples obtained by means of an **involuntary blood test** are **not** protected. *See Schmerber v. California.* The facts here are analogous to those of *Schmerber.* Therefore, the fact that the blood test was involuntary will not, in and of itself, be a bar to the use of the results as evidence against Adam.

Adam will also argue that the extraction of his blood violated his Fourth Amendment right to be free of "unreasonable" searches and seizure because the intrusion was severe and the government did not have a compelling need for the evidence.

But this assertion probably will fail because (1) the medical procedure involved is well established and can be (and was) accomplished in complete safety, and (2) the intrusion into Adam's body was minimal and relatively painless. *See, e.g., Winston v. Lee* (discussing the use of a balancing test to determine the reasonableness of the intrusion).

Adam will also claim that the admission of both the blood test and the chemical analysis violated his Sixth Amendment right to confront witnesses against him. He will argue that the forensic reports are testimonial evidence and that their admission requires both the witness's (the technician who prepared the reports) unavailability and the defendant's prior opportunity to cross-examine the witness. *See Bullcoming v. New Mexico* (blood test report); *Melendez-Diaz v. Massachusetts* (forensic drug analysis). Because the forensic technician was not made available at trial, and given that Adam had no prior opportunity to cross-examine, the results of the blood test and the chemical analysis would likely not be admissible against him.

Thus, assuming Adam's arrest was proper, the results of the blood test probably would be admissible against him.

Was Adam entitled to counsel at the preliminary hearing?

Once an individual has been charged with a crime, he is entitled to the assistance of counsel at every "critical stage" (any context in which substantial rights of the accused may be affected) thereafter. Since the purpose of the preliminary hearing was to test the sufficiency of the state's evidence, the hearing probably was a "critical stage" of the proceedings. If so, Adam was entitled to have counsel appointed for him. *See, e.g., Coleman v. Alabama.*

Was Adam deprived of his right to effective counsel?

Under the Sixth Amendment (applicable to the states via the Fourteenth Amendment), a person charged with a crime has a right to "effective" representation. To succeed with an ineffective representation claim, the accused must show that (1) his counsel's performance fell below an objective standard of reasonable representation; and (2) "but for" such unprofessional conduct, there is a "reasonable probability" that the result of the proceedings would have been different. *See, e.g., Strickland v. Washington.* Since, as discussed above, there are numerous arguments upon which the prosecution's case could reasonably and effectively have been attacked, the failure by Adam's counsel to raise any issues on appeal probably violated Adam's Sixth Amendment right to effective counsel.

Does Adam's conviction for heroin addiction violate the Eighth Amendment?

Adam will claim that his conviction for addiction to the use of a narcotic violated the Eighth Amendment prohibition on cruel and unusual punishment, applicable to the states via the Fourteenth Amendment. He will claim that the facts show no reasonable basis upon which to conclude that he was addicted.

It is well established that the imposition of criminal penalties for "status" (rather than for commission of a specific criminal act) violates the Eighth Amendment. *See, e.g., Robinson v. California.* Because addiction is a status or condition rather than a specific action, Adam probably will succeed with this claim. As a result, his conviction for addiction will be overturned.

Answer to Question 7

Are Dan's statements to the plainclothes detective admissible?

Dan will argue that the admission of his tape-recorded statement to Norma violated his Fifth Amendment right against self-incrimination (because he received no *Miranda* warnings), his Sixth Amendment right to counsel, and his Fourteenth Amendment right to due process. However, Dan probably will lose on each point.

No Fifth Amendment violation occurred by reason of the detective's failure to give Dan *Miranda* warnings because Dan was not in custody at the time the questioning took place. A reasonable person in Dan's position would have believed himself to be free to leave at any time during the discussion with the plainclothes officer, especially since Dan didn't even suspect that he was talking to a police officer. On these facts, custody did not exist when Dan's statements were made and recorded.

The right to counsel is triggered only by the institution of formal proceedings against a defendant. Therefore, no Sixth Amendment violation occurred here because Dan had not been formally charged with a crime when his statements to the detective were made.

Finally, enticing Dan into a discussion about his crime did not violate his due process rights. Norma's conduct would not be viewed as the type of governmental overreaching that "shocks the conscience." Dan assumed the risk that the person he was speaking with might spread his statements to others.

Norma's testimony and the tape-recorded conversation between Norma and Dan (assuming it complied with any applicable state law on surreptitious recordings) would be admissible against Dan.

Was Dan's arrest valid?

Dan can claim that his arrest was invalid and that the statement he blurted out was, therefore, the fruit of the poisonous tree (the arrest). This claim would be supported by the argument that an arrest warrant was required and that the police lacked probable cause to arrest Dan.

Assuming the police officers who took Dan into custody did not have an arrest warrant, whether Dan's arrest was valid depends upon where it occurred. The facts are silent here. If Dan was arrested in his home, a warrant was required unless the officers had reason to believe exigent circumstances existed (e.g., Dan was about to flee the state). If Dan was not arrested in his residence, no warrant was required because bank robbery is a felony.

Whether or not a warrant was required, the police were required to have probable cause at the time they arrested Dan. That is, they were required to be aware of facts that made it more probable than not that Dan had committed the crime at issue. Because Dan had (1) been identified to the police as the likely killer and (2) made incriminating statements to the detective posing as a door-to-door salesperson, the "probable cause" test appears to be satisfied. Therefore, the arrest probably was valid.

If the arrest is found to have been invalid, the "fruit of the poisonous tree" doctrine probably would make the blurted-out confession inadmissible. The connection between the arrest and the confession was close in time and there was no significant intervening event to break the chain of causation (i.e., to "purge the taint"). *See, e.g., Taylor v. Alabama.*

Was the statement Dan blurted out admissible?

Dan will also argue that his statement, "I didn't mean to kill him," should be inadmissible because he had not been given *Miranda* warnings before he made the statement. The prosecution probably will reply successfully that (1) no interrogation had occurred, and (2) Dan's statement was voluntary. Therefore, the lack of *Miranda* warnings would not be fatal, and Dan's statement (assuming the arrest was proper) would be admissible.

Was the prosecutor's comment during his closing statement improper?

The prosecutor may not undermine the exercise of an accused's Fifth Amendment privilege (applicable to the states via the Fourteenth Amendment) by commenting upon the accused's refusal to testify. *See Griffin v. California.* The prosecutor's behavior was clearly improper. But the prosecution will argue that the comment should be tested under the "harmless error" standard (i.e., the error was harmless because it did not contribute to Dan's conviction). *See Chapman v. California.* The prosecution will point to the volume of direct evidence against Dan—particularly his own taped admission—and argue that in light of that evidence the jury probably attached little weight to the prosecutor's improper comments on Dan's refusal to testify. On these facts, the "harmless error" standard may be satisfied. Although a close issue, reversal of the verdict against Dan is unlikely.

Answer to Question 8

Was the stop of Don's car proper?

A warrantless vehicle stop is tested by the standard for a "stop and frisk" enunciated in *Terry v. Ohio*. Under that standard, the police need have only a reasonable suspicion, based on objective, articulable facts, that criminal activity may be afoot. In other words, something less than probable cause is required. The prosecution will contend that this standard was satisfied: (1) Don fit the description of the heroin smuggler reported to the police chief, and (2) Don drove through the town within the time frame (the next week) contained in the report.

Even if we assume that the information reported to the police chief originated in a reliable source (i.e., one known for accurate information about criminal activities in the past), it's unlikely that the vague description here would constitute a "reasonable suspicion" that Don himself was engaged in criminal activity. Because the town was located near an interstate freeway, numerous out-of-state vehicles would be likely to pass through it. If the "reasonable suspicion" standard was not satisfied—the probable result on these facts—the stop was a violation of Don's Fourth Amendment rights. Therefore, all of the evidence derived from the illegal stop (i.e., Don's driver's license, the illegal pills, and the marijuana) would be inadmissible as "fruits of the poisonous tree."

On the assumption, however, that our conclusions will be rejected by the Court, we will discuss the other issues that can arise under these facts.

Was the request to see Don's driver's license proper?

Assuming Jones had a reasonable suspicion to stop Don, Don will contend that Jones had no right to request his driver's license. However, when the police make a valid auto stop, they are always free to verify that the driver is licensed. Therefore, Don will almost certainly lose on this issue, and the resulting arrest of Don for violation of the license statute will not be thrown out.

Was the warrantless arrest of Don valid?

An arrest outside the suspect's home, even for a misdemeanor (presumably driving without a proper driver's license would be a misdemeanor rather than a felony), may be made without a warrant when probable cause exists (this result being consistent with the Fourth Amendment). As such, the lack of an arrest warrant would not invalidate Don's arrest.

Don will contend his equal protection rights were violated. He will argue that Jones's insistence on placing him under arrest (instead of merely issuing a citation) constituted unlawful, selective enforcement. But to assert this theory successfully, a defendant must show that (1) the defendant was, in fact, selected for prosecution while others who were similarly situated were not; and (2) the determination to prosecute the defendant was arbitrary or unreasonable. Although Don apparently can show that drivers who lived in the town were merely cited, the decision to imprison (at least until bail could be obtained) out-of-town drivers probably would not be unreasonable. Out-of-town drivers would be less likely to appear for trial or sentencing. Also, presumably, fines would be more difficult to collect (i.e., out-of-state personnel might be needed to pursue collection). If the stop and the request to see Don's driver's license were valid, then Jones's decision to arrest (as opposed to merely cite) Don probably was proper also. *Cf. Atwater v. City of Lago Vista.*

Was the "pat-down" of Don proper and the evidence derived therefrom admissible?

When the police make a valid **arrest** (even for a misdemeanor), they may search the suspect incident to that arrest. *See, e.g., United States v. Robinson.* Therefore, if the arrest was valid, the pills taken from Don were properly seized.

Even if the arrest was invalid (e.g., suppose Don won on the "selective enforcement" argument), the prosecution could argue that Jones still had grounds for a *Terry* "stop" of Don's car, the pat-down of Don, and the subsequent search of Don's pocket and seizure of the pills under the "stop-and-frisk" doctrine. But when the police conduct a pat-down in a stop-and-frisk situation, they are permitted to check only for weapons, not for contraband. An officer may nevertheless seize nonthreatening contraband discovered during a pat-down authorized by *Terry* as long as the officer does not exceed the proper bounds of that pat-down. *See, e.g., Minnesota v. Dickerson.* When Jones conducted the pat-down, he discovered something small and round. Based on the facts, Jones could not have thought it was a weapon and could not have immediately concluded it was contraband. Many legitimate things—such as over-the-counter vitamins or breath mints—could have been in the vial. In fact, the pills at issue could have been possessed legally if Don had a prescription. In short, Jones could not have immediately concluded that the vial contained contraband during the lawful *Terry* pat-down. For this reason, Jones probably did not have the right to reach into Don's pocket and did not have probable cause to seize the pills. The facts are similar to those in *Dickerson, supra*, where the seizure of the contraband was found to be unlawful.

Is Don's statement that he did not have a prescription for the pills admissible against him?

Don can argue that he was entitled to *Miranda* warnings before he admitted that he didn't have a prescription for the pills. Don was entitled to *Miranda* warnings if Jones was conducting a *custodial* interrogation. Because Don had already been placed under arrest when Jones asked his question about a prescription, the inquiry probably would be considered custodial. If Jones neglected to give Don his *Miranda* warnings before he asked the question, Don's response would be inadmissible.

Did Don consent to a search of his car's interior?

The prosecution will contend that Don voluntarily gave permission to search the car. The prosecution will argue that in *Schneckloth v. Bustamonte*, permission by the occupants of a car to search the vehicle after a stop for a minor traffic violation was deemed to be voluntary. Don will argue that in *Schneckloth*, the occupants had not been arrested and a congenial atmosphere existed between them and the officer who had detained them. Here, by contrast, Don had already been arrested. But Don probably will lose on this point—most consent searches following arrest have been upheld, as long as the police didn't assert or imply that they had a right to make the search. If, however, the previous arrest or detention was unlawful, the subsequent consent to search will ordinarily be invalid. *See, e.g., Florida v. Royer* (plurality opinion).

Was the search of the vehicle's interior valid (even if Don did not consent to it)?

If Don was properly arrested, the search of the vehicle's interior was legal as incident to arrest. *See New York v. Belton*. Therefore, so long as the arrest was valid, the search was valid, even if Don's "consent" is found not to have been voluntarily given.

What is the effect of the state X constitutional provision?

States may give greater procedural protection to persons accused of a crime than the protection required by the U.S. Constitution. It's possible—as is sometimes but not always the case—that state X's version of the Fourth Amendment has been interpreted by state X courts to require stricter police conduct than the conduct required by the U.S. Constitution as interpreted by the U.S. Supreme Court. If so, Don can assert these decisions to preclude evidence that might otherwise be introduced against him.

Answer to Question 9

1. The gun taken from Mike's pocket:

Donna will argue initially that because the police did not have a search warrant for the gun, it is not admissible against her.

The prosecution will reply that Donna **lacks standing** to contest the discovery of her gun (i.e., a suspect must have a reasonable expectation of privacy in the area intruded upon to object to a warrantless search). Because (1) Donna had dropped the gun on a public street, and (2) the gun was obtained from the clothing of another individual, Donna probably has no standing to object to seizure of the gun. *See, e.g., Rawlings v. Kentucky; Rakas v. Illinois.*

It may be, however, that this jurisdiction (under the state constitution or an applicable law) gives an accused standing to object to any unlawful police conduct. In that case, Donna will contend that Mike's hesitation in responding to the officer's question did not reasonably create sufficient suspicion to cause him to order Mike out of the vehicle. A driver may be ordered out of a vehicle even for a minor traffic violation. *See Pennsylvania v. Mimms.* Furthermore, the prosecution will argue that, given the matching color of Mike's car and his hesitation and unusual nervousness in answering a relatively straightforward question, the police officer was reasonable in his suspicion that Mike was involved in the shooting. The prosecution probably would prevail on this issue.

Finally, Donna will contend that since Mike had not yet been arrested, the officer had no right to reach into Mike's pocket and seize the gun. But a warrantless frisk of a suspect's outer clothing may be made when the officer has reason to believe the suspect may be carrying a weapon. The officer had observed the bulge in Mike's pocket. Given the violence with which the crime had been committed (i.e., use of a gun and then of a motor vehicle as homicidal weapons), the officer's actions were lawful if he reasonably believed the bulge was a weapon (as opposed to, say, contraband). Thus, even if Donna had standing to contest the police seizure of her gun from Mike's pocket, the firearm probably would be admissible against Donna.

2. The Shorecliff envelope and its contents:

As with the gun taken from Mike's pocket, Donna would have to show that she has standing to oppose the admission of the evidence found in Mike's car. Because Donna has no justifiable expectation of privacy with respect to Mike's car or its contents, she probably lacks standing, and the evidence will be admitted, even if it was seized in violation of Mike's rights.

Even if Donna is found to have standing to contest the search of Mike's car, the prosecution can still assert that the search was proper because the interior of a vehicle may be searched in the course of a valid, full custodial arrest of its occupants. *See, e.g., New York v. Belton.* The fact that the vehicle was towed back to the police station before the search actually occurred would be immaterial. *See, e.g., United States v. Johns.*

Thus, the Shorecliff envelope and its contents probably will be admissible against Donna, even though they were obtained without a warrant.

3. *Mike's statement:*
Mike's statement to the police cannot be introduced against Donna. It would be a violation of Donna's confrontation right. *See, e.g., Crawford v. Washington.* However, Mike can—and apparently will—testify at Donna's trial about Donna's involvement in the crime. Donna's attorney will then have the ability to cross-examine Mike on the witness stand before the jury.

4. *Donna's admission:*
Once an accused requests counsel, all questioning must cease until she is provided with an attorney. *See, e.g., Edwards v. Arizona.* Questioning may proceed only if the suspect (1) *initiates conversations* with the officers interrogating her and (2) makes a "knowing and intelligent *waiver* of the right to counsel." *See Oregon v. Bradshaw.* There is no indication that these conditions were satisfied here. Thus, Donna's statement is inadmissible.

Answer to Question 10

Issues Pertaining to Dee and Jay

Dee and Jay would first challenge the officers' entry into their apartment. Any such entry into a home must be supported by probable cause and ordinarily conducted pursuant to a judicially approved warrant. Probable cause exists where facts and circumstances known to the officer, and of which they have a trustworthy belief, would support a reasonable person's conclusion that the home may contain evidence of or actors involved in criminal activity. Officers possessing probable cause may only dispense with the warrant process if the search falls within the scope of one of several specifically delineated exceptions to the warrant requirement.

Dee and Jay would likely argue that the officers' entry was made without probable cause because they had no information whatsoever regarding the activities taking place inside the apartment. Even though the officers may have had reason to chase Henry, they had at best a 50/50 chance of guessing which apartment he may have entered. The State will likely counter by arguing that probable cause, as a flexible assessment of the totality of the circumstances, does not require absolute certainty or perfect accuracy of law enforcement actors. Probable cause is meant to measure probabilities, and officers who possess sufficient information to justify their probable cause determination do not violate the Fourth Amendment if their otherwise reasonable judgment turns out to be incorrect. Here, the officers had abundant cause to pursue Henry for arrest, and it was reasonable for them to believe that he had just run into one of two apartment units.

The ultimate determination with respect to probable cause will likely turn on the court's assessment of Officer Louis's "hunch." Depending on the testimony adduced at trial, the hunch may appear to have been no more than a blind guess, or it may have been a careful, reasoned and informed calculation. The reasonableness of this determination will largely answer the initial probable cause issue.

Even if the officers lacked probable cause upon selecting the left door, the level of suspicion may have increased after the police knocked and identified themselves. When the officers heard the hushed voices and shuffling sounds inside the apartment, they may reasonably have understood the occupants to be actively trying to hide someone or something. Together with the circumstances that brought them to the door in the first place, these facts will likely amount to probable cause.

Assuming the officers had probable cause sufficient to justify their entry, Dee and Jay may still argue that the officers' entry was not supported by a warrant and was therefore unreasonable. While the law continues to recognize the presumption in favor of the warrant requirement, it has also developed numerous exceptions that excuse noncompliance with that requirement under a variety of circumstances.

The government might invoke the "hot pursuit" doctrine, which allows officers to make a warrantless entry into a home if they are actively chasing a fleeing felon. *Warden v. Hayden.* Here, Henry had just engaged in an illegal firearm transaction with undercover agents and was being actively pursued into the building. However, the officers admitted that they lost sight of Henry in the hallway and did not know which of the two apartments he had entered during this flight. The hot pursuit doctrine would appear to support an officer's decision to enter a home in order to effectuate the arrest of a fleeing felon without first getting a warrant, but it does not similarly bear on the question of whether a warrantless entry is permitted when there is uncertainty as to whether the felon has retreated into the home to be searched.

The government may additionally invoke the "exigent circumstances" doctrine, which creates an exception to the warrant requirement where overriding law enforcement justifications—such as officer safety, the prevention of escape, or the loss of evidence—make time of the essence and the warrantless entry necessary. The officers in this case heard furtive movements and efforts to conceal activities inside the apartment as soon as they identified themselves. This undoubtedly raised a reasonable concern in the officers' mind that either an offender or evidence might be lost if they did not enter immediately.

Dee and Jay will likely argue that any exigency here was created by the officers' conduct, and that they should not be permitted to "manufacture" the circumstances that would justify such an exceptional intrusion into their home. Dee and Jay will argue that a contrary rule would permit police officers to knock on random doors and then listen for suspicious responses, thereby creating suspicion and exigent circumstances where otherwise none exists.

The court will likely reject this argument and allow the government the benefit of the exigent circumstances doctrine. In *Kentucky v. King*, the Supreme Court determined that, where officers do not create the circumstances that justify a warrantless entry through actual or threatened Fourth Amendment violations, the fact that their presence or actions may have precipitated the behaviors that contribute to the urgency does not undermine their decision to enter. In this case, the officers were surely entitled to knock on the door and identify themselves. Dee and Jay were not obligated to respond, but when they did respond by engaging in suspicious activity, they created a constitutional basis for the officers to force their way in.

Once inside the apartment, the officers observed behavior and circumstances readily suggesting that underage drinking was occurring in the presence of the two adults. It may be unclear whether Officer Louis had reasonable suspicion necessary to conduct pat-down searches of the subjects, but no suppressible evidence was discovered as a result. Because a suspect's identity is never subject to suppression, it does not matter whether it may have been discovered in the course of an unlawful search. *INS v. Lopez Mendoza.*

Issues Pertaining to Otis

Because the officers arrived at Otis's door under the same circumstances that brought them to Dee and Jay's apartment, the same probable cause analysis will generally apply. The distinguishing factor about the officers' suspicion regarding Otis's apartment is that they had just eliminated the first apartment as the one that Henry might have retreated into. This fact increased the apparent likelihood that Henry would be found within, and should satisfy a court as to the threshold probable cause requirement.

The next question is whether the officers were entitled to enter without a warrant. Again, as in Dee and Jay's case, the government may successfully invoke either the hot pursuit doctrine or the exigent circumstances doctrine. With respect to the latter, the apparent exigency may have increased to the extent that officers had reason to believe that the occupants of the second apartment might already be alert to their presence.

The overriding issue is whether Otis's arrest for possession of the illegal videos was valid. If so, then the search that revealed the cocaine in the desk might have been justified as a valid search incident to his arrest. The search incident to arrest doctrine authorizes Officers to search the person of an arrestee, and the area within his immediate control, contemporaneously with a lawful custodial arrest. The cocaine was discovered in the top drawer of the desk at which Otis was sitting. This space was actually and constructively well within Otis's "wingspan" and thus within the scope of the search that is categorically permitted upon arrest. It will be admissible if Otis was properly taken into custody.

While officers had abundant probable cause to suspect Otis of illegal video possession, the statute that defined the crime has since been invalidated. This would necessarily prevent his prosecution and conviction under the statute, and Otis would argue that this change in law destroys the basis for his arrest. If the arrest was not lawful because the activity for which he is arrested is not a crime, Otis would argue that the subsequent search incident to that arrest was also unlawful and that the cocaine should be excluded from evidence.

The government would argue that the officers relied on the existence of the statute reasonably and in absolute good-faith. They had no reason to know, at the time of the arrest, that the legality of the statute they were enforcing would be challenged or that the Supreme Court would ultimately strike it down. This argument should prevail. An officer's good faith reliance on a law or legal opinion that was valid at the time of a search—or arrest—and supported by probable cause is not otherwise unconstitutional even if the underlying law or legal opinion on which the officer relies is later rejected. *Davis v. United States.*

Answer to Question 11

1. Issues Dave can raise on appeal:

Was Dave's Sixth Amendment right to effective counsel (applicable to the states via the Fourteenth Amendment) violated?

Dave will certainly make an "effective assistance of counsel" claim. This claim is not easy to establish. To succeed, the accused must show that (1) his attorney's performance fell below the reasonable norm of competence for attorneys in the area generally; and (2) "but for" the lawyer's lack of professionalism, there is a reasonable possibility the results of the proceedings would have been different. *See Strickland v. Washington.*

Dave will argue that his lawyer did not meet this standard for the following reasons: (1) the lawyer failed to conduct his own investigation to determine whether there were other witnesses than Witt; (2) he failed to question Witt to determine the extent of Witt's knowledge (if he had done this, he would have learned that Witt was not a witness to the shootings, but only to Dave's presence in the bar and to his drunkenness; (3) he apparently failed to make a formal request to the prosecution for *any* evidence that might be helpful to his client's case and for specific types of evidence (*see Brady v. Maryland*); and (4) he failed to argue the *Miranda* issue raised by the introduction of Officer Leslie's testimony (discussed below).

The prosecution will reply that Dave's attorney did not act unreasonably in accepting its statement that Witt was the only witness to the shooting and that Witt would testify that Dave was sober at the time. It will also argue that Dave's attorney could reasonably have concluded that the court was not likely to accept any arguments based on the *Miranda* rule on these facts.

Dave may succeed on the issue of lawyer incompetence (although the direct *Brady* claim, discussed below, is probably stronger). Most significantly, his lawyer failed to even attempt to interview Witt. If he had interviewed Witt, he would have learned that Witt was not a witness to the shooting and that Witt would testify that Dave was quite drunk, not sober.

Were Dave's due process rights violated by the prosecution's failure to advise Dave's attorney of Witt?

As we have seen, an accused's attorney has the due process right under *Brady* to request and obtain from the prosecution any evidence that is material and favorable to his client. Dave will contend that because the prosecution failed to inform Dave's attorney of the true substance of Witt's testimony, reversal is required. *See, e.g., United States v. Bagley.*

Although the prosecution did disclose that Witt was a witness, it had the affirmative duty to disclose not only the names of witnesses but also the *substance* of their testimony, if exculpatory. The prosecution failed to do that here. Thus, the *Brady* claim has a good chance of success.

Was the jury properly instructed with respect to whether Dave had attempted to perpetrate a robbery?

Under the Due Process Clause of the Fourteenth Amendment, if a jury in a criminal trial is improperly instructed on a material issue of law, the conviction must be reversed. Dave's conviction for first-degree murder required one of two critical premises: either (1) he intended to kill or seriously injure Babs, or (2) the killing occurred in the commission of a robbery. Dave's *mens rea* would be critical in determining whether either premise was satisfied. The prosecution would have to show a specific intent either (1) to kill (or seriously injure) Babs, or (2) to commit a robbery (i.e., permanently deprive Babs of property by force or the threat of force). In light of these factors, the court's instruction was incorrect because (1) Dave may have been so intoxicated as to make it impossible for him to form the requisite specific intent for first-degree murder, and (2) Babs's state of mind was irrelevant on the issue of Dave's intent.Because the court's instruction probably influenced the jury improperly, Dave's conviction should be reversed.

Was Dave's statement to Officer Leslie admissible?

Dave can argue that Officer Leslie's testimony about his confession to her should not have been admitted. Statements made to police officers during a custodial interrogation are ordinarily inadmissible unless preceded by *Miranda* warnings. Because Officer Leslie entered the bar with her revolver drawn, her question arguably constituted a custodial interrogation (i.e., was reasonably calculated to elicit an incriminating response). The prosecution will reply, however, that (1) Dave was not in custody; (2) Officer Leslie drew her gun only because she had previously heard shots; and (3) Officer Leslie's question was more in the nature of a general, spontaneous, on-the-scene inquiry directed at no one in particular, rather than an attempt to obtain a response from Dave that might implicate him in a crime. The prosecution should prevail on this issue.

Summary:

Because Dave's due process rights were probably violated, reversal of his conviction on appeal would be proper.

2. Can Dave be constitutionally convicted for the murder of John?

The Double Jeopardy Clause of the Fifth Amendment (applicable to the states via the Fourteenth Amendment) prohibits a person from being retried for the same crime after jeopardy has attached. But Dave's conduct with respect to John constitutes a separate and distinct offense from his conduct against Babs, and the mere fact that John was killed in the same incident would not bar retrial.

However, the double jeopardy doctrine also encompasses the doctrine of **collateral estoppel**. But this doctrine applies only when acquittal on one charge *necessarily* demonstrates that the suspect cannot be guilty on the other charge. *See Ashe v. Swenson.* Thus, if Dave were retried for Babs's murder and the jury acquitted Dave after finding that he had become so intoxicated as to be incapable of forming the specific intent to (1) kill, (2) cause serious bodily injury, or (3) perpetrate a robbery, the prosecution would be bound by these findings in a subsequent prosecution of Dave for John's murder.

However, unless we know for certain that the basis for acquittal on the Babs charge was Dave's lack of the requisite "specific intent" (instead, for example, because the jury found that Dave had acted in self-defense against an attack by Babs), we can't say that a trial for John's murder would be inconsistent with the acquittal on the Babs charge. (The valid self-defense claim with respect to Babs wouldn't necessarily compel a finding of self-defense in the trial for John's killing; the facts might be different.) Consequently, collateral estoppel, and thus double jeopardy, may not apply.

Answer to Question 12

1. (a) The state X conviction:

The Fifth Amendment to the Constitution prevents criminal defendants from being tried twice "for the same offense." This generally is called the double jeopardy doctrine and is applicable to the states by means of the Fourteenth Amendment. But arguably, Ashley's conduct with respect to the other tellers constitutes separate and distinct offenses from her conduct against the first teller, and the mere fact that the other tellers were robbed in the same incident would not bar those trials. However, the double jeopardy doctrine also encompasses the doctrine of *collateral estoppel*. But this doctrine applies only when acquittal on one charge necessarily demonstrates that the suspect cannot be guilty on the other charge. *See Ashe v. Swenson.* Here, the facts establish that the first jury acquitted Ashley because they believed her alibi, triggering the doctrine of collateral estoppel. Furthermore, because the facts constituting the alibi would be the same for the first count as for the other two counts, a conviction in the second trial could not logically be sustained. The prosecution is never permitted to appeal a jury acquittal. Similarly, it cannot retry the defendant on the same facts again. Ashley cannot be prosecuted for robbery with respect to the two other tellers. Thus, the state X conviction should be reversed.

(b) The federal sentence:

Under the dual sovereignty doctrine, a conviction or acquittal by one jurisdiction does *not* bar prosecution by *another jurisdiction on the same facts*. Therefore, the federal government can also indict and try Ashley for armed bank robbery, even though the facts presented by the prosecution will be essentially the same as in the state trial. The federal government brings such prosecutions only upon a finding that they will advance compelling federal interests. *See, e.g., Petite v. United States.*

In a criminal jury trial, jeopardy attaches when the jury is sworn in. This fact becomes important when a mistrial occurs. Usually, the prosecution is not prevented from retrying the defendant after a mistrial. But there are circumstances in which a mistrial will preclude a new trial. If the defendant moves for mistrial, the prosecution may always retry. But if the prosecution has been guilty of "overreaching" (i.e., "pushing" or "goading" the defendant to move for a mistrial), a new trial may not be permitted. *See, e.g., Downum v. United States.* Here, the facts don't tell us anything about the reason for the jury discharge. Presumably, the judge was annoyed by the prosecution's request for an adjournment after the jury was sworn. On the other hand, we have the objection to the jury's discharge by the defendant's lawyer. Presumably, the defendant's lawyer would not have objected if he had believed a mistrial would preclude further prosecution.

Generally, if the prosecution asks for a reasonable delay and there is no evidence that its request is designed to get an unfair tactical advantage, it's unlikely that a mistrial will be a bar to a new trial. *Cf. Illinois v. Somerville.*

Was Ashley's guilty plea valid?

A defendant cannot change a guilty plea that was made voluntarily and with knowledge of its consequences. In determining whether this standard is satisfied, the judge must be assured that the defendant is competent and that she understands (1) that she has the right to plead not guilty, (2) that she is waiving the right to a trial by jury, (3) the nature of the charge as to which the plea is offered (i.e., the elements that must be proved for the prosecution to be successful), and (4) the maximum possible penalty for the offense. *See, e.g., McCarthy v. United States.* In federal cases, the judge must engage in a specific colloquy with the defendant describing key aspects of the guilty plea process, and this colloquy must be transcribed on the record. Fed. R. Crim. P. 11. Because the judge merely asked Ashley whether she wanted to change her plea from guilty to not guilty, these requirements were *not* satisfied. Additionally, the facts fail to indicate that Ashley's attorney explained the necessary information to her.

On these facts, the Supreme Court probably would vacate the guilty plea and order that Ashley be retried.

2. Can Ashley be prosecuted under "the Statute"?

Because Ashley was never charged (placed in jeopardy) for shooting and killing Fred, she can be prosecuted under the Statute without invoking double jeopardy.

Ashley can argue that because the robbery of the tellers and the shooting of Fred arose from the same set of actions, they constituted the "same" offense and that prosecution under the Statute is barred by the Double Jeopardy Clause. However, when a second crime can be proved by at least one additional fact that is not present in or common to the first crime, the two crimes are not the "same" for double jeopardy purposes. *See, e.g., Brown v. Ohio.* Here, the Statute requires proof that a federal officer was assaulted while in the pursuit of his duties; the robbery charge required proof of the taking of property from the persons of three other people. The "additional fact" test of *Brown* would appear to be satisfied, and the prosecution is not prevented from trying Ashley under the Statute.

Answer to Question 13

1. Constitutional objections to the admission of Dan's confessions:

A confession obtained during a custodial interrogation before the suspect has received his *Miranda* warnings is ordinarily inadmissible. Dan will argue that the statement by police officers that the gun had been identified as his constituted an "interrogation" (i.e., no statement implicating him in the events should have been made to him before he was given the *Miranda* warnings), and that, therefore, his response was not admissible. Whether the statement constitutes an "interrogation" will depend upon whether the police should have recognized that their conduct was likely to elicit an incriminating response by the defendant. *See, e.g., Rhode Island v. Innis.* While the prosecution will argue that no direct questioning occurred (that Dan "blurted out" his initial confession after being told the simple facts as the police knew them), Dan probably will prevail on this issue.

The police will then insist that even if the initial statement is inadmissible on *Miranda* grounds, the second confession was properly preceded by *Miranda* warnings and, therefore, was valid. Dan would respond that the two confessions cannot be separated from each other because there was not enough of a time gap between them. He would argue that he was influenced by his first pre-*Miranda* response to continue with his admissions, and that the second confession was not truly "voluntary" (i.e., it was tainted by the original confession). But the Supreme Court has held that when a Mirandized second confession follows an un-Mirandized first confession, the second confession will not normally be deemed "tainted fruit" of the first. *Oregon v. Elstad.* Unless the police deliberately question the suspect first, provide *Miranda* warnings "midstream," and then repeat the same interrogation process with the objective of undermining the Fifth Amendment's safeguards, *Missouri v. Seibert*, all that's required is that the second confession be "knowingly and voluntarily made." *Elstad.* Based on the absence of any strategic law enforcement behavior, the second confession likely will be admissible under this standard even if the first is not.

2. Entrapment defense:

The defense of entrapment exists when the police have instigated or induced the crime for which the defendant is charged and the defendant was not predisposed to commit the crime (i.e., the police caused the defendant to perpetrate a crime that he was not otherwise predisposed to commit). This so-called subjective approach reflects the view of the majority of courts. Because Dan had several prior convictions for burglary and larceny, his predisposition to commit another similar crime is manifest. It is unlikely that Dan will succeed in asserting this defense.

A growing minority of courts have held that the defense of entrapment will be recognized when a reasonable person (regardless of his previous disposition) would, under the circumstances, be induced to commit the crime in question because of governmental action. If this jurisdiction subscribed to this so-called objective approach, Dan would argue that the average person, given the opportunity to obtain merchandise with very little risk of apprehension (i.e., an employee of the place to be burglarized had promised and arranged easy access to it), would be tempted to commit the offense. But this argument probably would not work either. While many people arguably might agree to buy or sell stolen merchandise when an apparently risk-free profit could be made, many people probably would not be willing to break into a warehouse in the dark of night.

In sum, Dan probably will not prevail on an entrapment defense.

3. What objections should Betty make to the admission of the stamps?

Betty will contend that the federal officers were required to obtain a search warrant before seizing the stamps from her.

The prosecution will make two arguments in response. There is no expectation of privacy with respect to items voluntarily delivered by one person to another. Therefore, the stamps that were sold by Betty to the federal officer should be admissible against Betty. Second, the stamps in the cabinet were seized incident to a valid arrest (i.e., they were within Betty's immediate control). Betty will reply that items inside (as opposed to those on top of) the display cabinet were *not* within her immediate control at the time of the arrest. The Supreme Court has held that a seizure is not incident to arrest unless the suspect has some opportunity at the time of arrest to get control of the item. *See, e.g., United States v. Chadwick; Arizona v. Gant.* Betty probably will prevail with respect to the stamps in the cabinet.

4. What objections should Betty make to the admission of the gun?

Because the gun was obtained by the police without a warrant, Betty could contend that it is inadmissible. It is well established that a hotelkeeper cannot consent to the search of a room occupied by a guest. *See Stoner v. California.*

But the prosecution will make two arguments in reply. First, Betty has no standing to complain of an unlawful search of her aunt's hotel room (i.e., she had no expectation of privacy with respect to that room). Second, even if we assume that this jurisdiction extends standing to anyone affected by unlawful police conduct, here, a person who was not a police officer—he was a hotel employee—conducted the search (and did so on his own initiative, rather than at the instigation or request of the government). Under these circumstances, the defendant has no constitutional right to object if the nongovernmental employee notifies the government about contraband or other evidence of criminality he may have found. *See, e.g., United States v. Jacobsen.* By the time the police saw the suitcase, they had probable cause (obtained without police violation of Betty's rights) to seize it and to arrest Betty.

Therefore the gun should be admissible against Betty.

Answer to Question 14

Does Joe have standing to object to the introduction of the incriminating books and records found in Eddy's home?

When a defendant has no expectation of privacy with respect to an area searched by the police, he lacks standing to complain about alleged police misconduct within the area. Because all of the possible police misconduct (the observation of the rooms from the roof, the subsequent entry into Eddy's home, and the seizure of gambling paraphernalia) was allegedly a violation of Eddy's rights, not Joe's, the prosecution can contend that Joe has no standing to assert any rights under the Fourth Amendment (applicable to the states via the Fourteenth Amendment). The fact that the books and records of the gambling operation referred to Joe is probably not enough to give him any expectation of privacy with respect to those records. However, a few states grant inherent standing to anyone whose rights are affected by police misconduct, even though the majority view would deny Joe standing. Although it is unlikely that Joe will be given standing, we will discuss the other issues on the assumption that he will.

Was the observation into Eddy's home a search?

Joe will point out that Eddy's windows were nine feet above the ground, creating an expectation of privacy and immunity from observation. That expectation of privacy, therefore, dictated that the police obtain a warrant before observing into the building from a place above the ground. Without a warrant for the observation, all of the evidence derived from it would be inadmissible. But the prosecution will respond that no one can have an expectation of privacy in areas that can be observed by the public. Eddy's neighbor was free to climb onto his own roof and peer into Eddy's window. If the neighbor could do it, then a police officer could do it without violating Eddy's right of privacy (and, by arguable extension, Joe's). Joe will reply that it's unlikely that Eddy's neighbor would climb onto his roof just to look into Eddy's window, and, in fact, it's unlikely that Eddy's neighbor would climb onto the roof himself for *any* purpose. Furthermore, because Able and Baker had to trespass and go through a lot of effort (perhaps an indication that this vantage point was not ordinarily used by the public or the neighbor) just to look in the window, Joe has a decent argument that Eddy had an expectation of privacy in his quarters. Although it may be a close question, Joe would appear to have the better of these arguments and is likely to prevail on this issue.

Was the police entry into Eddy's home valid?

The prosecution will argue that the police officers acted reasonably in ringing Eddy's doorbell to ask a few preliminary investigative questions. They will assert that their brief questioning at the door of the residence—which did not involve detaining Cathy or anyone else—did not rise to the level of a Fourth Amendment "stop." The prosecution probably will succeed with this argument.

Joe will claim that the entry into Eddy's home was unlawful in the absence of a warrant to search the premises. Furthermore, Joe will argue that the consent to the officers' entry by Cathy did not constitute effective permission to enter and search because (1) the police had misrepresented themselves and their purpose (instead of identifying herself as a police officer, Officer Able stated that she knew Eddy, thus implying that he would be pleased to see her and talk to her); and (2) a 14-year-old lacks authority to consent to entry into premises owned by her parent.

The prosecution will respond as follows: First, no warrant was required, because the police merely wanted to question Eddy about what they had seen from the roof, not to arrest him or search his house (so there was, therefore, no Fourth Amendment stop or search at all). Second, their statements to Cathy were not dishonest (i.e., Officer Able had known Eddy for several years and did desire to question him). Third, a 14-year-old can consent to entry into her own home (especially when, as in this instance, her father apparently permitted her to answer the door, and especially because the visitors were given access only to a common room in the house rather than, say, to a study or a bedroom).

The prosecution probably will win on the issue of entry—most courts hold that deception by undercover agents as to their identity doesn't nullify consent, and most courts also allow a teenager to consent to entry into at least the common areas of her parent's house. Deception (even of a sort more blatant than present in this situation) is not grounds to invalidate a consent search. *See, e.g., Hoffa v. United States.* Cathy's age arguably presents a closer question and one that would benefit from additional facts about her maturity. Nevertheless, depending on the facts, several courts have approved of consent searches authorized by children approximately this age. *See, e.g., State v. Griffin.* As noted, the prosecution's argument benefits from the fact that the consent was for entry into a common area—the living room.

If their entry into Eddy's home was valid, Able and Baker probably were (1) entitled to open the door to the room in which the bets were being taken (the words being spoken in the room were in "plain sound" and justified Able and Baker in inspecting the area from which they came) and (2) permitted to seize evidence of Eddy's gambling activities under the plain view doctrine.

Is Joe's statement ("I want to bet $1,500 on Citation") admissible?

Joe can contend that his statement is inadmissible because Officer Able's question was not preceded by *Miranda* warnings. But, because Joe was not in custody at the time of Able's inquiry, this contention should fail.

Answer to Question 15

Juvenile delinquency adjudication:

The argument by Debbie's attorney that Debbie was entitled to a jury trial will *not* be successful. The Supreme Court has held that this right does not extend to delinquency proceedings. *See McKeiver v. Pennsylvania.*

The admissibility of the marijuana:

The facts raise complex issues surrounding searches of students and their effects in public schools. So long as there are "reasonable grounds for suspecting that the search will turn up evidence that the students has violated or is violating either the law or the rules of the school," a warrantless search is permitted. *New Jersey v. T.L.O.* The search may be conducted by an authorized agent of the school (e.g., the principal). As is relevant to this case, it remains an open question under *T.L.O.* whether individualized suspicion is required as part of the reasonableness standard, and even "whether a schoolchild has a legitimate expectation of privacy in lockers, desks, or other school property provided for storage of school supplies." *New Jersey v. T.L.O.* Some lower courts have concluded that students do have an expectation of privacy in their school-owned lockers, which are then subject to search pursuant to the standards of *T.L.O. See, e.g., State v. Michael G.*

Debbie may argue that it wasn't necessary for the principal to open any locker. She would argue that even assuming the lockers were waterlogged, the consequence would be damage to student property, not to any interest of the school. In any event, before he opened lockers, the principal was required to obtain a warrant, especially as it might relate to any specific locker. Debbie's signature on the consent form is a difficult fact for Debbie's attorney to overcome. She may contend that the consent was intended to apply only when circumstances would indicate on some reasonable basis that her individual locker might contain a weapon, some item of contraband, or another object that would violate the school's rules. On these facts, there was nothing that would justify any suspicion of Debbie by the school authorities.

The prosecution will argue that as a general matter Debbie did not have a legitimate expectation of privacy in the locker and that there was no "search." The prosecution will also assert that the principal acted reasonably in an emergency circumstance in response to damage (and a substantial threat) to school property (e.g., the lockers and the walls in which they were located), as well as student property. It arguably furthers the prosecution's reasonableness claim that the principal was not seeking to uncover evidence that might implicate anyone in a crime. As noted above, the prosecution will also rely on Debbie's signed consent that authorized members of the high school staff to inspect her locker at any time and assert that this form negates any legitimate expectation of privacy that Debbie may have otherwise had in the school-owned locker. The prosecution would also respond that Debbie's interpretation of the consent form would render it superfluous under *T.L.O.*

While this is a complicated area, it seems likely that Debbie's claim will fail.

Answer to Question 16

Did the police legally arrest Cindy?

If the police did not have probable cause to arrest Cindy or if an arrest warrant was required, much of the evidence described below probably would represent "fruits of the poisonous tree." As such, the evidence would be inadmissible.

Cindy will contend that the police lacked probable cause to arrest her based solely upon Sylvia's description and upon the documents and records found on Allen's dining room table. Alternatively, she will argue that even if the police had probable cause to arrest, they were required to obtain an arrest warrant before they would be permitted to arrest Cindy in her home.

On the probable cause issue, the prosecution will rely on (1) the fact that Allen had financial documents pertaining to stock transactions strewn on his dining room table and (2) the statement concerning the Stock Exchange made by Cindy. These were enough to arouse reasonable suspicion that Allen's stockbroker was responsible for the attack. When they arrived at Cindy's home and she fit the description given by Sylvia, their suspicion ripened into probable cause. As to the lack of a warrant, the prosecution will first assert that no warrant was needed because Cindy was in a "public place," the doorway of her home, when she was arrested. *See United States v. Santana.* Additionally, the prosecution can assert that no warrant was needed because they were in hot pursuit (i.e., they arrived at her house only five minutes after her) and exigent circumstances existed (i.e., realizing that the police suspected her, Cindy might flee the jurisdiction if not arrested immediately).

The prosecution probably would prevail on validity of Cindy's arrest.

1. *The hospital room identification:*

Cindy will argue that Allen's hospital room identification was inadmissible because her due process rights were violated. The appropriate test requires that the procedure used for identification not be "so unnecessarily suggestive and conducive to irreparable mistaken identification" as to deny the suspect her due process. *See, e.g., Stovall v. Denno.*

Under the circumstances (the time span involved), we can assume that Cindy was the only person shown to Allen and that she was still wearing her blood-splattered clothing. Cindy has a plausible argument that the procedure under which Allen identified her was indeed "unnecessarily suggestive" and "conducive to irreparable mistaken identification." The prosecution will reply that (1) it was conceivable that Allen would die at any moment (i.e., there was no time to conduct a formal lineup in the hospital room); and (2) because Allen had known Cindy for a long period of time and she was alone with him at the time of the stabbing, there was little likelihood of misidentification. An in-hospital identification by a critically ill victim was upheld in *Stovall*. Allen's hospital room identification, therefore, probably would be admissible.

Cindy will argue that her Sixth Amendment right of confrontation (applicable to the states via the Fourteenth Amendment) would be violated by the introduction at trial of Allen's statement because (1) Allen's statement would be proved by the testimony of the police officer who heard it (i.e., hearsay), and (2) Allen would not be available for cross-examination. The Supreme Court invigorated the Sixth Amendment confrontation right in *Crawford v. Washington*. However, it specifically reserved judgment on the status of testimonial "dying declarations." *Id.* at 56 n.6 ("Although many dying declarations may not be testimonial, there is authority for admitting even those that clearly are. . . . We need not decide in this case whether the Sixth Amendment incorporates an exception for testimonial dying declarations. If this exception must be accepted on historical grounds, it is *sui generis*."). Before *Crawford*, "dying declarations" (i.e., statements by an individual who sincerely believes that death may be imminent) generally were deemed to contain sufficient indicia of reliability to overcome an accused's Sixth Amendment objections. Now, their status is uncertain, and lower courts are divided.

Lastly, Cindy will assert that she had a Sixth Amendment right to counsel during the hospital-room identification. But this argument will fail. A suspect has no right to the presence of counsel at a show-up or other identification procedure unless formal proceedings have been instituted against her. *See Kirby v. Illinois* (plurality opinion).

If Cindy does succeed in having the in-hospital ID ruled illegal, she will then argue that many of the other items of evidence (e.g., the bloodstains on Cindy's clothing or Cindy's incriminating statements to Paula) were the fruits of the poisonous identification. That is, the police would never have gotten—or at least, they would not have had probable cause to get—these other pieces of identification without first getting the ID. If she prevails in attacking the ID (which is unlikely), Cindy has a respectable chance of succeeding on this "poisonous fruits" argument. But the prosecution could attempt to show that it would have obtained these pieces of evidence anyway, so that the taint should be deemed "purged."

The rest of our discussion assumes that the in-hospital ID will be found valid.

2. Sylvia's visual identification of Cindy at the lineup:

We assume that (1) the lineup was properly conducted (i.e., the other persons taking part in the lineup were of relatively similar height and weight as Cindy), and (2) Sylvia will be available to testify as to her identification of Cindy at the lineup. If these assumptions are accurate, then Sylvia's identification at the lineup will be admissible. If the lineup was not properly conducted, Cindy's due process rights may have been violated. If Sylvia will not testify and thus will not be available for cross-examination, a Sixth Amendment right-of-confrontation issue will arise.

Again, Cindy had no Sixth Amendment right to have an attorney present since she had not yet been formally charged with a crime.

3. Sylvia's voice identification of Cindy at the lineup:

Again, it will be assumed for our discussion that (1) each person at the lineup was required to state the words, "What will I ever do? What will the Stock Exchange do with me?" and (2) Sylvia will testify at Cindy's trial.

Cindy will argue that her Fifth Amendment rights (applicable to the states via the Fourteenth Amendment) were violated by requiring her to repeat the words that Allen's assailant was heard to scream as she left the apartment. But the prosecution will contend that the Fifth Amendment applies only to "communications" or "testimony," not to real or physical evidence, even evidence taken forcibly from the suspect's body. *See, e.g., Schmerber v. California.* Several cases have permitted forced statements by the suspect for the purpose of identifying his voice. *See, e.g., United States v. Dionisio.* The prosecution will prevail on this issue.

4. The results of the laboratory analysis performed on Cindy's clothing:

Cindy will assert that because they never obtained a search warrant, the police had no right to seize the clothing she was wearing and do a laboratory analysis on the blood found on it. On the assumption, however, that the prosecution convinces the court that the arrest was lawful, the police search probably would also be permitted as a full inventory search of the suspect's person and clothing. The seizure of Cindy's clothing and the results of the laboratory analysis matching Allen's blood to the blood on her clothing would then be admissible.

If Cindy does establish that her arrest was unlawful, her "fruits of the poisonous tree" argument as it applies to the lab results would be quite powerful. In that event, the seizure would be the direct result of the arrest, and the lab results would be the direct result of the seizure; assuming an unlawful arrest, the court probably would find the lab results inadmissible.

5. Cindy's statement to Paula while awaiting trial:

Cindy will contend that Paula was a police informant who was deliberately put into her cell, thus violating Cindy's Sixth Amendment right to an attorney at all "critical stages" of the proceedings. However, because Paula was strictly instructed to be a "passive" or "listening post" informant and to refrain from asking Cindy any questions, and followed these instructions, Cindy's statement to Paula probably will be admissible against Cindy. *See Kuhlmann v. Wilson.* These circumstances are distinguishable from situations in which a cellmate/informant deliberately elicited statements from the defendant. *See United States v. Henry.*

Answer to Question 17

1. Is Doug's gun admissible into evidence?

Are Bus Co. personnel considered governmental agents?

The Fourth Amendment proscription against unreasonable searches and seizures (applicable to the states via the Fourteenth Amendment) applies only to *governmental* action. Here, the person who seized Doug's gun worked for a private bus company, and the prosecution will argue that Doug had no right to complain about the search, especially since he had chosen to use the bus instead of some other means of transportation. Doug will reply that (1) the terminal itself was publicly operated; (2) mass transportation is a quasi-public function; and (3) the security personnel were, in effect, carrying out a police function (i.e., preventing criminal acts that might threaten Bus Co.) pursuant to governmental regulations. For these reasons, the guards who had seized Doug's gun likely will be viewed as governmental agents.

In dealing with the other issues presented by these facts, we will assume that the court would find that the bus guards should be treated as government agents.

Did use of the metal detector constitute an unreasonable search?

Doug will assert that the metal detector constituted an illegal (i.e., warrantless) search. As a result, the gun would be inadmissible as "fruit of a poisonous tree." This argument should fail because the search is likely to be viewed as part of an acceptable regulatory scheme of administrative screening and/or because Doug will be deemed to have consented to the search (presuming the presence of the metal detector was or should have been known to him). Thus, the gun likely will be admissible against Doug.

Was it proper to detain and search Doug after the metal detector was activated?

When police officers have a reasonable suspicion that someone may be carrying an illegal weapon, they may stop and frisk that individual. Doug will assert that because metal detectors are activated by any number of lawful objects (keys, belt buckles, etc.), the security personnel did not have sufficient "reasonable suspicion" to search his pockets. However, activation of the metal detector probably justified a search of Doug's pockets (at least if Doug insisted on boarding the bus). Ordinarily, in searches of people in mass facilities (airports, courthouses, etc.), the people are asked to empty their pockets as part of the search. Arguably, reaching into a person's pocket would be no more intrusive.

Assuming that the search of Doug's pockets was proper, retention of the gun by Bus Co. security personnel probably was also valid—at that point, they had probable cause to believe that the gun was evidence of a crime (the murder of Thompson), especially since the guard had followed the Thompson story in the newspapers and knew that Doug's gun fit the description of the gun used in the killing. The ballistics test and its results would also be admissible because once an item is validly in police custody, it may ordinarily be subjected to any type of reasonable test or analysis.

2. The bloodstains on the front seat of the car:

Doug will argue that he was unlawfully stopped and detained. The prosecution will respond that driving with a broken taillight is a violation of the vehicle code. Because Officer West had probable cause to believe that a traffic violation was occurring, he was justified in stopping Doug. *See, e.g., Delaware v. Prouse.* It does not matter that Officer West's subjective intent (investigating the hazard lights, perhaps with the intent of helping Doug) was a more questionable basis for the authorizing the stop. *See, e.g., Whren v. United States.*

Because the initial stop of Doug was valid, inspection of the bloodstains on the front seat of Doug's car did not require a warrant. Under the plain view doctrine, when a police officer is positioned at a vantage point that he has a right to occupy and sees evidence of criminal activity, he may seize the evidence without a warrant. In the case of evidence attached to or within an automobile, he may seize the auto itself for further investigation.

Thus, the laboratory analysis indicating that the bloodstains matched those of Thompson would be admissible. Note, however, that the analysis would not be admissible at trial if the lab technician who conducted the analysis is unavailable for cross-examination, as this would violate Doug's rights under the Confrontation Clause.

3. Doug's statement to Officer West:

Assuming the stop of Doug's car is held to be proper, Doug will nevertheless argue that Officer West's comment about Doug's probable guilt was a custodial interrogation (i.e., reasonably calculated to elicit an incriminating response). Because it was not preceded by *Miranda* warnings, it is arguably inadmissible. However, even if the comment was reasonably likely to elicit an incriminating response, the court is likely to hold that Doug was not in "custody." The test is an objective one—would a reasonable person in the suspect's position believe he was free to leave? *See Berkemer v. McCarty*. While Doug will argue that an individual ordinarily does not feel free to drive away from a police officer who is leaning against his car, the prosecution probably would prevail on this issue too.

Answer to Question 18

1. What evidence is admissible?

Was the initial stop of Tony valid?

If the initial stop was not valid, all of the evidence subsequently obtained would be inadmissible as "fruits of the poisonous tree."

A police officer may stop the driver of a vehicle when she has a reasonable suspicion that he is engaged in criminal activity. To satisfy this standard, the prosecution must show that Officer Meane had an objective, articulable basis for her belief (rather than a mere hunch). Tony will argue that because (1) he was driving legally, and (2) Officer Meane was not in a position to observe the "weird smile" on his face for more than a moment, no "reasonable suspicion" of criminal activity could have been formed. The prosecution will argue, however, that Officer Meane was an experienced highway patrol officer and her experience would tell her when a weird smile and a vehicle's slow speed combined to raise a reasonable suspicion that the driver was under the influence of an intoxicant. Although this is a close question, the prosecution probably will prevail. (If Tony prevails, the case against him should be dismissed because all of the evidence against him was derived from the illegal stop.)

Was the field sobriety test valid?

The field sobriety test constituted an additional search that was not justified without probable cause. The factors (described above) that constituted the basis for stopping Tony, plus the likely odor of beer on Tony's breath, were enough to give Officer Meane probable cause to believe that Tony was drunk, thereby justifying the field sobriety test. If so, the results of that test would also be admissible. Alternatively, the court may reasonably conclude that Tony implicitly consented (by undergoing the test without an objection) to taking the test. If so, probable cause for the test would not be necessary.

Is Tony's initial conversation with Officer Meane admissible?

A custodial interrogation must be preceded by *Miranda* warnings. Because these were not given to Tony, he will contend that his statements are inadmissible. However, the prosecution could argue that Tony was not in custody when his conversations with Officer Meane took place. In *Berkemer v. McCarty*, the Supreme Court ruled that one who has been stopped on a public road for a minor traffic violation is normally not in "custody" for *Miranda* purposes. Additionally, a cordial atmosphere apparently prevailed at first between Tony and Officer Meane. While Officer Meane could have arrested Tony immediately after Tony failed the sobriety test (in which event Tony would have been in custody), there was no constitutional requirement that she do so.

Tony will then argue that, even if *Miranda* warnings were not required in this context, his statements to Officer Meane were involuntary, and, therefore, violated both his Fifth Amendment privilege against self-incrimination and his Fourteenth Amendment right to due process. This argument will be supported by the fact that Tony was under the influence of intoxicants and was incapable of understanding the devastating effect that his statements would have in his subsequent trial. Although not a specious argument, it is unlikely to succeed given Tony's general ability to behave coherently. In *Colorado v. Connelly*, the Supreme Court ruled that statements made by a suspect who suffered from an unfounded paranoia that he would be punished if he failed to answer the police's questions were nevertheless admissible. The Court reasoned that as long as no police overreaching had taken place, a suspect's inherent condition did not make his statements involuntary. The theory of *Connelly* would indicate that Tony's statement here, even if arguably the product of his drunkenness, was not involuntary. (This same reasoning would likely doom Tony's claim that his subsequent waiver of his *Miranda* rights to Officer Meane was invalid.)

Thus, Officer Meane can probably testify with respect to her initial conversation with Tony.

Was Tony's statement at the station house admissible?

If the court should rule that Tony's initial conversation with Officer Meane is inadmissible, Tony will argue that his confession at the station house is also inadmissible. That is, Tony would argue that this confession was tainted by the first; he reasoned that because he had already made one incriminating statement, and another after he had waived his *Miranda* rights (i.e., by admitting his use of marijuana and offering Officer Meane his last marijuana cigarette), he had nothing left to lose by repeating and amplifying his first confession. But the Supreme Court has rejected this "cat out of the bag" theory and has ruled that an earlier illegal confession does not *per se* invalidate a subsequent one. *Oregon v. Elstad. Cf. Missouri v. Seibert* (suppressing the second statement only when produced by deliberate use of two-step interrogation process designed to undermine *Miranda* protections). The station house statements probably would be ruled untainted and, thus, admissible against Tony. Furthermore, Tony's confession in the station house only confirmed the confession he had already made when he handed Officer Meane a marijuana cigarette and admitted his use of marijuana after waiving his *Miranda* rights.

Is the marijuana cigarette admissible?

Because Tony voluntarily gave this item to Officer Meane after waiving his *Miranda* rights, he would have no viable argument against its admissibility. In any event, it presumably would inevitably have been discovered by the police anyway, either by Officer Meane as a search incident to a valid arrest or at the station house pursuant to a "booking" (or inventory) search.

2. What other issues are available on appeal?

Tony should contend that his Sixth Amendment right to represent himself (applicable to the states via the Fourteenth Amendment) was violated by the court's order to appoint counsel for him. *See Faretta v. California.* In most circumstances, a person has the right to represent himself in a criminal proceeding. This right applies even though the trial judge reasonably believes that the person will do an incompetent job of representing himself. Tony, therefore, probably will have the right to retrial on this basis.

Answer to Question 19

1. Were the arrest and search warrants validly issued? Were the radios admissible?

To arrest an individual or search an area in which that individual had a reasonable expectation of privacy, probable cause must exist. (That is, it must be more probable than not that the defendant committed a crime or that evidence of criminal activity will be located in the area to be searched.) When tips from an informant are the sole basis for probable cause, the sufficiency of the tips is measured by the "totality of the circumstances." The reputation of the informant as a generally reliable witness and the informant's basis for knowing the particular facts at issue will both be considered in assessing the "totality of the circumstances." *Illinois v. Gates.*

Dot would argue that the affidavit presented to the magistrate was insufficient because (1) there was no statement telling why the source was reliable (i.e., had he given accurate information in the past? Did he actually see the radios? If so, when and under what circumstances?); (2) the affidavit failed to indicate that Dot had any part in the theft of the radios or knew that they were stolen; and (3) the fact that Dot had been convicted previously of grand larceny and associated with convicted felons was irrelevant to this specific crime. However, the prosecution will reply that (1) implicit in the words "who knows Dot" is that the informant had personal knowledge that Dot was involved in the crime in question; and (2) the affidavit did say that the radios were in Dot's apartment, and this supported the charge that she was in possession of stolen property.

In conclusion, the information contained in Officer Brown's affidavit is likely to be insufficient to establish probable cause to arrest Dot or search her apartment.

Is the "good faith" exception to the exclusionary rule applicable?

The prosecution will contend that, even if probable cause did not exist, the "good faith" exception to the exclusionary rule applied. Under that exception, when police officers reasonably and in good faith rely upon a facially adequate warrant, however deficient, the fruits of that search are admissible. *United States v. Leon.* Because Officer Brown was acting in good faith and may be presumed to have believed that his affidavit supporting the warrants was adequate, the radios found at Dot's apartment are arguably admissible. While Dot would assert that Officer Brown should have realized that the warrant was facially insufficient (i.e., he had prepared the warrant himself), the prosecution probably would prevail on this issue. Thus, the radios should be admitted against Dot.

Even if the "good faith" exception is inapplicable, are the radios nevertheless admissible against Dot under the plain view doctrine?
Even if Dot was successful with respect to the issues discussed above, the prosecution can still argue that the radios are admissible against her.

Its argument would proceed along the following lines: (1) the police may arrest without a warrant and outside her home someone who may have committed a felony (provided probable cause exists); (2) although insufficient information may have been provided to the magistrate, Officer Brown (personally) had enough information to arrest Dot (i.e., a statement by a participant in the crime that he was assisted by Dot); (3) Dot voluntarily let Officer Brown into her apartment (she must have been aware that Officer Brown was accompanying her as she entered the apartment to make a telephone call); and (4) the radios were in *plain view* (i.e., they were observed by Officer Brown from a vantage point he had a right to be in). For these reasons, the radios are admissible.

Dot will reply that (1) probable cause did not exist because the statements of Hal, her ex-husband, might have been prompted by ulterior motives, such as vindictiveness or an effort to get a lighter sentence; and (2) because Officer Brown had to leave Dot's side and walk over to the boxes before he could determine that they contained radios, they were not in plain view from the place where he had a right to be (at Dot's side). But the prosecution should prevail on this issue for the following reasons: (1) Hal's statement probably could be taken as trustworthy, in light of the fact that he had confessed to a crime for which he had not been arrested; (2) an officer is permitted to accompany a suspect who has been lawfully arrested, even in his home (*Washington v. Chrisman*); (3) while he's accompanying her, he may continue to observe those areas and inspect those articles that come into view; (4) Officer Brown could see enough as he walked beside Dot to arouse his suspicion that the boxes contained radios, thus justifying his detour; and (5) Officer Brown had a right to visually inspect the outside of the boxes to confirm his suspicions.

The prosecutor probably gets the better of these arguments. Thus, the radios are probably admissible against Dot.

2. Was the in-court identification of Dot by Grace admissible?
When a witness identifies a suspect through the use of photos under circumstances involving the police, due process requires that the process not be "unnecessarily suggestive." *Simmons v. United States.* A suggestive identification can undermine the witness's ability to make a fair in-court

identification of the suspect during the trial. This will happen when the identification is so suggestive as to create a substantial likelihood of irreparable misidentification. *Simmons.*

Dot will argue that it was improper to limit Grace's identification to Dot's photo and not to show the photos of the other women who worked at Store. Fifty women worked at Store. When Marsh showed Grace only Dot's photo, it suggested to Grace that Dot was already a suspect in the robbery. That was enough to cloud Grace's identification. Because a substantial likelihood of misidentification had been created, Dot's due process rights were violated. But the prosecution will reply that (1) no governmental action was involved because it was Marsh (not Officer Brown) who presented the photograph to Grace, and (2) Grace's response to the photograph ("She could be the one") was not a positive identification of Dot. (The significance of the latter point is that witnesses are sometimes reluctant to recant their previous identifications; if the first identification is ambiguous, as here, the witness will be more apt to discount her identification and testify accurately at trial, especially because she will consider her testimony at trial to be more significant to the proceeding than her earlier identification.) Because Grace saw the person talking to the delivery clerk from a distance of only 30 feet, the identification probably was reliable.

On this reasoning, Grace's in-court identification of Dot is admissible. This would be true even if Officer Brown was the one who had asked Grace to look at Dot's photo.

3. Did the court properly admit Marsh's testimony as to Dot's statement to him?

The court permitted Marsh to testify as to Dot's statement to him at the store on the day of the crime (that she was in the store during the time of the robbery). Dot will argue that Marsh should not be permitted to testify about the statement because Dot was not given *Miranda* warnings before she made it. But this argument will fail for several reasons. First, the inquiry was made by Marsh (rather than Officer Brown), so no governmental conduct was involved. Even assuming that the inquiry could somehow be attributed to Officer Brown because Marsh asked his question in Brown's presence, Dot was not in custody at the time of the interrogation. Finally, statements that do not satisfy a suspect's *Miranda* rights but that are voluntarily made may be used for purposes of **impeachment**. *Harris v. New York.* Marsh's testimony here was used to impeach Dot's denial of having been in the store at the time of the theft (rather than as part of the prosecution's case-in-chief).

Answer to Question 20

The existence of probable cause to arrest Dunn will be central to the resolution of the motion to suppress the marijuana.

Can the results of the police surveillance of Dunn's apartment be considered in determining whether the police had probable cause to arrest Dunn?

Dunn will argue that the police surveillance of Dunn's apartment should be regarded as a search. Because no search warrant was obtained, Dunn will argue that the fruits of the search (the observation of Sally's and Dunn's conduct) must be disregarded in determining whether probable cause to arrest Dunn existed. The prosecution will reply that an individual has no expectation of privacy with respect to conduct that can be observed by the general public. Because people from an adjoining apartment were able to see Dunn and Sally, Dunn cannot complain that police officers (rather than his neighbors) were the ones who undertook to observe them. Under the Fourth Amendment (applicable to the states via the Fourteenth Amendment), an individual has no right to object to the search of an area in which he does not have a reasonable expectation of privacy. The prosecution will contend the surveillance was simply not a Fourth Amendment search at all.

Dunn will respond that, although he may have surrendered his expectation of privacy with respect to observation by the naked eye, he had not agreed to be observed through high-powered binoculars, especially by the police. The prosecution will contend that binoculars can easily be purchased by the general public and are often used to observe the stars and events around them; if the public can use them, so can the police. The police will rely on the line of cases permitting observation of suspected areas from airplanes flying overhead. *See, e.g., Florida v. Riley; Dow Chemical v. United States; California v. Ciraolo.* These cases hold that the aerial observations were not searches at all because the areas observed were in plain view from the air. However, the use of a very unusual or sophisticated spying device to see something that couldn't be seen by the naked eye from public space might make a difference. *Cf. Kyllo v. United States* (discussing the use of sense-enhancing technology to learn information about the *interior* of a home that would not be otherwise available without physical intrusion).

The information obtained from the surveillance is likely to be properly considered, although its probative value may be questioned.

Should Dunn's letter to Sally be considered in determining whether probable cause to arrest him existed?

Dunn will also assert that, because the search of his wastepaper basket was made without a warrant, the letter was the fruit of an illegal search and, thus, cannot be relied upon in assessing probable cause to arrest him. The prosecution will make two arguments in reply. First, the search was consented to by Dunn's employer. The employer arguably had equal access and control with Dunn to all nonenclosed areas (i.e., everything but the contents of Dunn's desk drawers) where Dunn worked. Second, Dunn had no reasonable expectation of privacy in the trash can because: (1) the contents were, in effect, "held out" to others (i.e., persons who collected and discarded the office refuse); and (2) Dunn did not have exclusive control over the trash can (it was shared with another employee). The prosecution probably will be successful on at least one of the foregoing arguments. *See, e.g., California v. Greenwood* (no privacy expectation in trash left outside home).

The letter probably would be considered on the issue of probable cause to arrest. The question, of course, is what weight to attach to this information. Two people can have "another hot night" without having sexual intercourse.

Was there probable cause to arrest Dunn at all?

Whether probable cause exists depends upon the "totality of the circumstances." *Illinois v. Gates.* The Supreme Court has stated that the "probable-cause standard is incapable of precise definition or quantification into percentages because it deals with probabilities and depends on the totality of the circumstances." *Maryland v. Pringle.* There needs to be a "reasonable ground for belief of guilt." *Id.*

Dunn will argue that there was no probable cause to arrest him at all. What the police saw with their binoculars was only two people kissing and, then, one person being picked up and carried by the other. Neither of these acts confirms the crime of statutory rape, which requires proof of sexual intercourse between an adult and an underage person. Dunn will similarly point to the ambiguity of the recovered letter. The police may argue that when a man carries a woman into a room after they've been kissing, it's reasonable to conclude that they will engage in intercourse. It will also claim that the charge against Dunn is supported by Buck's statement that Sally had stayed in Dunn's apartment overnight on two occasions. It will point to the letter as corroboration that intercourse occurred. But none of these arguments are likely to be sufficient to establish probable cause to arrest for the crime of statutory rape.

If the court determines that there was no probable cause to arrest Dunn, the fruits of the resulting search will be suppressed.

Assuming there was probable cause, was it proper to arrest Dunn without a warrant?

Assuming that there was probable cause for the arrest, the fact that the police failed to obtain an arrest warrant before arresting Dunn would be immaterial. A suspect who has committed a felony may be taken into custody from a public place without prior judicial approval, provided probable cause exists.

Assuming the arrest was proper, was the search of Dunn's car proper?

Dunn will contend that even if there was probable cause to arrest him, the police had no right to search underneath the front seat of his car. But the prosecution will make two arguments in reply. First, incident to a valid arrest, the area within a suspect's immediate control may be searched. Because Dunn had just begun to enter his car, the area under the front seat was within his reach.

Dunn will reply that the area under the front seat of his car was not within his immediate control (presumably, he would need to stoop down and extend his arm under the front seat; this would be difficult with the police standing at his side). This argument is likely to fail—the Supreme Court allows the police to search the entire passenger compartment of a car, even closed containers and places that the suspect cannot possibly reach. *See, e.g., New York v. Belton.*

Dunn will also contend that he had not been driving the vehicle before his arrest (he was arrested *as he was entering it*), so the right of the police to inspect the car had not arisen. But the automobile exception has been interpreted broadly to include cases in which the suspect was entering or leaving the car rather than driving it. *Cf. Thornton v. United States.* Therefore, the search of the car probably would be upheld—assuming, again, that the arrest was proper.

Answer to Question 21

The GPS Evidence

The first issue to be resolved is whether the officers' warrantless use of a GPS device to track the Godfather's whereabouts violated his right to be free from unreasonable search and seizure. The Fourth Amendment is triggered whenever law enforcement actors intrude upon an individual's reasonable expectation of privacy. A search or seizure must be supported by probable cause and a warrant, unless their actions are subject to a recognized exception to the warrant requirement. Above all, any search or seizure must be reasonable in light of the law enforcement needs and surrounding circumstances.

In this case, the GPS tracker relayed information about the Godfather's changing location over time, allowing officers to create a detailed history and spatial map of his movements. The key question is whether the defendant had an objectively reasonable expectation of privacy in that information. In previous cases, courts have generally permitted warrantless electronic collection of location evidence as a suspect travels about in public. *See, e.g., Knotts v. United States.*

However, in *United States v. Jones*, the Supreme Court held that the physical intrusion occasioned by the installation of a GPS tracking device constituted a search or seizure for purposes of the Fourth Amendment. The Court's opinion indicated that this sort of encroachment on an "effect" is expressly protected by the terms of the amendment, and would have been considered a search at the time of the amendment's adoption. Because the officers in this case engaged in a similar encroachment on the Godfather's property, *Jones* strongly counsels the court against admission of the GPS tracking information.

The Anonymous Tip

The Godfather may seek to challenge the admission of the 911 report regarding Sam's attack as a violation of his Sixth Amendment right to confront witnesses against him. The Confrontation Clause prohibits the admission of an unavailable witness's prior testimony unless the witness is both unavailable and the defendant has had a previous opportunity to cross-examine. *Davis v. Washington.* Testimonial evidence is that which is focused on proving past events potentially relevant to later criminal prosecution. The Godfather would argue that the 911 call is offered in its testimonial capacity, and that his right to confront the witnesses against him requires that all testifying witnesses be made available for cross-examination. The

911 report itself cannot be examined, and thus the caller would need to take the stand.

Unfortunately for the Godfather, the 911 report most likely falls within the "ongoing emergency" exception to the Confrontation Clause and is therefore admissible. Where the unavailable witness's testimony is given for the purpose of assisting police in resolving an ongoing emergency, a court will construe that evidence to be given in a non-testimonial capacity and will admit the evidence even though the witness does not appear at trial and has not previously been cross-examined. *Michigan v. Bryant.*

The Incriminating Statements

The Godfather would likely also challenge the admission of his incriminating statement regarding the attack on Sam as the product of unlawful interrogation. As indicated in the *Miranda* warnings, an individual has the right to consult with an attorney during any custodial interrogation. Moreover, when an individual invokes the right to counsel, all questioning must cease until counsel is present or the suspect voluntarily reinitiates. The prohibition on further questioning applies to all officers to interrogation about any crime. *Edwards v. Arizona.*

The Godfather would argue that he was subject to custodial interrogation. He was forcibly detained in a police-dominated environment, and he faced direct questioning by law enforcement officers. He would further argue that he invoked the right to counsel in clear and unambiguous language by telling the officers that he wanted no communication them without his attorney present. The government would respond that, even if his invocation of the right to counsel was effective initially, the invocation had lapsed by the time that the stationhouse interrogation took place. Invocation of the right to counsel during police questioning is meant to offset potentially coercive pressures inherent in custodial interrogation, and those coercive pressures naturally dissipate over time. The limitations on post-invocation questioning should not last longer than necessary to effectively prevent compelled self-incrimination.

While the *Edwards* rule, as initially articulated, was a blanket prohibition on any questioning after invocation of the right to counsel, the doctrine has since been relaxed in order to permit subsequent interrogation where the inherent concerns regarding coercion have been sufficiently dispelled. The dissipation of those coercive pressures is understood to occur (1) after the passage of a sufficient period of time between the interrogation triggering the invocation and the follow up interrogation and (2) where the subsequent questioning is preceded by fresh *Miranda* warnings. *Maryland v. Shatzer.* Consistent with this approach, the Court has declared that fourteen days is a sufficient amount of time, and has limited the effect of the *Edwards* rule to that period.

In this case, the Godfather's stationhouse questioning occurred a full three weeks (21 days) after his invocation of his right to counsel, and it was preceded by a new set of *Miranda* warnings. In light of the bright line drawn regarding the duration of an *Edwards* invocation, his effort to exclude the statements must be rejected because they fall outside the scope of protection provided by the rule.

Answer to Question 22

1. Was Dan's initial stop at the checkpoint lawful?

Because each of the contraband items discovered in Dan's possession were collected as a direct consequence of Dan's initial stop at the checkpoint, this initial stop must have been constitutional if the evidence is not to be suppressed as "fruits of the poisonous tree." The Supreme Court has dealt with suspicionless stops at roadblocks or checkpoints on three relevant occasions, and has determined the legality of such suspicionless stops by reference to the purpose for which the roadblock is used. For example, in *Michigan v. Sitz*, the Court upheld this sort of brief, nonthreatening stop when conducted for the purpose of reducing the number of intoxicated drivers on the road. The Court reasoned that the law enforcement interest served by the roadblock (over and above the ordinary interest in criminal enforcement) outweighed the intrusion, in terms of restraint, fear, and surprise, borne by the stopped motorists. Then, in *Indianapolis v. Edmond*, the Court invalidated a roughly similar roadblock that was erected for the purposes of identifying and apprehending illegal drug smugglers using the same balancing test. Finally, in *Illinois v. Lidster*, the Court permitted police officers to use a traffic checkpoint to make suspicionless stops of motorists for purposes of identifying potential witnesses to a recent hit-and-run accident.

Here, the state would certainly argue that *Lidster* supports the conclusion that the officers' reliance on a checkpoint to search for and identify possible witnesses to the arson attacks was a sufficiently compelling justification to excuse the otherwise suspicionless stop. Given the brevity of the interview, and the generally orderly and nonintrusive nature of the roadblock, it is likely that the state would prevail on this issue.

2. Was Sergeant Smalls' "dog sniff" inspection of Dan's vehicle lawful?

The Fourth Amendment prohibits unreasonable searches and seizures, and ordinarily a search must be supported by probable cause. Here, the facts clearly indicate that Officer Olsen had no reason to believe Dan was involved in criminal activity, and thus the dog sniff was conducted without any basis in suspicion. However, the Court has categorically excluded dog sniffs from the scope of the term "search," and therefore such inspections need not be justified at all. *United States v. Place*. During a lawful traffic stop, police may subject a suspect's vehicle to a dog sniff without any suspicion of wrongdoing if it does not extend the length of time otherwise necessary to conduct the stop. *Illinois v. Caballes*. Precedent clearly supports the state on this issue.

3. Was Officer Olsen's decision to remove Dan from the vehicle and search the passenger compartment constitutional?

Police may order occupants of a lawfully stopped vehicle to exit the car when, in their judgment, doing so would be necessary to ensure officer safety. *Pennsylvania v. Mimms.* Further, if the officer has reasonable suspicion to believe that the person with whom they are dealing may be presently armed and dangerous, they are permitted to conduct a *Terry*-style pat-down to disarm the suspect. *Id.* The Court has concluded that even ordinary traffic stops carry an inherent potential for danger to the officer, and provide law enforcement officers wide latitude, such that the decision to remove Dan would likely pass constitutional muster. Likewise, given the close proximity between the officer and Dan, and the nature of the crime of which he was suspected (based on the assumption that drug crimes often entail use or possession of a firearm), the court would most likely conclude that the pat-down was proper.

Dan would likely argue that, once he was removed from his vehicle and placed in the back of the police cruiser, Officer Olsen could no longer justify her inspection of the car based on safety concerns. Whether Olsen had a reasonable suspicion that Dan might have a weapon concealed in his car would be a close factual question for the court to resolve. However, the state would almost certainly argue that Olsen was not acting in *Terry*-type capacity, but rather had developed probable cause to believe that the car contained contraband narcotics. Assuming the admissibility of the results of the dog sniff, probable cause would likely have been established, and Officer Olsen was therefore entitled to search the entire car and any container found inside. A court would thus conclude that discovery of the backpack, and the pipe therein, was the product of a lawful search.

4. Was Dan lawfully arrested?

Police may lawfully place a suspect under arrest if there is probable cause to believe that person has engaged in criminal activity. *Atwater v. City of Lago Vista.* The facts presented here would readily support the officer's conclusion that Dan had committed the crime of possessing drug paraphernalia. Assuming the admissibility of the dog sniff and the propriety of Officer Olsen's subsequent search, these facts would lead the court to conclude that Olsen had cause to arrest Dan.

However, Dan may seek to argue that his arrest was unlawful according to the state statute. Because the relevant provision criminalizing his conduct expressly mandates citation rather than arrest, Dan may argue that his arrest was rendered constitutionally unreasonable because the officer exceeded her authority. The state would respond that, although the arrest may have been contrary to state criminal law, this is not fatal to the reasonableness standard by which the constitutional provision is tested. Indeed, the Supreme Court has concluded that the probable cause determination that a crime has occurred renders such an arrest reasonable, notwithstanding the fact that the arrest itself is contrary to state law. *Virginia v. Moore.* Assuming that the state constitutional provision (which is identical to the Fourth Amendment) will be interpreted in the same fashion, the court will likely reject Dan's challenge.

5. *Was the second search of the automobile lawful?*

Dan may seek to suppress the drug evidence found in the trunk of the car during the second search. The court would be called on to assess whether the officers continued to have lawful justification for their actions. The state might argue that the search of the vehicle was legitimate as incident to Dan's arrest. Assuming, based on the above, that Dan's arrest was lawful, the state would argue that the officers were categorically permitted to search the car and any containers found therein. *New York v. Belton.* However, Dan may respond that the search-incident-to-arrest doctrine does not include the trunk of the car within the scope of the search, and that evidence found there would have to be suppressed. *Id.* Dan would also argue that the search-incident-to-arrest doctrine no longer permits warrantless searches of the automobile of an arrestee when that arrestee is secured away from the vehicle and poses no threat of harm to the officer. *Arizona v. Gant.* Either or both of these arguments would overcome the state's reliance on the arrest as a justification for the second search.

The state may also argue that the second search was supported by their ongoing probable cause to believe that the car contained narcotics. Dan might respond that the officers only had cause to believe that contraband was in the passenger compartment (this is where the dog alerted), and that their suspicion was dispelled once Olsen discovered the pipe with drug residue, such that the trunk should not have been opened. If the court were to agree, then the drug evidence from the trunk should be suppressed. If the court were to determine that the officers had ongoing probable cause, they would be permitted to engage in a search of any part of vehicle, including the trunk, that could reasonably be calculated to contain such evidence. *California v. Acevedo.* The admissibility of the crack cocaine thus depends on the resolution of this probable cause determination.

Answer to Question 23

1. Evidentiary issues pertaining to Freddie:

The first issue that may arise is whether Officers Pounce and John had lawful authority to initiate their contact with Freddie and Samson. Police may approach and address any person found in a public place without any suspicion of wrongdoing. The police may also briefly detain an individual if specific and articulable facts warrant their belief that criminal activity may be afoot. *Terry v. Ohio.* A court would therefore conclude that the officers need not justify the initial approach of the two men, and would likely conclude that Officer Pounce's order to Freddie to "freeze" was permissible given the activities and demeanor observed prior to the encounter.

If the court were to conclude that the officers had reasonable suspicion regarding Freddie and Samson's activities, then Pounce would have the authority to further investigate that suspicion by posing questions to Freddie on the porch. Although Freddie's freedom of movement was obviously curtailed, the detention did not at this time rise to the level of a formal arrest, and thus no *Miranda* warnings were required.

However, Freddie may argue that he was unlawfully detained after Officer John returned with Samson and the bag. When Officer Pounce told Freddie that he was not free to leave, the level of restraint may have exceeded that authorized for a *Terry* stop. The state could counter by arguing that Freddie was being detained in order to preserve the opportunity to secure and execute the search warrant. The court would likely conclude that Freddie could be detained while the warrant was obtained, and that they were entitled to exclude him from the house (or follow him closely within the home) until the warrant could be served. *Illinois v. McArthur.* Further, the police would be inherently authorized to detain Freddie, as a resident of the premises subject to the search warrant, during the search itself. *Michigan v. Summers.*

Assuming that the search warrant was properly issued and, and based on the fact that the drugs were found within Freddie's residence, his arrest would be adequately supported by probable cause. Moreover, assuming the validity of the initial detention, and the propriety of the extension of that detention during the warrant application and execution process, the drug evidence would likely be admissible in his criminal prosecution.

2. Evidentiary issues pertaining to Samson:

Samson may also challenge Officer Pounce's and Officer John's initial engagement with the two men, and resolution of this issue would proceed as described in the discussion pertaining to Freddie, above.

The question whether Officer John had authority to chase and then arrest Samson depends on the level of suspicion Officer John is determined to have possessed. As stated above, the officers likely had reasonable suspicion sufficient to initiate the encounter and investigate further. However, Samson's noncompliance with Officer John's attempt to interview him (through flight) precipitated his arrest before a *Terry*-style encounter could take place. The crucial question, therefore, is whether Officer John had probable cause to place Samson under arrest. At the moment of arrest, Officer John was unaware of the contents of the duffel bag, so that information may not factor into the analysis. The Supreme Court has held that "mere" flight from the police, without more, does not establish probable cause or even reasonable suspicion with respect to criminality, but that unprovoked flight under additionally suspicious circumstances may suffice to create reasonable suspicion. *Illinois v. Wardlow.* The trial court could conclude that Samson's flight, considered in conjunction with the previously observed conduct and the appearance of the duffel bags, together amounted to reasonable suspicion for Officer John to investigate further. However, no additional facts were learned during the encounter that would appear to provide probable cause for Samson's arrest. If the court were to reach this likely conclusion, Samson's arrest would be declared unconstitutional.

In the event that the court was to find probable cause for Samson's arrest, the next issue would be whether the narcotics evidence was lawfully discovered. Pursuant to a lawful arrest, police may search the person of the arrestee and the area within his or her immediate control. *Chimel v. California.* Because the duffel bag was slung over Samson's shoulder and within arm's reach, it would fall within the permissible scope of a legitimate search incident to arrest. Assuming the arrest itself was lawful, the evidence discovered by opening the duffel would be admissible against him.

The next question is whether Samson's incriminating statements may be used against him. Statements made in response to custodial interrogation are inadmissible if not preceded by valid *Miranda* warnings and a knowing and intelligent waiver of *Miranda* rights. Samson was clearly in custody once formally arrested and continued to be in custody throughout his ride to and time at the police station. Interrogation occurs anytime an arrestee faces direct questioning or its functional equivalent, and the questions posed by the officers (both in the car and at the station) are sufficient to trigger *Miranda's* protections. Because Samson's incriminating statements made in the car were both unwarned and not preceded by a valid waiver, they may not be used in the prosecution's case-in-chief.

The state may seek to offer instead Samson's verbal and written confessions obtained at the station house. These incriminating statements were collected after valid warnings were given and a waiver was obtained, and this would ordinarily be sufficient to "purge the taint" of the earlier unwarned interrogation. *Oregon v. Elstad.* However, police may not deliberately use this "question-first" technique as a strategy for circumventing or undermining the value of *Miranda*'s prophylactic safeguards. *Missouri v. Seibert.* Under these circumstances, strategic and intentional withholding of *Miranda* warnings until after Samson had incriminated himself violated his Fifth Amendment rights and warrants suppression of Samson's station house confession.

3. Issues pertaining to Mary:

Assuming the validity of the search warrant, the only procedural issue Mary might raise at trial is whether the officers' decision to aggressively restrain Mary, and to allow that restraint to last for two hours, rendered her seizure unreasonable under the Fourth Amendment. Police may detain individuals found at locations subject to a search warrant, and may use that level of physical restraint necessary to safely achieve their lawful objectives. *Muehler v. Mena.* Here, the question would be whether the drug possession crime being investigated was serious and inherently dangerous enough to justify Mary's treatment. *Cf. Mena* (upholding nearly identical restraint for two to three hours where warrant was for weapons and evidence of gang activity). Whatever the court's conclusion this issue might be, because no evidence was discovered as a result of Mary's seizure (the drug evidence having already been collected upon execution of the warrant), this issue may only be presented if Mary were to bring a §1983 action alleging violation of her constitutional rights, and would not be a matter relevant to the admission of evidence.

Answer to Question 24

1. What evidentiary issues may arise on Blinken's appeal?

The first question is what significance to assign, if any, to the confidential informant's tip regarding Nod's involvement in the shooting. Although the contribution of the tip to a probable cause determination would be assessed against the totality of the circumstances (*see Illinois v. Gates*), and there is some ambiguity as to whether the tip was sufficiently detailed to be reliable overall, the tip actually played no role in the encounter with Blinken other than bringing Detective Friendly to Winken and Blinken's apartment door.

The central evidentiary issue on appeal is likely to be whether Detective Friendly was permitted to enter the apartment to speak with Nod without a warrant. If Detective Friendly were not authorized to enter, the discovery of the narcotics in Blinken's bedroom would necessarily be suppressed as the fruits of that unlawful entry.

Whether Detective Friendly's entry was justified depends on whether she was acting pursuant to an exception to the presumption against warrantless intrusions into the home. The consent of a party possessing authority over the property is ordinarily treated as an exception to the warrant requirement. *Schneckloth v. Bustamonte; United States v. Matlock.* However, where two parties with shared access to and control over property disagree over the rendering of consent, and both are physically present, officers must defer to the nonconsenting party in spite of the co-occupant's agreement. *Georgia v. Randolph.* Blinken could argue that he clearly communicated to the officers both his rights with respect to the apartment and his unequivocal nonconsent. In light of these facts, a court would likely conclude that Detective Friendly lacked a lawful basis for his entry, and the evidence discovered in Blinken's bedroom will be suppressed.

2. What evidentiary issues might arise during Nod's prosecution?

Although it may be that Detective Friendly entered the apartment unlawfully, unless Nod can show that he possessed a legitimate expectation of privacy therein (typically unavailable to such a short-term guest), he would lack standing to object to Detective Friendly's presence.

The court must therefore determine whether Detective Friendly had a right to interview Nod regarding the shooting. Officers may temporarily detain and question an individual for purposes of investigation any time they have specific and articulable facts supporting the belief regarding that person's involvement in criminal activity, and may continue this limited intrusion long enough to confirm or dispel their suspicion (although they may not compel answers to these questions). *Terry.* Here, a court could conclude that the conversation with Nod in the bedroom constituted a *Terry* stop, and that the confidential informant's tip furnished reasonable suspicion to support this action.

Assuming the validity of Detective Friendly's initial encounter with Nod, Nod's subsequent arrest must be supported by probable cause or else the discoveries and disclosures which followed may be suppressible as fruit of the poisonous tree. Nod would argue that the confidential informant's tip, without more, was insufficient to furnish Detective Friendly probable cause to arrest for the shooting. While the totality of the circumstances is designed to be flexible, it would not likely be satisfied by an anonymous tip so lacking in detail, and which is impossible to corroborate through independent investigation. *Cf. Gates.*

Alternatively, the state may argue that the arrest was justified by Detective Friendly's reliance on the outstanding arrest warrant. Nod would counter that a warrant for his arrest did not, in fact, exist and that the arrest was therefore without legal basis. However, where clerical error that is not the result of systematic failures or reckless record keeping leads to the mistaken belief that a warrant exists, and arresting officers reasonably rely on that belief in good faith, any evidence flowing from the arrest will not be subject to the exclusionary rule. *Herring v. United States.*

The final issue is whether Nod's incriminating statements to the undercover agent placed in his cell can be used to rebut his alibi defense. Law enforcement officers may not deliberately elicit incriminating statements from a suspect who has invoked the right to counsel and then use those statements as part of the prosecution's case-in-chief. However, if a criminal defendant chooses to take the witness stand in his defense, and testifies in a manner inconsistent with prior incriminating statements, such prior statements may be admissible for purposes of impeachment even assuming they were deliberately elicited after invocation of Sixth Amendment rights. *Kansas v. Ventris.* The trial court should, for these reasons, rule in favor of the government on its motion to permit introduction of the incriminating statements Nod made to the jailhouse informant.

Multiple-Choice Questions

1. Sub lived in a residential neighborhood over which planes often flew. Sub liked his privacy, so he erected a tall fence that completely enclosed his backyard. One reason he liked his privacy was that he grew marijuana in his yard. Unbeknownst to Sub, the police had received a tip as to his activities. They rented a plane, flew overhead, used binoculars, and took pictures of the marijuana. The police accurately submitted this information to a judge, who then issued a search warrant. Executing the warrant, the police seized Sub's marijuana, which was used at trial against him. Sub's pretrial motion to suppress the marijuana was denied.

   Under the U.S. Constitution, the trial court's ruling was

   A. incorrect, because individuals have a reasonable expectation of privacy with respect to items contained within the home.

   B. incorrect, because the marijuana was within the curtilage of Sub's home.

   C. incorrect, if the marijuana was not observable from ground level.

   D. correct, because Sub had no reasonable expectation of privacy in his backyard with respect to aerial surveillance.

2. Two police officers in a squad car received a radio message from headquarters to be on the lookout for a large green sedan occupied by two women who had just committed a bank robbery. An hour later they saw a car answering this description traveling down a main boulevard leading out of town. They pulled the car over to the side of the road and walked over to it. One of the officers told the occupants that they were under arrest for bank robbery. Doreen, the driver, suddenly put the car into gear and drove off. The officers, unable to overtake the car and afraid they would lose sight of it in heavy traffic, shot at the car. A bullet struck Valerie, the passenger sitting next to Doreen.

   Doreen was caught five minutes later. Valerie died from loss of blood. Doreen was taken to the police station.

   The bank robbers had handed the teller a handwritten note demanding money. Doreen was asked to write out the words of the note and have her fingerprints taken. Doreen complied. She was then, for the first time, allowed to telephone a lawyer, who thereafter represented her.

   Doreen was charged with the bank robbery and the murder of Valerie.

   At trial, the prosecution, after introducing the robbers' note to the teller, also offered into evidence Doreen's exemplar of the words of the note written at the demand of the police. On appropriate objection, the court should rule that this evidence is

A. admissible.

B. inadmissible, if Doreen was not advised that her handwriting sample could be admitted into evidence against her.

C. inadmissible, if Doreen was not advised that she could refuse to give a handwriting sample.

D. inadmissible, if Doreen had not been informed that she had a right to have counsel present.

3. Jack and Paul planned to hold up a bank. They agreed that Paul would drive the car (owned by Jack) during the getaway. Jack entered the bank while Paul remained as lookout in Jack's car. After a few moments, Paul panicked and drove off.

Soon after leaving the scene, Paul was stopped by the police for speeding. Noting his nervous condition, the police asked Paul if they could search the car. Paul reluctantly agreed. While Paul looked on, one of the police officers reached into the ignition and removed the keys. These keys were used to open the trunk, where heroin was found.

In the trial against Jack for bank robbery, the prosecution's BEST argument to sustain the validity of the search of Jack's car would be that

A. the search was reasonable in light of Paul's nervous condition.

B. the search was incident to a valid arrest.

C. Paul consented to the search.

D. exigent circumstances, including the inherent mobility of a car, justified the search.

4. A grand jury was investigating a murder. The only information known to the prosecutor was a rumor that Suspect might have been involved. The grand jury subpoenaed Suspect. Without specifying why, Suspect refused to answer questions about the murder. Suspect was found in contempt and has appealed this determination. The finding of contempt will be

A. affirmed, because a subpoenaed grand jury witness must answer all questions.

B. affirmed, because Suspect did not specifically invoke the Fifth Amendment privilege against self-incrimination.

C. reversed, because grand jury witnesses are not legally obliged to answer questions.

D. reversed, if Suspect's answer might have implicated him in a crime.

5. Dillon held up a gasoline station. During the robbery he shot and killed a customer who attempted to apprehend him. Dillon was prosecuted for deliberate, premeditated murder, but was acquitted. Thereafter, he was indicted for armed robbery of the station. Dillon's attorney moved to dismiss the indictment on the ground that further proceedings were unconstitutional because of Dillon's prior trial.

The motion to dismiss should be

A. granted, because once Dillon was acquitted on any charge arising out of the robbery, the prosecution was constitutionally estopped from proceeding against Dillon on any other charge resulting from the same transaction.

B. granted, because the Double Jeopardy Clause prohibits a subsequent trial on a lesser included offense.

C. denied, because there is no constitutional requirement that all known charges against Dillon be brought in the same prosecution.

D. denied, because estoppel never applies when the defendant is charged with committing two different crimes.

Questions 6–7 are based on the following fact situation:

Nancy was a developmentally disabled adult who was serving a two-year sentence for burglary when police detectives received an anonymous tip implicating her in the unsolved killing of a police officer during a traffic stop several years earlier. Investigators pursued their suspicion and soon had collected a varied body of evidence linking her to the crime.

Two detectives arranged for Nancy to be brought from her cell at the state correctional facility and into a small interview room. There, she was questioned over a period of six hours about her suspected involvement in the unsolved murder. Her questioners did not advise her of her *Miranda* rights or otherwise indicate that she was not obligated to answer them, but they did tell her that she could choose to leave and return to her cell.

After indicating on a number of occasions that she was "done talking," but without ever asking to be brought back to her cell, Nancy began to make incriminating statements in a misguided effort to deny responsibility. Once officers confronted her with the accumulating inconsistencies in her answers, Nancy became confused and eventually provided a detailed confession describing her role in the (formerly) unsolved killing.

Based on the forensic and testimonial evidence gathered by homicide detectives, including her confession at the correctional facility, Nancy is indicted for and convicted of first-degree murder under aggravated circumstances for causing the death of a peace officer in the performance of their official duty. She is ultimately sentenced to death.

6. Defense counsel's effort to have Nancy's confession thrown out will likely

    A. fail, because she was not in custody for purposes of *Miranda* during the prison interrogation.

    B. succeed, because being incarcerated is the quintessential custodial condition.

    C. fail, because she never invoked her right to silence.

    D. succeed, because her statement that she was "done talking" was an unambiguous invocation of her right to silence.

7. If Nancy cannot invalidate her conviction, the best argument in seeking to overturn her sentence would be

    A. that there is an emerging international consensus that the death penalty violates standards of human decency.

    B. that the death penalty has been shown to be ineffective as a deterrent and disproportionately applied to certain groups of offenders.

    C. that imposing the death penalty on developmentally disabled or "mentally retarded" offenders is cruel and unusual punishment.

    D. that litigation over capital sentences ultimately impose excessive costs on taxpayers, and that cases often languish for years while the expenses accumulate.

Questions 8–12 are based on the following fact situation:

After a series of muggings within a four-square-block vicinity, police conducted a comprehensive sweep of the area. The mugger was described as a white male, about six feet tall, with blond hair and a goatee. While on patrol in this area, uniformed Officer O'Leary noticed Byron walking nervously down the street with his hands in his pockets. O'Leary could tell that Byron was white, about six feet tall, and had blond hair, but could not, from her angle of view, determine if he had a goatee. When O'Leary attempted to approach Byron for the purpose of determining if he had a goatee, Byron (having spotted O'Leary) hurriedly entered the apartment building that was closest to him. O'Leary followed him. When she saw Byron on the lighted stairway, O'Leary noticed that Byron did have a goatee and arrested him on the spot. After handcuffing and putting him in the squad car, but before reading Byron his *Miranda* rights, O'Leary asked Byron where he'd been at 9:00 P.M. on the preceding night (the date and time of the most recent mugging). Byron broke down and confessed to that mugging and several others.

O'Leary then searched Byron's pockets and found a diamond ring, which was later identified as the one taken from a recent mugging victim.

At the station, Byron initially claimed his innocence. However, when he considered his earlier confession and the ring, he agreed to plead guilty, based on a promise by the prosecutor of a reduced sentence. Soon afterward, however, Byron made a motion to permit withdrawal of the guilty plea and the entry of a not guilty plea. The court granted Byron's motion.

At his trial, Byron took the stand and was asked just one question by his attorney, "Did you commit the robberies with which you are charged?" Byron answered, "No." The prosecution then attempted to cross-examine Byron. However, the prosecution was prevented from doing so by the court when Byron's attorney asserted the Fifth Amendment privilege against self-incrimination. The court also prevented the prosecution's attempt to introduce evidence of Byron's confession to O'Leary for the purpose of impeachment.

8. Which of the following statements describes most accurately Byron's standing to object to the introduction into evidence of the diamond ring?

A. Byron has standing, because he was inside a residential structure when the ring was seized.

B. Byron has standing, because the ring was in his pocket.

C. Byron does not have standing, because he was unlawfully on the premises of the apartment house.

D. Byron does not have standing, because he did not own the ring.

9. If Byron contends that the search that produced the ring violated his Fourth Amendment rights, the most accurate statement is which of the following?

A. Byron is correct, because exigent circumstances did not exist.

B. Byron is correct, because there was no probable cause to arrest him.

C. Byron is correct, because there was no probable cause to believe Byron had the ring on his person.

D. Byron is incorrect, because O'Leary had probable cause to make the arrest.

10. Assume, for the purpose of this question only, that Byron's confession and the ring were inadmissible. On which of the following grounds, if factually true, could the court properly allow Byron to withdraw his plea of guilty prior to sentencing?

I. A criminal defendant is permitted to withdraw a guilty plea at any time.

II. Byron was under the mistaken impression that the confession was admissible when he pleaded guilty.

III. The guilty plea was "involuntary" because it was induced by the promise of a lighter sentence.

A. I only

B. II and III only

C. II only

D. None of the above

11. Did the trial court correctly prevent the prosecution from cross-examining Byron based on the Fifth Amendment's privilege against self-incrimination?

A. Yes, because Byron did not make an incriminating statement when he took the stand.

B. Yes, because by taking the stand merely to deny guilt, Byron did not waive the privilege.

C. No, because by taking the stand to deny guilt, Byron waived the privilege.

D. No, because Byron's right to rely on the privilege did not arise unless and until he was actually asked a question that could incriminate him.

12. Did the trial court correctly prevent the introduction into evidence of Byron's confession?

A. Yes, because the confession was made in violation of the *Miranda* rule.

B. Yes, because the confession was made pursuant to an invalid arrest.

C. No, because the confession is admissible for all purposes.

D. No, because the confession is admissible for impeachment purposes.

Questions 13–14 are based on the following fact situation:

Lynn, a lawful permanent resident of the United States, was involved in a heated argument with her partner in which words came to blows, and she was eventually arrested after neighbors called the police to report the domestic disturbance. Unfortunately, shortly after being released on bail for this initial offense, she returned home where she promptly got into another altercation and was arrested again. After a brief investigation following the second arrest, the local prosecutor charged Lynn with two counts of felony domestic assault and successfully argued to have her detained pending trial.

As her trial date approached, Lynn's appointed counsel and the deputy prosecutor handling her case met to discuss a potential plea agreement. The prosecutor offered to reduce the charges to simple assault in exchange for Lynn's guilty plea. Lynn discussed this with her attorney, and she was informed that she would probably serve six months on the reduced charges, and as much as two years on the felony counts, but that there was otherwise no difference for her to consider. Unwilling to admit her guilt, Lynn rejected the offer and decided to take her chances at trial.

Unfortunately, her gamble was a bad one. At the close of the case, the jury spent only two hours deliberating before returning guilty verdicts on both counts. At her sentencing hearing, the state trial court judge reviewed the jury's findings and sentenced Lynn to two years (the statutorily recommended term) for each offense. The judge then made the further determination that each count was a separate and independent offense, and he therefore invoked a provision in the sentencing statute that allowed him to order that her sentences be served consecutively. To make matters worse Lynn was informed that, due to her lawful permanent resident status, her conviction would provide the basis for her removal from the country after serving out her sentence in prison.

13. Which of the following statements best describe the sentencing decision in this case?

   A. The decision is invalid because it was arbitrary and capricious, or not supported by substantial evidence.

   B. The decision is valid because it was based on proof beyond a reasonable doubt.

   C. The decision is invalid because the term of Lynn's imprisonment was increased based on a fact found by the judge rather than the jury.

   D. The decision is valid because the choice of whether multiple sentences should be served concurrently or consecutively is traditionally within the province of the trial court.

14. If Lynn were to challenge her conviction as being tainted by the ineffective assistance of counsel, her best argument would be that

   A. her attorney should have been more aggressive during plea negotiations.

   B. her attorney failed to submit mitigating evidence showing that she had been subject to abuse as a child.

   C. her attorney failed to inform her of the immigration consequences of her conviction.

   D. her attorney failed to object to the introduction of the 911 call as a violation of the confrontation clause.

Questions 15–16 are based on the following fact situation:

Lucky was tried and convicted of arson in a state X court. She appealed her decision to the state X Supreme Court. Yesterday, the U.S. Supreme Court issued a decision indicating that peremptory challenges, when used by the prosecution to systematically exclude blacks from a jury, require automatic reversal. Lucky's jury was identical in composition to the jury that was invalidated in the U.S. Supreme Court case.

15. Lucky's appeal will be

    A. successful, because Supreme Court decisions pertaining to criminal procedure are ordinarily given retroactive effect in cases pending on direct appeal.

    B. successful, because improper jury formation is always grounds for reversal.

    C. unsuccessful, if the new decision is a "clear break" from previous precedent.

    D. unsuccessful, if reversal would cause a serious disruption to the administration of criminal justice.

16. If Lucky's appeal was predicated on a writ of *habeas corpus*, whether the recent Supreme Court decision would be given retroactive effect would depend on

    A. whether the new decision was a "clear break" from the past.

    B. the purpose of the new rule, reliance on the old rule, and the effect that retroactive application would have on the criminal justice system.

    C. applicable state law.

    D. none of the above.

17. After Dexter was arrested and formally indicted for rape, Dexter's photograph (along with several photos of other persons with similar features) was shown to Sally, a rape victim. Sally identified Dexter as her assailant. The prosecutor failed to notify Dexter's attorney that he was going to conduct a photographic identification by Sally. Have Dexter's constitutional rights been violated?

    A. No, because there is no right to counsel at photo displays.

    B. Yes, if Dexter's counsel had specifically requested to be present at any photo displays.

    C. Yes, because Dexter's Sixth Amendment right to counsel was violated.

    D. Yes, because this particular photo display was overly suggestive.

18. Trish went to a public high school. One of her rivals saw her smoking marijuana in the girl's room and informed the principal, who immediately asked Trish to see him. When the principal was advised that Trish was not at her assigned class, he searched Trish's locker (without obtaining Trish's permission to do so). There was no lock on the locker, so it was easily opened. The principal found a gun and other illegal drugs in Trish's locker. In a criminal prosecution against Trish, the gun and drugs will be

    A. admissible, because Trish had not reached the age of majority.

    B. admissible, because Trish was not in her assigned classroom.

    C. admissible, because the locker was in plain view.

    D. admissible, because the principal had a reasonable suspicion that Trish had engaged in criminal conduct.

19. Detective received information from Informant, who had given reliable information many times in the past. Specifically, Informant said that, two days before, he had visited Harry's apartment with Bill. Informant said he saw Harry sell Bill some heroin at the apartment and that there was more heroin still in the apartment when Informant left. Detective knew that Informant, Harry, and Bill were friends. Thereafter, Detective put this information into affidavit form, appeared before a magistrate, and secured a search warrant for Harry's apartment. The search turned up a supply of heroin. Harry's motion to suppress introduction of the heroin into evidence probably will be

    A. granted, because a search warrant cannot validly be issued solely on the basis of an informant's information.

    B. granted, because the information supplied to Detective concerned an occurrence too remote in time to justify a finding of probable cause.

    C. denied, because there was reasonable cause to believe a crime had been committed.

    D. denied, because there was probable cause to issue the warrant.

20. The police had reason to believe that the four Jones sisters had committed a robbery. This suspicion arose because they all claimed to have been out of town when the crime occurred. To check their suspicions, the police arrested all four and fingerprinted them. The sisters demanded to see an attorney before the fingerprinting occurred, but their demands were ignored. The fingerprinting procedure was

    A. unlawful, because it was done pursuant to an unlawful seizure.

   B. unlawful, because the police rejected the Jones sisters' request for an attorney.

   C. lawful, because fingerprints are nontestimonial in nature.

   D. lawful, because an individual has no reasonable expectation of privacy in her fingerprints.

Questions 21–25 are based on the following fact situation:

Willy was validly arrested on a charge of drunken driving. Over Willy's objection, the police took Willy's car to a lot that was owned by the police department and inventoried the contents of the car. Under the front passenger seat, the police found a plastic bag containing heroin. On the rear seat, there was a suitcase that was sealed by a zipper. The police unzipped the suitcase, opened it, and found two illegal machine guns. In the locked trunk of the car (which the police broke into), the police discovered a dead body.

21. The police impoundment of Willy's car was

   A. lawful, because Willy was lawfully arrested.

   B. lawful, because Willy impliedly consented to this action.

   C. lawful, if done pursuant to standardized police procedures.

   D. all of the above.

22. Is the heroin admissible against Willy in a criminal prosecution for unlawful possession of that substance?

   A. No, because the vehicle was not searched at the time Willy was arrested.

   B. Yes, if the impoundment was lawful.

   C. No, because the police did not have probable cause to search the interior of the vehicle.

   D. No, because while probable cause existed to search the car, no warrant was ever obtained by the police.

23. In a prosecution against Willy for unlawful gun possession, the firearms discovered in his car are

   A. admissible, because Willy was validly arrested.

   B. admissible, because the police had probable cause to believe the vehicle contained evidence of criminal activity.

   C. inadmissible, because the police lacked probable cause to believe the vehicle contained evidence of criminal activity.

   D. inadmissible, because the contents of the suitcase were not in plain view.

24. In a prosecution of Willy for murder, the body that was discovered in the trunk is

    A. inadmissible.

    B. admissible under the inventory exception.

    C. admissible under the homicide scene exception.

    D. admissible under the "search incident to arrest" exception.

25. For this question only, assume that (1) in a single trial, Willy was tried for possession of heroin, possession of an illegal firearm, and murder; (2) the body found in the trunk of the car was admissible; (3) the prosecution proved that Willy's victim was poisoned (i.e., she was killed in a deliberate, premeditated manner); and (4) as part of the guilty verdict, the jury sentenced Willy to death. On appeal, Willy's BEST argument for overturning the death sentence portion of the verdict is

    A. the murder charge should have been tried separately from the possession charges.

    B. the death sentence is cruel and unusual punishment.

    C. a sentence of death in these circumstances would violate the principle of proportionality.

    D. there was not a separate sentencing phase on the death sentence.

26. John and Diana rob a liquor store. As they leave, Diana turns and shoots the shopkeeper, Bill. John is caught by the police a few hours later, but Diana is never caught. John is indicted, tried, and convicted of first-degree robbery, a felony. Three months after the conviction, Bill dies from the injuries he suffered during the robbery. Immediately after Bill's death, John is indicted, tried, and convicted of felony murder for the death of Bill. John appeals his conviction for felony murder, arguing that the second indictment and trial were prohibited by the Double Jeopardy Clause. The appellate court will

    A. uphold the second conviction, because the conviction for robbery establishes that John is responsible for any murder committed during the course of the robbery.

    B. overturn the second conviction, because the Double Jeopardy Clause prohibited John's prosecution for felony murder following his conviction for robbery.

    C. uphold the second conviction, because Bill died after John's trial for robbery.

    D. overturn the second conviction, because both the robbery and the felony murder arose from the same event.

27. The police observed what appeared to be a drug transaction between Joe Seller and Bill Buyer on a sidewalk corner. When they approached Buyer to arrest him, he swallowed his purchase and began to run. After three blocks, however, the police caught and arrested Buyer. Within a two-hour period, the police obtained a warrant (based on the foregoing facts) that authorized them to inject Buyer (against his will) with a solution that would cause him to vomit violently. Laboratory analysis of the vomitus revealed partially digested heroin. Assuming there was probable cause to issue the warrant, the heroin would probably

    A. be suppressed.

    B. not be suppressed, because the heroin would dissipate within Buyer's system without injection of the solution (i.e., exigent circumstances existed).

    C. not be suppressed, because the police had obtained a warrant.

    D. not be suppressed, for the reasons in both **B** and **C**.

Questions 28–32 are based on the following fact situation:

The police received an anonymous telephone call that Paul was engaged in illegal gambling operations consisting of betting on professional sporting events. The informant did not say how he knew any of this information. Officers Laverne and Shirley went to Paul's place of business (Joe's Restaurant, where Paul worked as a waiter) and were given permission to speak to him. They advised Paul that they had full knowledge of his involvement in illegal gambling operations and that he probably would be sent to jail as a consequence of these activities. When Paul responded, "I've got nothing to say to you gals," he was told that he should consider himself under arrest. Before Paul was advised of his *Miranda* rights, Officer Shirley told Paul, "Confession is good for the soul," and asked Paul if he would like to make a statement about his illegal activities. Paul hesitated, but then informed the officers that he did "take" bets on sporting events.

He then voluntarily led the officers to the garage adjacent to his home, where he showed them notebooks in which were written the names of bettors, the amounts of money they had wagered, and the corresponding events. The police also searched Paul's person and found a pocket notebook that revealed bets that had been placed with Paul that day. The police then advised Paul that they were too busy to take him to the station house for booking then, but that they were confiscating the notebooks as evidence. Paul did not protest this action.

About two weeks later, Paul was subpoenaed to appear before a grand jury investigating illegal gambling. He appeared with an attorney whom he had retained, but was advised that he was not entitled to have counsel present. In a rage, Paul walked out. He has refused to return until his lawyer is allowed to be with him, even though he has been warned that he could be cited for contempt.

28. In the grand jury proceedings, Paul's confession as to his involvement in illegal gambling is

    A. admissible, because a *Miranda* rights violation does not result in suppression.

    B. admissible because Paul was not taken into custody.

    C. inadmissible, because it was given after Paul was improperly arrested.

    D. inadmissible, because it was obtained in violation of Paul's *Miranda* rights.

29. Can Paul be compelled to appear as a witness at the grand jury proceedings?

    A. No, because the police initially lacked probable cause to arrest him.

    B. No, because he was not given *Miranda* warnings.

    C. Yes, despite the lack of *Miranda* warnings.

    D. Yes, but only if the grand jury has reason to believe that Paul was involved in gambling operations, without reference to Paul's confession.

30. Which of the following statements is correct?

    A. Paul had an absolute right to have counsel present at the grand jury proceedings.

    B. There is no right to have counsel present at grand jury proceedings.

    C. Paul had no right to have counsel present at the grand jury proceedings if the evidence obtained from him was inadmissible in a criminal case.

    D. Paul had a right to have counsel present because he was arrested in connection with the purpose of the grand jury proceedings.

31. As a consequence of Paul's refusal to answer any questions, which of the following is correct?

    A. Paul could be convicted of perjury.

    B. Paul could be convicted of contempt.

    C. Paul cannot be convicted of any crime because the evidence obtained from him is inadmissible in a criminal case.

    D. Paul cannot be convicted of any crime because he was protected by the Fifth Amendment privilege against self-incrimination.

32. In the subsequent trial of Paul for the crime of participating in an illegal gambling operation, which of the following items of evidence obtained by the police officers would be admissible?

    A. Paul's confession, but nothing else.

    B. The regular-sized notebooks, but nothing else.

    C. The pocket notebook, but nothing else.

    D. None of the evidence.

33. Jay was angry with John for stealing his girlfriend, Sue. Jay wanted to get even. He called John up and told John there were no "hard feelings" and that he wanted to take over a bottle of wine. Actually, Jay had heard that John had some marijuana around and wanted to tell the police where it was located. John let Jay into his home on the assumption that Jay wanted to share a drink. After the two drank the wine, Jay asked John if he had any "stash." John obliged by going to his bookcase and taking some marijuana from a hollowed-out book. Shortly after they had begun smoking some marijuana cigarettes, John had to answer a telephone call. After he left the room, Jay grabbed the book that contained the marijuana and took it to police headquarters. He then told the police exactly how he obtained it from John. If John is charged with possession of an illegal substance on the basis of this evidence and Jay's testimony, John would probably

    A. win, because the marijuana is inadmissible (Jay gained entrance into John's home through a ruse).

    B. win, because this type of conduct "shocks the conscience."

    C. lose, because the evidence would be admissible.

    D. win, because the evidence, even if admissible, would be insufficient as a matter of law.

34. Officer Donald obtained a valid warrant to search Vic's apartment for a stolen television. When he arrived at Vic's apartment, Vic was home. After Officer Donald announced his authority and purpose, Vic permitted him to enter. Vic stated, however, that he had an important business meeting to attend and therefore wanted to leave. Officer Donald advised Vic that he was obliged to remain until the search was completed. When Officer Donald discovered the television set in question, Vic blurted out, "Okay, I took it. How else was I going to see the World Series?" Vic's confession is

    A. inadmissible, because he had specifically requested to leave.

B. inadmissible, because no arrest warrant for Vic had been obtained.

C. inadmissible, because Officer Donald had no reasonable suspicion that Vic had engaged in criminal activity when he forbade Vic to leave the premises.

D. admissible.

35. Sharon's phone was bugged by federal agents for 90 consecutive days on the strength of a court order that authorized a "tap" for four months. The tap revealed that Sharon was engaged in unlawful vice activities. Sharon wishes to exclude the electronically obtained evidence. Assuming the warrant authorizing the tap was based on probable cause and necessity, Sharon's best argument is that

A. electronic surveillance violates the Fourth Amendment.

B. a federal wiretap can be for a maximum period of only 30 days, unless there is a renewal.

D. the wiretap did not exceed the period authorized by the order.

E. a federal wiretap can be for a maximum period of only 60 days, unless there is a renewal.

36. Huffer was involved in illegal gambling activities, but the government had never been able to assemble enough evidence to prosecute him. Insider, who had been indicted for a similar offense, offered to help the government prosecute Huffer in return for a lighter sentence in her case. The FBI agreed. Insider purposefully engaged Huffer in several conversations, during which Huffer made incriminating statements. If the government seeks to have Insider testify about these conversations, her testimony will be

A. admissible, because Huffer spoke to Insider voluntarily.

B. admissible, because Insider was a private party.

C. inadmissible, because there was no court order authorizing the governmental action.

D. inadmissible, because the conversations violated Huffer's Sixth Amendment rights.

Questions 37–38 are based on the following fact situation:

Dr. Carla (a private physician) saw Jones loitering on the public street in front of her house. Assuming that Jones was "casing" her home for a future robbery, Dr. Carla went outside and ordered Jones to remain there while she summoned the police. When Jones started to walk quickly away, Dr. Carla tackled Jones and told a passerby to call the police. While Jones was struggling to extricate himself from

Dr. Carla's hold, a vial of heroin dropped from Jones's jacket. Dr. Carla grabbed the vial and held it until the police arrived. Assume that under applicable state law, (1) Dr. Carla had no legal right to restrain Jones under these circumstances; and (2) as a consequence of her actions, Dr. Carla could be liable to Jones for assault, battery, and false imprisonment.

37. The police subsequently arrived. They arrested Jones and confiscated the heroin. Jones was charged with possession of heroin. If Jones moved to suppress this evidence at trial, he probably would be

   A. successful, since it was derived from an invalid arrest.

   B. successful, since Dr. Carla had no legal right to restrain Jones.

   C. unsuccessful, if it could be proved by a preponderance of the evidence that Jones actually intended to burglarize Dr. Carla's home.

   D. unsuccessful, because the heroin was discovered as a consequence of Dr. Carla's actions.

38. Assume, for this question only, that the vial of heroin had not fallen out of Jones's jacket prior to the time the police arrived. Assume also that based on Dr. Carla's assertion that Jones had "attempted to rob" her, Officer Brown arrested Jones. The vial was discovered when the items in Jones's possession were inventoried, pursuant to standard police procedures, at the police station. Jones was then charged with possession of heroin. If Jones moved to suppress this evidence at trial, he probably would be

   A. successful, because it was derived from an invalid arrest.

   B. successful, because the search of Jones at the police station was conducted without a warrant.

   C. unsuccessful, because there was probable cause to arrest Jones.

   D. None of the above.

Questions 39–40 are based on the following fact situation:

While his mobile home was parked in the parking lot of a state-operated recreational park, Reggie solicited illegal drug sales. Buyers would make the actual purchase inside the motor home. Bill, an off-duty police officer vacationing at the campsite, heard about Reggie's activities from other campers. One individual, who had just left Reggie's motor home, showed Bill amphetamines that he had bought from Reggie. When Reggie left to pick up some supplies in town, Bill (taking his badge and gun) searched Reggie's motor home. Bill found illegal amphetamines in a closed suitcase. When Reggie returned from town, he was placed under arrest by Bill. Reggie was taken to the police station and strip searched. He was then put in a jail cell and formally charged.

39. The search of Reggie's motor home was

   A. lawful, because Bill was off duty when the search was made.

   B. lawful, because Bill had probable cause to believe it contained contraband.

   C. unlawful, because Reggie had a reasonable expectation of privacy in his motor home.

   D. unlawful, because the amphetamines were in a sealed container.

40. The strip search of Reggie at the station house was

   A. lawful, as a "booking" search.

   B. lawful, because "exigent circumstances" existed.

   C. unlawful, if it revealed nothing.

   D. unlawful, because Reggie's arrest was invalid.

41. Officer Jane, having obtained a valid arrest warrant for Defendant, went to Defendant's home. There, Defendant's wife told Officer Jane (1) that Defendant was visiting Friend and (2) Friend's address. Officer Jane then went to Friend's home. Friend answered the door-bell and, after Officer Jane announced her authority and purpose, said to Officer Jane, "Beat it, I've got no love for cops." Officer Jane then advised Friend that unless he opened the door, it would be broken down. Friend let Officer Jane enter. Inside, Jane arrested Defendant and seized heroin belonging to Friend (the heroin was on the table next to which Defendant was sitting). Friend is now being prosecuted for heroin possession. If Friend moves to suppress the heroin, his motion should be

   A. granted, because Officer Jane unlawfully entered Friend's house.

   B. granted, because the heroin was inadvertently discovered by Officer Jane.

   C. denied, because Friend consented to Officer Jane's entry.

   D. denied, because the heroin was discovered incident to a valid arrest.

42. Officer Joe was walking his beat one day when Kathy (the local candy store owner) advised him that Billy (a 26-year-old who had the intel-ligence of a 15-year-old) had just taken $50 from Kathy's cash register. Billy had done this by locking Kathy in the supply room (where she had gone to obtain a candy bar requested by Billy). As Officer Joe and Kathy were talking, Billy appeared on the other side of the street. When Billy saw Kathy talking with Officer Joe, he turned and ran. Officer Joe gave chase and shouted at Billy to stop. Officer Joe, who was losing ground to Billy, fired a shot over Billy's head, but Billy kept running. Finally, Officer Joe fired at Billy's leg. The shot accidentally hit Billy in the back, causing him to become permanently paralyzed. Assume that Billy's actions in Kathy's store constituted burglary (a felony) under applicable state law. The shooting of Billy was

A. lawful, because Officer Joe had probable cause to arrest Billy.

B. lawful, because Billy's prior conduct constituted a felony.

C. unlawful, because Officer Joe's conduct was unreasonable.

D. unlawful, because shooting Billy under these circumstances constituted cruel and unusual punishment.

Questions 43–44 are based on the following fact situation:

Defendant, a 17-year-old, was arrested (as she walked to school) for setting fire to a building on Main Street. She was given *Miranda* warnings and then asked if she would like to make a statement about the Main Street arson. Defendant answered, "I'll talk to you, provided you don't start hasslin' me." In the course of the interrogation, Officer Bill asked Defendant about a fire at a store on First Street. Defendant admitted committing that arson. The police then told Defendant that someone had died as a result of the fire. Defendant was subsequently charged with felony murder.

43. Defendant's admission is

A. admissible, if the police had probable cause to arrest Defendant for the Main Street fire.

B. inadmissible, because prior to her confession she was not told that anyone died at the First Street fire.

C. inadmissible, because she had not fully waived her *Miranda* rights.

D. inadmissible, because she was arrested only for the Main Street fire.

44. Assume, for purposes of this question only, that Defendant was validly arrested, but that she suffered from an unreasonable delusion that Officer Bill would kill her if she didn't answer his questions. Under these circumstances, Defendant's admission is

A. admissible.

B. inadmissible, because she was a minor.

C. inadmissible, because her delusion would invalidate her *Miranda* waiver.

D. inadmissible, because she was arrested only for the Main Street fire.

45. A gun and bullets were stolen from a gun shop. The owner immediately called the police. They combed the area, searching for the person who met the description furnished by the owner. About two hours after the theft, Jack emerged from a children's movie house. Because he closely fit the description of the person who had robbed the gun shop, Officer John accosted Jack with his revolver drawn. Jack froze when he saw Officer John approach and placed his hands behind the back of his head. Officer John then asked Jack, "Where's the gun?" Jack said, "I'm not answering any questions. I know my rights." Officer John responded, "Come on, there are kids inside that movie." Jack then led Officer John to the gun, which he had taped to the underside of a seat in the theater. At Jack's trial, the gun should be

  A. admissible, if Jack had committed a felony.

  B. admissible, because Officer John was concerned about a threat to the public safety.

  D. admissible, because Jack, who had not been arrested, was not in "custody" for *Miranda* purposes.

  E. inadmissible, because the police had no right to question Jack without prior *Miranda* warnings.

46. Although no arrest warrant had been obtained, Pat was arrested by the police as she walked home from work. She was told, "You have the right to remain silent. You have the right to have an attorney present during questioning. Anything said to us may be used against you." Pat then asked for a drink of water, which she received. Officer Jones then asked, "Would you like to make a statement? It might make you feel better." Pat responded, "I know I got a right to a free lawyer, but I want to tell you the truth anyway." She then confessed to shooting Arthur. The confession is probably

  A. inadmissible, because the waiver of *Miranda* warnings was not voluntary.

  B. inadmissible, because *Miranda* warnings were not given effectively.

  C. inadmissible, if there was no probable cause to arrest Pat.

  D. admissible, whether or not probable cause existed to arrest Pat.

47. Locust was convicted of murder in a state X court. The evidence used to convict him at trial was illegally obtained. However, Locust's attorney neglected to make the proper motions to suppress the improper evidence. After Locust had exhausted his direct appellate rights, he filed a writ of *habeas corpus* with the proper federal court. Locust asserted that his Fourth Amendment rights had been violated by admission of the illegally obtained evidence. The writ probably will be

A. granted, because Locust's counsel had negligently failed to raise a Fourth Amendment violation.

B. granted, if there was a fair showing that Locust's conviction would have been overturned but for the admission of the illegal evidence.

C. denied, because Fourth Amendment issues will not be considered in a federal *habeas corpus* proceeding if the defendant had a full and fair opportunity to raise them in the state proceeding.

D. granted, because Locust's Sixth Amendment right to effective counsel may have been violated.

48. Defendant was arrested and charged with distributing controlled substances. As part of its case, the prosecution wanted to show that a huge quantity of illegal drugs had been seized at a summer cabin owned by Defendant. However, at a suppression hearing that preceded the trial, the evidence discovered at the cabin was excluded because no search warrant had been obtained. At trial, Defendant took the stand and testified that although his brother was heavily involved in the drug trade, Defendant was completely innocent of the charges against him. When Defendant was asked on cross-examination if he ever had drugs in his possession, on advice of counsel, he claimed that he was privileged to refuse to answer since it might "tend to incriminate him." Although the judge ordered Defendant to answer the prosecution's question, Defendant still refused. The prosecution was then permitted to introduce into evidence the drugs that had been illegally seized at Defendant's summer home. The prosecution's use of the illegally seized evidence was

A. proper, because it was used to impeach Defendant.

B. proper, because Defendant improperly refused to answer the prosecution's question.

C. improper, because the evidence had been suppressed at a pretrial hearing.

D. improper, because Defendant's refusal to answer the prosecution's question was on the instructions of his attorney.

49. At the request of the police, a pen register was installed at a privately owned telephone company. The register listed all of the telephone numbers dialed from Darlene's residence. The police suspected that Darlene was selling drugs. No warrant was obtained by the police to install this pen register. The telephone numbers subsequently disclosed by the pen register suggested that Darlene was associating with several known drug addicts. As a result of this information, the police questioned the drug addicts and obtained incriminating evidence against Darlene. Darlene was charged with distribution of illegal drugs.If Darlene moves to suppress the evidence attributable to the pen register, her motion should be

A. granted, because the telephone company acted as a governmental agent.

B. granted, because no search warrant was obtained.

C. denied, because Darlene had no reasonable expectation of privacy in the resulting evidence.

D. denied, if the police acted in good faith.

Questions 50–51 are based on the following fact situation:

Bob was convicted in the state of Midwest. The main evidence used against Bob was the result of a warrantless entry upon his land and search of a fenced-in area located about 50 feet away from his house. Bob had grown marijuana within the enclosure and was successfully prosecuted under a Midwest law for possession of an illegal substance. However, the Midwest Supreme Court reversed the conviction, concluding that "pursuant to the Midwest Constitution, Bob had an expectation of privacy in the area searched."

50. The state has appealed the decision to the appropriate federal court. The appeal will be

A. successful, if there was a "No Trespassing" sign on the fence that surrounded the marijuana.

B. successful, because there is no expectation of privacy in "open fields."

C. unsuccessful, because Bob was afforded greater constitutional protection from the state than that given by the U.S. Constitution.

D. successful, because the area invaded was completely fenced.

51. Assume, for this question only, that the decision of the Midwest Supreme Court was upheld by the federal court. The federal government then indicted Bob for an identical offense under U.S. law. The federal prosecution

A. violates due process.

B. violates the Double Jeopardy Clause.

C. is precluded by the principle of collateral estoppel.

D. is permissible.

52. Officer Judy validly arrested Defendant and gave Defendant correct *Miranda* warnings. Defendant stated, "I want to see my lawyer." The police then allowed Defendant to call his attorney, who was out of his office. Defendant then said to Officer Judy, "You know, I've heard confession is good for the soul. I think I'd like to make a statement after all." Officer Judy stated the *Miranda* warnings again. Defendant then confessed. The confession is

   A. admissible, because Defendant waived his *Miranda* rights.

   B. admissible, if Defendant had been arrested for a misdemeanor only.

   C. inadmissible, because Defendant had requested to talk to his attorney.

   D. inadmissible, because the police were obligated to provide Defendant with another attorney until the first lawyer arrived.

Questions 53–56 are based on the following fact situation:

Informant was known to be reliable. He had given information to Officer Joe on several occasions. Informant told Officer Joe that (1) he had talked to Suspect a few minutes before, and (2) there was a bulge in the pocket of her suit, which probably indicated that Suspect was carrying an illegally concealed weapon. Officer approached Suspect (who was seated in her parked car) and asked, "May I see some ID, please?" Suspect shrugged and began to reach toward her pocket, saying, "I'll show you my license." Officer grabbed Suspect's hand and held it. Officer then patted the outside of the pocket, felt what he reasonably concluded was a gun, reached into Suspect's pocket, and pulled out what was indeed a gun. Officer Joe then arrested Suspect. Suspect was prosecuted for concealing an illegal weapon (a misdemeanor).

53. If Suspect moves to suppress the gun, her motion will be

   A. granted, because the weapon was the product of an unlawful detention.

   B. granted, because Officer Joe had failed to obtain a warrant.

   C. denied, because there was a valid detention and frisk.

   D. denied, because Officer Joe had probable cause to believe Suspect was engaged in criminal activity.

54. Suspect was convicted of the misdemeanor, which is punishable by a maximum term of three months imprisonment. Prior to her trial,

Suspect asked to be tried by a jury, but her request was denied. If Suspect appeals the conviction on this basis, the trial verdict will be

A. affirmed, because there is no constitutional right to a jury trial in criminal cases.

B. affirmed, because the right to a jury trial exists only when the offense is punishable by a prison term of at least six months.

C. reversed, because there is a right to a jury trial in all criminal cases.

D. reversed, because there is a right to a jury trial whenever a criminal defendant affirmatively requests it.

55. Assume Suspect had requested that an attorney be appointed for her, but one was not. Suspect appeals upon the ground that she was denied the right to counsel. Her appeal is based on an assumption that is

A. correct, because there is a right to counsel in all criminal cases.

B. correct, because Suspect's crime was punishable by imprisonment.

C. correct, if Suspect was actually imprisoned.

D. incorrect, because there is no right to counsel for crimes punishable by imprisonment of six months or less.

56. For purposes of this question only, assume that (1) Suspect was sentenced to three months imprisonment, but was immediately paroled; and (2) she filed a writ of *habeas corpus* with the appropriate U.S. district court, contending that the failure to appoint counsel for her constituted a Sixth Amendment violation. Suspect's appeal should be

A. denied, if she has not exhausted all of her state court remedies.

B. denied, because one must be in custody to assert *habeas corpus.*

C. denied, because there is no right to petition for *habeas corpus* from a state court to a federal court.

D. granted, because there is a constitutional right of *habeas corpus* review by a federal court with respect to all state court criminal cases.

Questions 57–59 are based on the following fact situation:

Susan was a 13-year-old eighth grader who attended her local public school. In the fall semester Susan decided to audition for the middle school marching band and was eventually selected to join the ensemble. In keeping with school district policy, all students participating in after-school sports or other extracurricular activities were required to submit to a urinalysis to screen for illegal substances. Susan's test results were returned to the school Vice Principal, Mr. Brown, showing high levels of opiates.

While considering what to do about this, Mr. Brown received an anonymous student letter stating that "Susan has been dealing oxy(contin) on campus all semester." Deciding that the time to act had come, he called Susan into his office and asked Mrs. Green, the school nurse, to join them. When Susan arrived, Mr. Brown immediately accused her of using and possessing drugs on campus and demanded that she "hand them over." When Susan denied the accusations and refused to surrender anything, he instructed Mrs. Green to observe Susan as she was forced to undress and submit to an inspection for concealed contraband. During that inspection, Mrs. Green discovered two capsules of oxycontin, a narcotic painkiller for which a doctor's prescription is required, and which is subject to the school's zero tolerance policy on possession.

57. Under these circumstances, Mr. Brown's decision to investigate Susan was most likely

   A. appropriate, given that he had a reasonable basis for his suspicion in light of the test results and anonymous letter.

   B. appropriate, because schoolchildren traditionally have no expectation of privacy when they are at school.

   C. inappropriate, because the anonymous letter was insufficient to establish either the informant/author's veracity or the basis of their knowledge.

   D. inappropriate, because random drug tests fail the particularity requirement of probable cause.

58. If Susan were subsequently prosecuted for unlawful possession of a controlled substance, the capsules discovered by Mrs. Green are most likely

   A. admissible, because Mrs. Green and Mr. Brown were careful to respect her modesty.

   B. admissible, because the search was based on a reasonable belief that it would uncover contraband.

   C. inadmissible, because Susan was confronted with the allegations of drug dealing without being allowed to call her parents.

   D. inadmissible, because it is unreasonable for school officials to strip search a student even if they have a well-grounded suspicion that the student may possess illegal drugs.

59. Now assume that Susan returns to class until the end of the school day, at which time she is escorted by her teacher into a small conference room near the main school office. There, without her parents or other adults present, two uniformed School Resource Officers question her regarding the allegations of drug dealing. They do not precede their

questioning with any warnings, and neither do they advise Susan that she is free to leave. After she initially denies any involvement, she ultimately confesses to selling prescription drugs on campus after the officers tell her that she's "too young to throw her life away." Only then did the officers inform Susan that she did not have to answer their questions and that she could leave whenever she wanted. Admitting that she probably did have too much to lose, Susan wrote out and signed a statement incriminating herself in the sale of a controlled substance. If these incriminating statements were offered into evidence during her criminal prosecution, their admissibility would most likely be

A. analyzed according to a standard, objective custody analysis.

C. analyzed according to a modified custody analysis that takes into account the suspect's age.

C. analyzed in light of the fact that Susan had just been strip searched.

D. Both A and C.

Questions 60–61 are based on the following fact situation:

Denise was charged with the crime of aggravated battery (a serious felony) in state X. She asked Lawyer Lon to defend her. Lon agreed. Lon was a highly qualified lawyer who was licensed to practice law in two states, but not in state X. Lon applied to the state X Supreme Court, requesting to defend Denise on a *pro hac vice* basis. This application was denied. Denise then chose Ron, an in-state attorney. Denise had some reservations about Ron's approach to her case, but the strategy was competent. A 9-to-1 verdict of guilty was returned against Denise by the ten-member jury.

60. The state X Supreme Court's denial of Lon's petition to defend Denise

    A. violated Denise's right to effective counsel.

    B. violated Denise's right to a fair trial.

    C. violated Denise's due process rights.

    D. did not violate any of Denise's rights.

61. Denise has argued on appeal that her Sixth and Fourteenth Amendment jury trial rights were violated. Her appeal should

    A. succeed, because she did not have a 12-person jury.

    B. succeed, because the jury's verdict was not unanimous.

    C. succeed, because she was not represented by counsel of her choice.

    D. fail.

62. Linda was charged with committing arson. She was indigent, so a public defender, Mary, was appointed for her. Linda was convicted. Mary appealed Linda's case to the state intermediate appellate court (as was Linda's right under existing law), but the appeal failed. Linda requested Mary to appeal her case gratuitously to the state X Supreme Court. Mary, due to her own time constraints, refused Linda's request. Linda filed her own petition for review with the state X Supreme Court. Under state X law, there is no right of appeal in criminal cases to the state X Supreme Court. Linda's petition was denied. Linda was

  A. denied the right to effective counsel, because Mary refused to pursue the case to the state X Supreme Court.

  B. denied the right to effective counsel, because no attorney appealed her case to the state X Supreme Court.

  C. denied the right to counsel, if she can show that her appeal probably would have been successful if conducted by an attorney.

  D. not denied the right to effective counsel, since this was a discretionary appeal.

Questions 63–65 are based on the following fact situation:

Wanda was prosecuted for petty theft (a misdemeanor). She was indigent and requested that counsel be appointed for her. This request was denied. Wanda was convicted and immediately put on probation.

Two months later, Wanda was arrested for shoplifting a diamond ring and indicted for grand theft. She was offered a public defender, but refused. Against her wishes, a standby attorney was appointed who occasionally coached Wanda at trial. Wanda was again convicted.

Under the state's sentencing statute, repeat theft offenders are obliged to serve an additional three years in prison. Wanda was sentenced to a term of five years imprisonment for the second offense.

63. When the state denied the right to counsel to Wanda in her petty theft trial

  A. there was a reversible constitutional error.

  B. there was error, but it will be deemed harmless unless Wanda can prove she would have prevailed.

  C. there was no error, because Wanda was charged only with a misdemeanor.

  D. there was no error, because no imprisonment resulted.

64. When the state appointed "standby" counsel for Wanda in her grand theft trial

    A. she was denied the right to defend herself.

    B. she was denied her due process rights.

    C. she was denied the right to effective counsel.

    D. there was no constitutional error.

65. Wanda's five-year sentence is

    A. a violation of the principle of proportionality.

    B. a violation of the Double Jeopardy Clause.

    C. a violation of her right to effective counsel.

    D. constitutionally permissible.

Questions 66–67 are based on the following fact situation:

Bill killed Tom. He was tried originally in a state X court on a charge of voluntary manslaughter. Although the prosecution introduced sufficient evidence to support a determination of guilty, the jury was unable to reach a verdict. Bill was then retried for the same offense. This time, the jury returned a verdict of guilty. However, their determination was overturned by the trial judge, based on the weight of the evidence.

66. Bill's retrial was

    A. barred by the Double Jeopardy Clause, because jeopardy had previously attached.

    B. barred by the Double Jeopardy Clause, because the jury had been impaneled and sworn.

    C. not barred by the Double Jeopardy Clause, because there was a hung jury in the first trial.

    D. barred by the Double Jeopardy Clause, because a verdict had been returned in the first trial.

67. Can Bill be retried a third time?

    A. No, because the initial trial ended in a hung jury.

    B. No, because retrial is barred after a reversal resulting from insufficient evidence.

    C. Yes, because a retrial is not barred after a reversal based on the weight of the evidence.

    D. No, because only a single retrial is permissible.

68. Six workers had just cashed their weekly paychecks in a liquor store when they were robbed at gunpoint in the liquor store's parking lot. The state X prosecutor charged and prosecuted Jim with the robbery of Joe, one of the workers. Jim's sole defense was an alibi defense. Jim

was acquitted. The state X prosecutor has now charged Jim with the robbery of Allan, another of the workers. Jim

A. can have the charge dismissed, because the prosecution is obliged to bring all criminal charges arising from a single incident, transaction, or occurrence in one case.

B. can have the charge dismissed, because he was successful in the initial case based on an alibi defense, equally applicable to the second case.

C. cannot have the charge dismissed, because the charge against Jim for robbery of Allan constitutes a different case for purposes of the Double Jeopardy Clause.

D. cannot have the charge dismissed, because there are different issues in this instance.

Questions 69–71 are based on the following fact situation:

The police in the city of Smud were conducting a lineup as part of a murder investigation. Wanting to conform to constitutional safeguards, Officer Green decided that they would need five persons in the lineup in addition to the suspect, Jones. Jones had been arrested without a warrant one hour earlier while walking home from work. Jones had not yet been charged with the murder in question. Because Jones was white and there were only three other persons at police headquarters who were white, Officer Green walked outside to find a citizen who would "volunteer" to be in the lineup.

Green spotted Mr. Bad Lad sitting on a bench. He approached Bad Lad and asked him to volunteer. Bad Lad refused. However, when Green taunted him about not fulfilling his civic duties, Bad Lad agreed to be placed in the lineup.

Jones, the suspect, was 6′ 5″, Bad Lad was 6′ 2″, and the rest of the participants were 5′ 9″ to 6′ 0″.

Green placed Bad Lad next to Jones and then brought Witness into the room. As soon as Witness saw Bad Lad, he pointed at him and shouted, "Hey, that guy robbed my store this morning." Green immediately asked, "What about the guy standing to his right [referring to Jones]?" Witness replied, "He looks like the guy who shot my brother, yeah, that's him."

Bad Lad tried to run from the elevated stage, but Green grabbed him by the wrist. Green told other officers to take Jones away. Green searched Bad Lad and found a small handgun on him. Bad Lad then exclaimed, "Man, this ain't my day. I might as well confess." Green then read Bad Lad his *Miranda* warnings, after which Bad Lad refused to speak.

Bad Lad and Jones were indicted shortly thereafter.

69. Jones objected to the lineup. That objection should be

    A. sustained, on the grounds that Jones did not have assistance of counsel at the lineup.

    B. sustained, on the grounds that Jones's right to due process of law was violated because the lineup procedure was impermissibly suggestive.

    C. overruled, because no constitutional violation occurred in obtaining this evidence.

    D. overruled, whether or not the police lacked probable cause to arrest Jones.

70. If Bad Lad was tried for the robbery of Witness's store, the gun would be

    A. admissible, because Bad Lad's arrest was valid.

    B. inadmissible, because no warrant had been obtained for Bad Lad's arrest.

    C. inadmissible, because Bad Lad had not been given the *Miranda* warnings.

    D. inadmissible, because Bad Lad had been illegally detained.

71. If Bad Lad was tried for the robbery of Witness's store, Bad Lad's statement ("I might as well confess") would be

    A. inadmissible, because he had not been given the *Miranda* warnings.

    B. admissible, because *Miranda* warnings were not necessary.

    C. inadmissible, because it was the product of an illegal detention.

    D. inadmissible, because counsel was not appointed for Bad Lad immediately after Witness's identification.

Questions 72–79 are based on the following fact situation:

Mel, an FBI agent, was advised by a reliable informant that she had personally seen Ann printing counterfeit money in her house. Mel went to the office of the assistant U.S. attorney on the same day and asked her whether she felt there was enough evidence to arrest Ann. The assistant U.S. attorney answered affirmatively.

Mel then went to Ann's house. As he arrived at Ann's door, Mel realized that he had once heard from a source he could not remember that Ann had a violence-prone boyfriend. As a consequence, Mel decided to be careful. He knocked on the door. A young female voice asked, "Who's there?" Mel replied, "A friend of Ann's." The door was opened by Ann's 17-year-old daughter, Suzy. Mel started into the house but, less fearful now, told Suzy before he crossed the threshold that he was an FBI agent who wanted to arrest Ann. Suzy then tried to close the door, but Mel was able to push into the house before Suzy was able to slam the door shut.

Mel found Ann taking a nap in her bedroom and placed her under arrest. Mel saw a small, but sophisticated machine (which could be used to print counterfeit money) next to the bed where Ann was napping. He thought about seizing it, but decided against it.

After taking Ann to the jail to await arraignment, Mel obtained a search warrant. It authorized him to search Ann's bedroom for and to seize the machine. As Mel left to execute the search warrant, the assistant U.S. attorney said, "Mel, seize anything else that looks good while you're out at Ann's." (Although probably not the case, you may assume that the search warrant was validly issued.)

When Mel arrived back at Ann's house, he knocked on the door. Suzy answered. Mel properly identified himself and told her he had a warrant to search the house. Suzy then let Mel in. On the way to the bedroom, Mel saw a closed door in the living room (which he thought led to a closet, as indeed it did). Thinking that Ann's boyfriend might be hiding there, he opened the closet door. No one was inside, but Mel saw a sawed-off shotgun on a shelf. Because possession of such a firearm violated federal law, he seized it. He next went to the bedroom and saw that the machine was no longer on the floor. Mel opened a jewelry box on Ann's desk and found chemicals and dyes used in counterfeiting. He seized them, too. Mel then opened the bedroom closet door and saw the machine sitting on the floor along with a number of bills (which later proved to be counterfeit). Mel seized the machine and the bills.

72. Mel's arrest of Ann was

    A. invalid, because he had failed to obtain an arrest warrant.

    B. valid, because the assistant U.S. attorney had approved the arrest.

    C. valid, if Mel had probable cause to arrest her.

    D. valid, if Ann's conduct constituted a felony.

73. Mel's first entry into Ann's home was

    A. valid, if there was probable cause to arrest Ann.

    B. invalid, because Suzy's consent to Mel's entry was vitiated because she was a minor.

    C. valid, since sufficient exigent circumstances existed.

    D. invalid.

74. When Mel saw the machine at the time he arrested Ann

    A. he could legally have seized it, because it was in plain view.

    B. he could not seize it, because he did not have a warrant for Ann's arrest.

C. he could not seize it, because it was located beyond Ann's immediate control.

D. he could not seize it whether or not the arrest was proper, because he did not have a search warrant for the machine.

75. Mel's seizure of the sawed-off shotgun was

A. invalid, because his second entry into Ann's house was invalid.

B. invalid, because the sawed-off shotgun was not connected to the counterfeiting scheme.

C. valid, because the sawed-off shotgun was contraband.

D. invalid, because the search was outside the scope of the warrant.

76. Mel's seizure of the chemicals and dyes in Ann's jewelry box was

A. invalid, because police officers executing a proper warrant may not seize items not described in the document.

B. valid, because the jewelry box was in plain view.

C. invalid, because the machine could not reasonably have been contained in the jewelry box.

D. valid, because Mel was entitled to seize any evidence pertaining to the counterfeiting scheme found in Ann's bedroom.

77. Mel's seizure of the machine in the bedroom closet was

A. invalid, because it was not in plain view.

B. invalid, because it was not where Mel had previously seen it.

C. valid, because Suzy's consent to Mel's entry into the house entitled him to search the entire premises.

D. valid, because the machine was found while Mel was in the process of properly executing the warrant.

78. Mel's seizure of the counterfeit bills on the floor of Ann's bedroom closet was

A. invalid, because he had no reason to believe that the bills were evidence of a crime.

B. valid, because they were in plain view.

C. invalid, because an assistant U.S. attorney has no authority to expand the scope of a search warrant.

D. valid, because Mel had a warrant covering the evidence.

79. Assuming Ann moved to suppress the chemicals and dyes found in her jewelry box, their seizure could best be attacked on the grounds that

  A. they are privileged under the Fifth Amendment.

  B. the seizure was in violation of the Sixth Amendment

  C. the seizure was in violation of the Fourteenth Amendment.

  D. the seizure was in violation of the Fourth Amendment.

Questions 80–85 are based on the following fact situation:

Badluck called FBI Agent Hoover and told him that he had (1) participated in a bank robbery the previous day with Eddie Fingers and (2) since seen in Eddie's living room closet both the gun that Eddie used in the bank robbery and the stolen money. The bills were marked. Badluck described Eddie's home as a one-story frame house located at 823 Howard Street. Badluck also told Hoover that he had heard a rumor that Fingers had given his brother-in-law, Donald Doyle, some of the proceeds of the robbery to repay a debt and that Doyle had joked about the money feeling "kinda hot to the touch."

Later the same day, Hoover saw Doyle standing outside a massage parlor downtown. Hoover approached Doyle, identified himself, and told Doyle that he was a suspect and to raise his hands. Doyle complied. Hoover then "frisked" Doyle, feeling what Hoover thought to be a wallet in his back pocket. Hoover told Doyle that he wanted to see the contents of the wallet, and Doyle handed it over. After Hoover found in the wallet a map of the bank that had been robbed, he arrested Doyle. As he was leading Doyle to his unmarked police car, Hoover passed Doyle's car and noticed that it matched the description and bore the license plate of the robbery getaway car. Peering through a rear window, Hoover saw pants and a shirt on the floor. These items matched the description of those worn by one of the robbers. Hoover opened the closed (but unlocked) back door and seized the clothes.

After depositing Doyle at the federal jail, Hoover obtained a search warrant for the living room of Fingers's home. The probable cause affidavit detailed the information given to him earlier in the day by Badluck. A warrant was issued, but it mistakenly described Fingers's address as 823 Harold Street.

Hoover went to Fingers's home at 823 Howard Street without noticing the mistake in the warrant regarding the street name. He knocked on the door. When Fingers asked who it was, Hoover replied, "Fuller Brush." Fingers opened the door. Hoover then stated that he was really an FBI agent with a search warrant. Fingers told him to come in and was promptly arrested by Hoover. Following Fingers's arrest, Hoover searched the hall closet and found on the floor money that had been taken from the bank. He seized the money and then opened the living room closet, where he found the gun described in the warrant. On the floor of the living room, Hoover saw an unopened envelope addressed to Fingers from Doyle. Hoover opened the envelope and found a letter to Fingers from Doyle, thanking Fingers for the bank robbery opportunity.

Fingers asked to be allowed to go to his bedroom in order to bring his wallet to the police station. Hoover agreed and accompanied Fingers (who was handcuffed) to the bedroom. At Fingers's direction, Hoover retrieved Fingers's wallet from Fingers's nightstand. As he was picking up the wallet, Hoover noticed and seized a wig that protruded from underneath the pillow. The wig matched the description of one worn by one of the robbers.

80. Hoover's initial detention of Doyle was

    A. proper, as incident to a valid arrest.

    B. proper, because Doyle consented.

    C. proper, because of reasonable suspicion.

    D. improper.

81. Hoover's search of Doyle's car and seizure of the pants and shirt was

    A. valid, as incident to Doyle's arrest.

    B. valid, because there was a suspect at large who might have access to the car.

    C. invalid, because no warrant had been obtained.

    D. valid, because probable cause to search the car existed.

82. Hoover's arrest of Fingers was

    A. proper, assuming the Hoover was present pursuant to the execution of a valid search warrant and Hoover already had had probable cause to arrest Fingers.

    B. improper, because Hoover had sufficient time to obtain an arrest warrant and failed to do so.

    C. proper, because Hoover had probable cause to arrest Fingers.

    D. proper, because Fingers committed a bank robbery.

83. The entry of Hoover into Fingers's home was

    A. invalid, because he obtained entry by ruse.

    B. valid, because the error in the address would not make the warrant invalid.

    C. valid, because the presence of the gun in the house constituted exigent circumstances.

    D. invalid, because the street address was incorrect.

84. Assuming Fingers moved to suppress the contents of the envelope, Hoover's seizure and search of the envelope was

    A. invalid, because only items described in a search warrant may be seized by police.

    B. valid, because it was in plain view.

    C. valid, as incident to Fingers's arrest.

    D. invalid, because Hoover had no probable cause to believe that the envelope contained evidence of a crime.

85. The seizure of the wig was

    A. valid, because it was in plain view.

    B. invalid, because it was outside the scope of the warrant.

    C. invalid, because the warrant was defective.

    D. valid, because the wig was within Fingers's control.

86. Brawler was suspected by the FBI of illegal gambling. The FBI convinced Brawler's brother, Smitch, to place a bet through Brawler and to wear a recording device during the attempt. Smitch arrived at Brawler's home on July 4 and told Brawler that he would like to make a wager. Brawler said, "Okay, even though, as a patriot, I don't normally do this type of thing on national holidays." Brawler accepted the bet and was later prosecuted. The federal prosecutor introduced the taped recording of the conversation into evidence at Brawler's trial. Smitch's recording of his conversation with Brawler was

    A. constitutionally valid.

    B. done in violation of Brawler's Fourth Amendment rights.

    C. done in violation of Brawler's Fifth Amendment rights.

    D. done in violation of Brawler's Sixth Amendment rights.

Questions 87–90 are based on the following fact situation:

Percy, a 30-year-old adult, and Maynard, his 16-year-old sidekick, felt that they had a number of grievances against their local City Council that had not been satisfactorily addressed. They hatched a plan to "exact revenge" on the council by detonating an explosive device at the council's chambers. Alan, an FBI Agent, had been posing as a black market chemical dealer when he was approached by Percy and Maynard seeking the chemical ingredients for their bomb-making activities. Alan agreed to meet them at 8 P.M. the following night to deliver their requested materials.

The next evening, Alan, Percy, and Maynard met as planned. Alan delivered what appeared to be all the necessary materials for their explosive, but he had secretly substituted the contents of one of the containers with a nearly identical but inert substance that would prevent any explosive reaction.

While loading the goods into Percy and Maynard's truck, Alan (who was wearing a concealed recording device) began to ask Percy and Maynard questions about their plans and offered his help, "for a fee of course." Percy responded that their plans would better be kept secret for the time being but added that "everyone will soon see, in a flash of light, my message." With that, Percy and Maynard finished loading the trunk, paid Alan, and drove off.

Unbeknownst to Percy and Maynard, Alan had placed an electronic beeper inside one of the chemical containers. This beeper allowed Alan and his associates to track the movement of Percy and Maynard with the chemicals in their car throughout the night and the following morning. The beeper continually transmitted Percy and Maynard's location as they traveled to several hardware stores, and back and forth to a motel where they had rented a room. Using information from the beeper, Alan eventually determined that the chemicals had finally been unloaded and brought into Percy and Maynard's room.

Several hours later, without being seen by the officers who were tailing them, Percy and Maynard exited the motel by a side door and left in their car with the explosive device in hand. They placed the device against the outside wall of the City Council building, immediately adjacent to the dais where the councilmembers would all be sitting during their meeting that evening. Percy and Maynard set the timer to detonate the device 20 minutes into the meeting and then left. At the preset time, a huge explosion and flash of light tore into the building, killing four councilmembers and injuring the remaining three. As investigators later learned, it turned out the Percy and Maynard had already acquired some of the bomb-making materials from another source and had used the "active" version of the ingredient Alan had surreptitiously replaced.

Percy and Maynard (who was tried as an adult) are both convicted of multiple counts of aggravated murder and eventually sentenced to death. By the time that the date for carrying out their sentence arrived, Maynard had turned 18 while Percy, who was originally declared competent to stand trial, had suffered a psychotic breakdown during his time on death row and was now so severely mentally ill that he was unaware of what was happening to him and unable to comprehend his external reality.

87. If defendants seek to challenge the admission of the evidence collected by the electronic beeper,

   A. the court will admit the evidence because it was installed with the consent of the container's owner *before* it was transferred to Percy and Maynard.

   B. the court will suppress the evidence because installation of the beeper interfered with Percy and Maynard's property interest in the container, which vested upon their purchase from Alan.

   C. the court will admit the evidence because the beeper never transmitted any sensitive, intimate, or confidential information.

   D. the court will have to determine how much of the evidence to admit, differentiating between beeper transmissions confirming what the officers could otherwise see and transmissions revealing private and otherwise inaccessible information.

88. Assume that Percy's counsel objected to the introduction of Percy's recorded statement that "everyone will soon see, in a flash of light, [his] message." The court will likely conclude that

A. the statement is inflammatory and likely to appeal to the passions of the jury.

B. the statement was collected in the absence of a warrant and therefore inadmissible.

C. the statement can only be admitted into evidence if the witness, Alan, is also called to testify.

D. the statement can be admitted as a voluntary disclosure, regardless of whether Percy knew his statement was being recorded.

89. If all other arguments fail, and the defendants fail to overturn their convictions, Percy will

A. not be able to avoid the death penalty because he was found competent for trial and that finding has not been disturbed.

B. not be able to avoid the death penalty because he knew right from wrong at the time of the killings.

C. be able to avoid the death penalty because he appears to be not guilty by reason of insanity.

D. be able to avoid the death penalty because execution of mentally ill offenders violates the prohibition on cruel and unusual punishment.

90. If all other arguments fail, and the defendants fail to overturn their conviction, Maynard will

A. be able to avoid the death penalty if he can show that it was Percy who actually built and armed the explosive device.

B. not be able to avoid the death penalty because he was an active participant in the crimes.

C. be able to avoid the death penalty because he was under the age of 18 at the time of the offense.

D. not be able to avoid the death penalty because he had turned 18 by the date set for the imposition of his sentence.

91. Over the years, Mark and his neighbor Phil have come to despise each other. Most recently, Phil has neglected to return a power saw borrowed from Mark. Mark has asked Phil to return the item many times. But each time, Phil merely replies, "No problem," and then fails to return the saw. Mark has became so angry, he decides to kill Phil. He makes a list called "Six Ways to Do Away with Phil." One entry on the list is "Buy new hammer to bash Phil's skull in." Mark finally decides he's had enough and buys the hammer.

The next day, Mark sees Phil lounging in his backyard hot tub. Mark shoves the "Six Ways" list into his pocket, grabs his new hammer, and creeps up behind Phil as the latter sits in the hot tub. Yelling "You lazy bum!" Mark strikes Phil in the skull with the hammer several times, killing him. Betty, Phil's wife, hears Mark's yell and rushes out to find Phil dead. She calls the police and tells them (1) that Phil and Mark hated each other and (2) that she heard Mark's yell and saw him near the body. The police then arrest Mark for murder. When Mark is booked at the police station, his clothes are searched, and the "Six Ways" list is found in his pocket.

If the "Six Ways" list is introduced into evidence by the prosecution at trial, it is most likely that

A. it is admissible, if Mark was validly arrested.

B. it is admissible, if Mark had waived his *Miranda* rights.

C. it is inadmissible, because a valid search warrant had not been obtained.

D. it is inadmissible, if Mark's prior consent to the search had not been obtained.

92. Jason is a Slurpee-aholic. He felt the need for a Slurpee fix but had no money. He grabbed his brother's toy handgun and walked into the local 7-Eleven store. Jason brandished his "gun" and demanded ten Slurpees. After guzzling the Slurpees, Jason pointed the gun at the cashier and demanded several Pogs. He put the Pogs in his pocket and ran out of the store. The cashier immediately called the police and gave them a physical description of Jason. She also told them what direction Jason had taken when he ran away. Officer Johnson started driving in Jason's direction. He saw Jason and immediately arrested him. He began to search Jason and found the Pogs in his pocket.

If the prosecution attempts to introduce the Pogs at trial, it is most likely that

A. the Pogs are admissible if Officer Johnson had a reasonable suspicion that Jason was the perpetrator.

B. the Pogs are admissible if Officer Johnson had, based on the cashier's description, probable cause to arrest Jason.

    C. the Pogs are inadmissible because no search warrant was obtained.

    D. the Pogs are inadmissible if Jason was not apprised of his *Miranda* rights prior to the search.

93. Jack and Maria were married for more than ten years. Their relationship was very volatile, and Jack hit Maria on several occasions. One time, Maria called the police and pressed charges. Maria and Jack finally divorced. Determined not to let any other man have her, Jack shot and killed Maria one night when she came home late from a date. There were no witnesses.

When the police searched Jack's room under a valid warrant, no weapon was found. But pants that appeared to have a speck of Maria's blood on them were found stuffed in a laundry hamper. At his trial, Jack did not take the stand.

The prosecution wishes to comment upon Jack's failure to testify at his trial. Which of the following is true?

    A. The prosecution may comment on Jack's failure to take the stand because this is a murder case.

    B. The prosecution may comment on Jack's failure to take the stand, but the defense can then request that the jury be advised that no adverse inference may be drawn from Jack's failure to testify.

    C. The prosecution is not allowed to comment, and, if requested to do so by the defense, the judge must advise the jury that no adverse inference may be drawn from Jack's failure to testify.

    D. The prosecution is not allowed to comment, but the jury need not be advised that no adverse inference may be drawn from Jack's failure to testify.

94. Cynthia and Phyllis are attorneys who work at Morgan, Taller & Jacobs, a large law firm in downtown Mindenville. Cynthia and Phyllis have been rivals for 12 years, ever since they attended the same law school. Cynthia knew that Phyllis was up for partnership consideration and deliberately sabotaged her chances by surreptitiously hiding files and destroying telephone messages. As a result, Phyllis was passed over for partnership. Sensing that Cynthia was responsible for her disappointment, Phyllis deliberately struck Cynthia with her car while Cynthia was crossing a street and then sped off.

There were several witnesses to the hit-and-run, and Phyllis was arrested. Minutes after the arrest and prior to receiving her *Miranda* warnings, Phyllis was confronted by a police officer, who said, "I'll bet that Cynthia was a real SOB, wasn't she?" Phyllis angrily replied, "You betcha! I'm only sorry that she dented my car."

If the prosecution tries to have the police officer testify as to Phyllis's incriminating statement at trial, it is most likely that

A. the statement is not admissible because police officers may not talk with a suspect prior to giving her *Miranda* warnings.

B. the statement is not admissible if the officer's comment was reasonably calculated to elicit an incriminating response by Phyllis.

C. the statement is admissible because Phyllis waived her *Miranda* rights by responding to the officer.

D. the statement is admissible because Phyllis's blurt-out occurred before the police officer had an opportunity to recite her *Miranda* warnings.

95. Gina is a favorite gown designer for many Hollywood stars. In fact, she has been called the "designer to the stars." Lately, however, a young upstart designer, McClaren, has been gaining popularity. In fact, several actresses who are up for an Oscar in the best actress category have ordered dresses from McClaren. One of these actresses was previously a long-standing client of Gina's.

The night before the Oscar award ceremony, Gina took several old dresses and drove to McClaren's shop. She put the dresses in a bundle near the door, and set them afire. Because the outside of the building was glass and metal, the fire did little damage. The fire department arrived several minutes later and extinguished the burning dresses. A witness identified Gina (who had remained at the scene), and she was immediately arrested but not questioned by the police.

Unaware that an arrest had been made, a firefighter on the scene held up one of the burnt dresses, shook his head, and said to Firefighter Cole, "Who would be so stupid as to start a fire with some old trashy dresses?" Gina happened to overhear this remark as she was being led away and spontaneously responded, "What do you know about dresses? They make a great fire. Go back to the Fire Academy, Bozo."

If the prosecution attempts to introduce Gina's statement at trial, it is most likely that

A. the statement is inadmissible because Gina was arrested without a warrant.

    B. the statement is inadmissible because it was made in response to a calculated effort to elicit incriminating information from Gina.

    C. the statement is admissible if we assume that Gina was given her *Miranda* warnings before her statement.

    D. the statement is admissible because it was not made in response to an interrogation.

96. Madolyn yearned for a suit in the window of The Chanel Shop. Unable to restrain her desire, she drove her Rolls-Royce to the shop, ran into the place brandishing a small pistol, took the suit from the window display, and then drove off.

    The store manager called the police and described Madolyn and her Rolls-Royce. The police immediately began to search for her. Meantime, a few blocks away, Madolyn double-parked outside her manicurist's shop and went inside for a quick touch-up. She had the gun in her purse and quickly hid the gun between the cushions of her chair. When the police entered the salon after spotting her Rolls-Royce, Madolyn ran toward the back door exit. She was tackled and arrested.

    Before Madolyn could be given her *Miranda* rights, a police officer sternly asked her, "Where's the gun? Give it to me before someone gets hurt." Madolyn walked to her chair, removed the gun, and handed it to the officer.

    If the prosecution attempts to introduce the gun into evidence at Madolyn's trial, it is likely that

    A. the gun is admissible because it represented a threat to the public safety.

    B. the gun is admissible because Madolyn impliedly waived her *Miranda* rights.

    C. the gun is inadmissible because the police lacked probable cause to arrest Madolyn.

    D. the gun is inadmissible because it was obtained in a coercive manner.

97. Marcus is fired by the manager of Marcy's Department Store after serving the store for over 30 years. Furious, Marcus hires "Mr. X" to kill the manager. Marcus's hired gun succeeds only in shooting the manager in the foot. Mr. X is arrested and implicates Marcus, who is then arrested and indicted for conspiracy to commit murder. Tony, a police informant, is put in the cell with Marcus and, at the government's direction, pretends to befriend Marcus. After Marcus makes bail, Tony and

Marcus are released together. Tony leads Marcus into a conversation about Mr. X and the wounding of Marcy's manager. During the conversation, Marcus says, "What a bungler I picked. Someone else will finish the job."

If the prosecution attempts to introduce this statement at trial, it is most likely that

A. the statement is inadmissible because Tony tricked Marcus into making it.

B. the statement is inadmissible because Tony's questioning is attributable to the police.

C. the statement is admissible because Tony was not a police officer.

D. the statement is admissible because Marcus was no longer in custody when he made it.

98. Baldonado, a local gangster, enters Joe's Butcher Shop. He tells Joe that unless Joe pays Baldonado "protection money" of $1,000 per month, his shop "might accidentally get burned to the ground." Unbeknownst to Baldonado, Joe is an undercover FBI special agent put in the store to investigate a local drug gang. Baldonado's threats are captured on both audio- and videotape. Baldonado is tried in state court for attempted extortion, but his "friends" manage to "talk" to several of the jurors, and he is acquitted.

If the U.S. Attorney's Office then proceeds to prosecute Baldonado under RICO and/or other applicable federal statutes, it is most likely that the

A. prosecution is not barred if the federal crimes have at least one additional legal element not existing in the state crime of extortion.

B. prosecution is not barred because double jeopardy principles are inapplicable.

C. prosecution is barred under double jeopardy principles.

D. prosecution is barred if there is at least one common legal element in both the state and federal crimes.

99. Madison is a dangerous serial killer. One night, three coeds from a sorority at Gregor University are brutally murdered. Witnesses at the scene observe a yellow "Bug" (identified as Madison's vehicle) driving quickly away. Using DMV records, the police arrest Madison. The coroner establishes the time of all three of the deaths at about 1:00 A.M. on January 5. At Madison's trial in state court for the murder of one of the coeds, a defense witness, Sheila, testifies that Madison was with

her from 9:00 P.M. on January 4 until 8:00 A.M. on January 5. Sheila also testifies that she lived two hours from the scene of the murders. Sheila is the only witness presented by the defense. The jury believes Sheila's alibi testimony, and Madison is acquitted.

The prosecution subsequently indicts Madison for the murders of the two other individuals.

Based on the foregoing,

A. Madison can be tried for murdering the other women because double jeopardy is inapplicable to a case involving different victims.

B. Madison can be tried for murdering the other women because the *res judicata* principles inherent in double jeopardy are inapplicable to different victims.

C. Madison cannot be tried for murdering the other women because the jury determined in the initial action that he was not at the scene.

D. Madison can be tried for murdering the other women if the prosecution can show that Sheila committed perjury.

100. Margot was arrested for shoplifting a red sweater from Marcy's Department Store. Shoplifting is a misdemeanor in this jurisdiction. At her arraignment, Margot told the judge that she couldn't afford an attorney and requested that one be appointed for her. The judge, who saw that Margot was dressed in expensive clothes and was carrying a designer purse, denied her request. Margot refused to hire a lawyer and represented herself at trial. She was subsequently convicted. Because it was her first offense, Margot was merely placed on one month's probation. Concerned about having a criminal conviction on her record, Margot appealed her conviction, claiming that her right to appointed counsel had been violated.

The appellate court will most likely rule that

A. Margot's right to counsel was not violated because she was not actually imprisoned.

B. Margot's right to counsel was not violated because the charge against her was only a misdemeanor.

C. Margot's right to counsel was violated when her request was wrongfully denied.

D. Margot's right to counsel was violated because she was convicted.

101. Mandy and Douglas had dated for over two years, at which point Mandy broke off the relationship. At first, in an effort to win her back, Douglas called Mandy several times a day and had flowers delivered to her house. Ultimately, Douglas began stalking her. But Douglas never threatened Mandy with physical violence or death. Several months after the breakup, Mandy was found shot to death in her bedroom. There were no signs of illegal entry into her home. On Mandy's bedside table was a card from Douglas that read: "I know it's over, and I know I'll never see you again until we meet in heaven." Policewoman Carla, Mandy's sister, knowing that Douglas had stalked her sister, immediately suspected him. She began to follow him during her off hours. One evening, after Douglas left a bar, she saw him commit several minor traffic offenses (e.g., exceeding the speed limit by 5 mph) for which imprisonment is not an authorized punishment. Carla put on her flashing lights just as Douglas arrived home. When he saw the flashing lights, Douglas ran into his home and locked the door. Carla ran after him and forced the door open. She walked into the kitchen where Douglas, distraught, was sitting. She advised Douglas that he was under arrest and recited his *Miranda* rights. She then asked him if he had anything to say. When Douglas looked up and saw that it was Carla, he whispered, "I'm sorry that I killed Mandy." Douglas's confession is

   A. inadmissible because Carla unlawfully broke into Douglas's house.

   B. inadmissible because Carla saw that Douglas was distraught.

   C. admissible because Douglas voluntarily waived his *Miranda* warnings.

   D. admissible because Carla had personally seen Douglas commit several traffic offenses.

102. Marcia, a high school honors student, is very nearsighted. One day, Marcia was on her way to attend the monthly chess club meeting at the home of a friend she'd never visited before. She was carrying a small duffle bag that she'd borrowed from her friend, Stan. Marcia had filled the bag with expensive chess pieces. Unfamiliar with the area, Marcia walked slowly down the street peering at addresses. Two police officers in an unmarked car observed Marcia. They accosted her and asked, "Do you have any stash?" Marcia thought the police had asked her, "Do you have any cash?" Marcia, who had $5 in her wallet, replied, "Yes." She was promptly arrested.

Unbeknownst to Marcia, Stan had placed several packets of cocaine within an inner lining of the duffle bag. The police found the cocaine, investigated all the circumstances, and arrested Stan.

If Stan is indicted but his attorney objects to admission of the cocaine, it is most likely that

A. it is inadmissible because Marcia misunderstood the police officer's question.

B. it is inadmissible because Marcia was never given her *Miranda* rights.

C. it is admissible because the police officers had a reasonable suspicion that Marcia was involved in criminal activity.

D. it is admissible because Stan had given the bag to Marcia.

103. Anita was driving five miles under the speed limit when she passed Officer Johnson in his patrol car. Officer Johnson observed that Anita was not wearing her seatbelt as required by the law of state X. Officer Johnson pulled Anita over because of her violation of the seatbelt law. Pursuant to the law of state X, failure to wear a seatbelt while driving is a misdemeanor punishable only by a $50 fine, and police officers have the authority (and the discretion) to either arrest the violator or issue the violator a citation. Officer Johnson, who was very concerned about seatbelt law violations, chose to arrest Anita. Officer Johnson then handcuffed Anita, put her in his patrol car, and took her to the police station to be booked. Officer Johnson's decision to arrest Anita was

A. constitutional because violations of the seatbelt law were of great concern to Officer Johnson.

B. unconstitutional because Officer Johnson could have just issued Anita a citation under state law.

C. constitutional because such an arrest does not violate the Fourth Amendment.

D. unconstitutional because such an arrest violates the Fourth Amendment.

Questions 104–107 are based on the following fact situation:

Officer Alvin responded to a noise complaint from the neighbor living next door to a home where a loud party was underway. Alvin approached the front door and noticed several boxes of empty beer cans on the porch, and could hear loud music and voices coming from within. The din of the party prevented anyone from hearing Officer Alvin's knock, so he went around to the back door. There, through an unobstructed window, he saw two women in a fistfight against a teenaged boy. Officer Alvin immediately entered through the unlocked back door and announced his presence, saying, "Police department—nobody move!" Alvin then separated the parties who had been fighting. "What's going on here?" he demanded. Donna, who had been involved in the fight, answered, "He's just mad that we got some acid [LSD] for the party and were willing to share it with our friends." "Oh, really?" replied Alvin. "Well, I'm placing you under arrest for possession of narcotics," he continued, and gave her the standard *Miranda* warnings. Alvin then searched Donna's pockets, finding five paper tabs of what was later proved to be LSD. Officer Alvin then conducted a brief pat-down of everyone else in the room—the two others involved in the fight and the remaining five guests. Officer Alvin found nothing of significance on anyone until he came to Ray, one of the attendees. When he felt Ray's left shirt pocket, he heard the sound of crackling plastic and touched what felt like a business card inside. Officer Alvin reached in to remove the object, and found a small sheet of LSD blotter paper wrapped in plastic. Ray is taken into custody along with Donna, and both are subsequently charged with possession of the illegal substance.

104. Assume that Donna is the occupant of the home, and seeks to suppress evidence on the grounds that Officer Alvin's warrantless entry of the home violated the Fourth Amendment. The court would likely declare the entry

    A. lawful, because the neighbor's complaint gave Officer Alvin reasonable suspicion to investigate further.

    B. lawful, because the fight Officer Alvin observed justified dispensing with the warrant process.

    C. unlawful, because a warrantless entry of the home is *per se* unreasonable.

    D. unlawful, because the neighbor's complaint did not furnish the officer with probable cause for his actions.

105. Donna's statement about the LSD is

    A. inadmissible because she was not properly Mirandized before Officer Alvin began his questioning.

    B. inadmissible because Donna was under the influence of hallucinogenic drugs.

    C. admissible because it gave the officer probable cause for the arrest.

    D. admissible because *Miranda* warnings were not required under these circumstances.

106. During Ray's criminal trial, he seeks to suppress the drug evidence discovered in his pocket. The strongest argument he could present in favor of suppression is that the motion should be

    A. granted, because the officer made a warrantless entry into the house.

    B. granted, because Ray was not acting suspiciously.

    C. granted, because Officer Alvin improperly questioned Donna.

    D. granted, because Officer Alvin had no reason to believe that Ray was armed or that the item in his pocket was or could be used as a weapon.

107. Assume for purposes of this question only that Officer Alvin had not seen a fight through the window, but had observed minors in possession of and consuming alcohol. Under these circumstances, the officer's entry would likely be

    A. unlawful, because underage drinking is not a serious crime.

    B. unlawful, because underage drinking is not an immediate threat to public safety.

    C. lawful, because criminal activity was taking place in plain view.

    D. lawful, because the officer still had reasonable suspicion to investigate and respond to the noise complaint.

Questions 108–109 are based on the following fact situation:

Armed with a warrant to search the premises for stolen electronics, police travel to defendant's home. As they approach the door to execute the warrant, they hear the defendant's voice inside, and the lead officer decides to force open the door without knocking or announcing their presence to anyone inside the home. Once inside, the police show the defendant the warrant and conduct their search in an orderly manner. The completed search of the home uncovers a large number of items fitting the precise description provided in the warrant. During the search, the officers also encounter a laptop computer, not listed on the face of the warrant, sitting open on a kitchen table. One of the officers revived the computer from power-saving mode with a keystroke, and the display immediately showed open image files depicting child pornography. Defendant was arrested and eventually charged with receiving stolen property and possession of child pornography.

108. Defendant's motion to suppress the stolen goods will likely be

    A. denied, because the search uncovered precisely those items anticipated in the warrant.

B. denied, because the failure to "knock and announce" during the execution of a warrant is not a basis for applying the exclusionary rule.

C. granted, because the "knock-and-announce" rule is inherent in Fourth Amendment reasonableness analysis.

D. granted, because the officers did not confront exigent circumstances that justified their behavior.

109. If the defendant were to request suppression of the digital images depicting child pornography, a court would most likely

A. grant the motion because the officers' examination of the laptop constituted an additional, unauthorized search.

B. grant the motion because the discovery of the images was not inadvertent.

C. deny the motion because the computer was found in plain view.

D. deny the motion because the officers could have reasonably concluded that the computer was within the scope of items for which they were entitled to search.

Questions 110–111 are based on the following fact situation:

Defendant was observed standing on a street corner known as a prime location for drug transactions when he recognized a plainclothes police officer coming toward him. Defendant turned and ran in the opposite direction. The officer yelled, "Freeze!" and gave chase. As he ran, the officer saw the defendant pull a plastic baggie from his pocket and throw it to the ground. The officer caught up with defendant a block later and tackled the defendant to the ground. The officer placed the defendant under arrest and, after handcuffing defendant's hands behind his back, uncovered a concealed handgun during a search of the defendant's person. The officer also walked back to retrieve the item tossed away by defendant during the chase, and recognized it as containing small glass vials of crack cocaine. Defendant is charged with firearms and narcotics possession offenses, and proceeds to trial.

110. Defendant's motion seeking suppression of the crack cocaine should

A. succeed because the officer lacked probable cause to arrest him.

B. succeed because the officer lacked probable cause to chase him.

C. succeed because the officer didn't know about the crack at the time he arrested defendant.

D. fail, because the discovery of the crack was not the result of a Fourth Amendment search or seizure.

111. Defendant's motion seeking suppression of the handgun should

   A. succeed because the officer seized him when he tackled him to the ground.

   B. succeed because the officer failed to properly identify himself.

   C. fail because the gun presented a threat to public safety.

   D. fail because the officer had probable cause to suspect criminal activity under the circumstances.

112. Defendant is indicted by a grand jury on capital murder charges. At his arraignment, the defendant is too dejected to answer any of the court's questions, and stands by silently as the court appoints counsel on his behalf. Thereafter, during pretrial detention, the defendant asks to see the detectives on his case. When they visit him in his cell, they remind him of his *Miranda* rights, and ask what he wanted to see them about. Defendant responds that, to clear his conscience, he has decided to tell them about his crime. The defendant proceeds to further implicate himself in the killing for which he is charged.

Consistent with the Sixth Amendment, these inculpatory statements would be

   A. inadmissible except for purposes of impeachment.

   B. inadmissible because defendant was already represented by counsel.

   C. admissible because the statements were wholly voluntary.

   D. admissible because the court's initial appointment of counsel during defendant's passive silence does not prevent subsequent waiver of his right to counsel.

113. Roommates Cain and Abel live in an apartment overlooking a public park where an attempted child abduction had recently occurred. Police officers were canvassing the neighborhood in order to identify witnesses or generate other leads, and they knock on Cain and Abel's door as part of the process. Cain answers the apartment door and, after hearing the reason for the officers' visit, begins to invite them inside. Just then, Abel arrives and categorically objects to the officers' entry. Under these circumstances

   A. the officers must resolve the disputed consent to enter in favor of the objecting co-occupant.

   B. the officers must resolve the disputed consent in favor of the co-occupant who has lived on the premises the longest.

C. the officers may rely on the disputed consent of one co-occupant so long as that party has joint access to and control over the premises.

D. the officers may rely on the disputed consent of one co-occupant so long as they are given consent by that party before the objecting co-occupant intervened.

Questions 114–115 are based on the following fact situation:

Carrie was traveling by plane from New York to California. While waiting to go through the security checkpoint, Carrie aroused the suspicion of police officers observing the airport terminal because of her nervous eye movements, her profuse sweating, and her constant clutching of her carry-on luggage. Observant officers pulled Carrie out of the security line and asked her to wait with them at the checkpoint while they inspected her ticket and identification. Although all her travel documentation was in order, the officers instructed Carrie to continue to wait while a canine officer had his specially trained dog "sniff" her luggage. Unfortunately, the canine officer on duty at that time was busy filling out paperwork for a promotion and did not reach the terminal until two hours later. When she did arrive, well after Carrie's flight had left, the dog sniff revealed the probable presence of either drugs or explosives. At that point, the officers opened the luggage and found an unregistered hand grenade inside and placed Carrie under arrest.

114. In seeking to suppress the hand grenade at her subsequent federal prosecution, Carrie's strongest argument is

A. that the officers had no basis to initiate the interview that ultimately led to the discovery.

B. that the officers lacked probable cause to subject the luggage to the dog sniff.

C. that the officers were permitted to conduct the dog sniff, but that they should have obtained a search warrant prior to opening it.

D. that, although the officers had reasonable suspicion to detain her, the length of the detention went beyond what was permissible based on that suspicion.

115. Assume for purposes of this question only that the officers had no reason to suspect Carrie of anything at the outset and that they simply approached her and asked about her travel plans at random. Assume further that the officers who approached her had the trained detection dog with them and that the dog alerted to the presence of contraband immediately upon encountering Carrie. Under these circumstances, the evidence discovered should be

A. suppressed, because the lack of any suspicion made the initial approach unlawful.

B. suppressed, because the approach was lawful but the dog sniff constituted a search without probable cause.

C. admitted, because a dog sniff without more is not a search for Fourth Amendment purposes.

D. admitted, because even though a dog sniff is a Fourth Amendment search, airports present a "special needs" circumstance where the Fourth Amendment does not apply.

Multiple-Choice Answers

1. D There is no reasonable expectation of privacy from aerial surveillance of an area over which there is an established aerial route. *See California v. Ciraolo.* The fact that the police used a relatively unsophisticated mechanical device like binoculars probably doesn't change this result. However, the use of a very unusual or sophisticated spying device to see something that couldn't be seen by the naked eye from public airspace might make a difference. *Cf. Kyllo v. United States* (discussing the use of sense-enhancing technology to learn information about the *interior* of a home that would not be otherwise available without physical intrusion). Since Sub had no reasonable expectation of privacy with respect to items in his backyard that were visible from the sky, use of the photos to obtain a warrant was proper. Choice **A** is legally true (there is a reasonable expectation of privacy with respect to items contained **within** one's home), but it's incorrect here because Sub had no reasonable expectation of privacy with respect to surveillance made from a plane within the established aerial route over his home. (Remember, just because an answer is legally true does not make it the best answer.) Choice **B** is incorrect because, despite the fact that the evidence was within the curtilage of Sub's home, it was viewable to anyone within the established air route. Finally, choice **C** is incorrect because the marijuana could be seen from the air. In the *Ciraolo* case, the defendant built a fence around the marijuana to prevent it from being seen from the ground, but the aerial evidence was nonetheless found admissible.

2. A The evidence is admissible. Because the evidence obtained from Doreen was of a **nontestimonial** nature, the Fifth Amendment privilege against self-incrimination was **not** applicable. *See, e.g., United States v. Mara.* Also, because Doreen had apparently not been formally charged, her Sixth Amendment right to counsel had not yet attached. In any event, the handwriting exemplars were obtained at a noncritical stage of the proceedings. *Gilbert v. California.* Finally, Doreen's due process (Fourteenth Amendment) rights do not appear to have been violated because the police did nothing that unfairly prejudiced her ability to defend against the outstanding charges. Choice **B** is incorrect because there is no legal requirement that a suspect be advised that a handwriting exemplar may be used against her. Choice **C** is incorrect because there is no legal requirement that a suspect be advised she could refuse to give a handwriting exemplar. In fact, Doreen could have been compelled to provide a handwriting exemplar pursuant to a grand jury subpoena. The Fourth

Amendment could not help Doreen here since there is no expectation of privacy in a person's handwriting. *See Mara.* Finally, choice **D** is incorrect because, as discussed above, Doreen had no right to have counsel present when the handwriting exemplar was requested.

3. **C** A search warrant is unnecessary where consent to a governmental search is voluntarily given by someone with authority to do so. *See Schneckloth v. Bustamonte.* Paul was driving Jack's car with Jack's consent and in furtherance of a criminal conspiracy. However reluctantly, Paul did voluntarily agree to the search and did allow the officer to remove the ignition keys and search the trunk. Paul will be deemed to have consented to the search. Even though Paul didn't own the car, his consent as co-conspirator probably would be enough to extinguish any complaint Jack might assert that his Fourth Amendment rights were violated. Choice **A** is incorrect because Paul's nervousness alone would not constitute sufficient "probable cause" to search the entire car. Choice **B** is incorrect because Paul had not been arrested at the time the search occurred. Finally, choice **D** is incorrect because Paul was stopped for a minor traffic violation and exigent circumstances did not exist.

4. **B** The Fifth Amendment privilege against self-incrimination may be invoked at a grand jury hearing. However, that privilege must be specifically claimed in order to become effective. Because Suspect failed to invoke the privilege specifically, the contempt finding probably will be sustained. Choice **A** is incorrect because the privilege against self-incrimination under the Fifth Amendment may be asserted at grand jury hearings. Choice **C** is incorrect because witnesses at grand jury hearings ordinarily must answer all relevant questions, unless they assert a privilege entitling them to refuse to answer. Finally, choice **D** is incorrect because while his answer may have implicated him in a crime, Suspect nevertheless was obliged to assert a legal basis for refusing to respond.

5. **C** The Double Jeopardy Clause does not (unless collateral estoppel is applicable) preclude a subsequent prosecution of the same defendant for a different crime, even though the latter crime may have arisen from the same transaction presented in the earlier trial. Because the crime of armed robbery contains at least one element that is different from the elements of premeditated murder, the prosecution would *not* be estopped from prosecuting Dillon for armed robbery. Choice **A** is legally incorrect. The prosecution may charge a defendant with different crimes resulting from the same transaction, if (1) the later prosecution involves a crime that contains at least one element that is

different from the earlier offense, **and** (2) no issue essential to conviction for the subsequent crime was actually litigated and necessarily resolved in the defendant's favor in the earlier case. Choice **B** is both legally and factually incorrect. The clause does not prohibit trial on a lesser offense if a new element is present at the second trial, and armed robbery is not a lesser offense included within the crime of premeditated murder; the two crimes are defined by different elements. Finally, choice **D** is legally incorrect (estoppel may apply when the defendant is charged with committing two different crimes if the double jeopardy doctrine is invoked). Prosecution for a second offense would not be possible if there was a finding in favor of the defendant in the first trial on a factual element essential to conviction on the second offense.

6. **A** *Miranda* warnings are required whenever an individual is subject to custodial interrogation. Custody exists where a reasonable person would not feel free under the circumstances to terminate their encounter with law enforcement. *Miranda* rights must be adapted to the context. Even though prisoners are not technically free to leave, that does not invariably mean that they are in custody and thus subject to *Miranda*'s protections if interrogated while in prison. The relevant question is whether a prisoner would reasonably feel free to terminate the interview, and being incarcerated is not dispositive of that issue. So long as Nancy knew she was free to return to her cell, and was not otherwise restrained from doing so, her freedom of movement was not constrained beyond that which is ordinary for life behind bars. *Howes v. Fields.* Choice **B** is incorrect because courts have refused to create a *per se* rule equating incarceration with custody. Choice **C** is incorrect because Nancy very well may have invoked the right to silence with her repeated comments, but the overriding factor is that she had no Fifth Amendment right to invoke. Choice **D** is incorrect because, even assuming that Nancy invoked her right to silence by saying she was "done talking," she was not questioned in a custodial setting.

7. **C** The execution of developmentally disabled offenders (those the Supreme Court has referred to as "mentally retarded") violates the Eight Amendment's ban on cruel and unusual punishment. Because these offender's mental disability generally prevent them from appreciating the significance or purpose of their punishment, taking their life serves no legitimate penological value. *Atkins v. Virginia.* Choice **A** is incorrect because, while international consensus against the death

penalty is increasingly strong, the United States has yet to agree with
the general proposition and instead has invalidated its use only in
specific circumstances. *See, e.g., Atkins; Roper v. Simmons; Kennedy v.
Louisiana.* Choice **B** is incorrect because, while the premises are likely
true, they have been rejected as reasons for invalidating the death
penalty under the Eighth Amendment. Choice **D** is incorrect for the
same reasons.

8. **B** A suspect has standing to object to the search of an area in which he
has a legitimate expectation of privacy. *See Rakas v. Illinois.* Because
the ring was in Byron's physical possession at the time of his arrest,
he had a legitimate expectation of privacy in the item. Choice **A** is
incorrect because Byron had no expectation of privacy in the apartment building, which was not his home. It's not his presence on
the stairway that gives him standing, but the possession of the ring.
Choice **C** is incorrect; the fact that Byron may have been trespassing when arrested does not lessen his expectation of privacy with
respect to items in his physical possession. Finally, choice **D** is incorrect because ownership is not a *per se* requirement of standing; here,
the key factor was possession.

9. **D** Probable cause to arrest exists when, considering all the circumstances, the police officer has reasonable grounds to believe that
the suspect has committed a crime. Because Byron fit the mugger's
description, was in the vicinity where the muggings had occurred,
and sought to avoid O'Leary as she attempted to approach him, it
is likely that probable cause was present. Therefore, the search of
Bryon's outer clothing was proper as a search incident to a valid
arrest. Choice **A** is incorrect because although exigent circumstances
may not have existed, O'Leary nevertheless had probable cause to
arrest Bryon. Choice **B** is factually incorrect (there was probable
cause to arrest Byron). Finally, choice **C** is incorrect because it is
not necessary to believe that a suspect has a particular item in his
possession in order to be able to use all the evidence discovered in a
valid search. Because the arrest was valid, any evidence found within
Byron's immediate control could be used against him.

10. **C** A court may permit a defendant to withdraw a guilty plea prior
to sentencing whenever there is a "fair and just reason" for doing
so. Fed. R. Crim. P. 11D. If Byron was under the mistaken impression that the confession and ring would be admissible against him
at a trial when he agreed to plead guilty, the mistaken impression

probably would constitute a "fair and just" reason for permitting him to withdraw his plea. (It is not clear that the court *would* so decide, but the court *could* decide this way without abusing its discretion, and the question asks you on what grounds the court could allow withdrawal.) Choice **A** is legally incorrect (a criminal defendant cannot withdraw a guilty plea that is fairly and voluntarily made). Choice **B** is incorrect because a guilty plea is not "involuntary" simply because it was induced by the prosecution's offer of a sentence that was lighter than might otherwise have been exacted under the circumstances. Finally, choice **D** is incorrect because, as described above, Byron probably would be permitted to withdraw his guilty plea under these circumstances.

11. **C** When an accused takes the stand to testify in his own defense, the Fifth Amendment privilege against self-incrimination is waived. When Byron chose to testify in his own behalf, he waived his Fifth Amendment right to refuse to answer questions about the crime charged. Choice **A** is incorrect. Byron did *not* preserve his Fifth Amendment privilege merely because he hadn't incriminated himself during his direct testimony. Choice **B** is factually incorrect (i.e., Byron did waive his Fifth Amendment privilege against self-incrimination by taking the stand to deny his guilt). Finally, choice **D** is incorrect because, having voluntarily chosen to testify in his own behalf, Byron could not subsequently refuse to answer questions that might tend to incriminate him. The right to assert the privilege arises when the defendant makes the decision to testify or not to testify.

12. **D** A voluntary statement obtained in violation of the *Miranda* rule may be used to impeach the accused. *Harris v. New York*. Byron's statement could not be used by the prosecution for its case-in-chief because it was not preceded by *Miranda* warnings. However, since it appears to have been made voluntarily, it may be used to impeach Byron's testimony. Choice **A** is incorrect because the confession is being used in cross-examination of Byron's testimony (rather than as part of the prosecution's case-in-chief). Choice **B** is incorrect because, as discussed above in the answer to question 9, Byron's arrest probably was valid. Finally, choice **C** is incorrect because statements obtained in violation of the *Miranda* rule are not admissible as direct evidence against the accused.

13. **D** Unlike the finding of facts that determine the length of an offender's sentence, which is the exclusive responsibility of the jury, the

determination as to how multiple sentences will be served is quite often a duty assigned to the judicial officer. In a series of cases beginning with *Apprendi v.New Jersey*, the Court has made clear that any fact (other than the fact of a prior conviction) that can serve to increase a defendant's sentence must be submitted to the jury and proven beyond a reasonable doubt, and it has enforced that requirement in exacting fashion in subsequent cases. *See also Blakely v. Washington*. However, the Court has also made a bright-line distinction between facts used to establish the maximum term of imprisonment, which belong to the jury, and those matters affecting whether sentences will run consecutively or concurrently. *Oregon v. Ice*. In light of the historical practice and the states' recognized authority over the administration of their criminal justice systems, the Sixth Amendment does not prevent states from assigning this responsibility to judges rather than juries. Choice **A** is incorrect both factually and as a matter of analysis—one should not discsuss the arbitrary and capricious standard in the context of a criminal trial. Choice **B** is incorrect because, while likely true, the quantum of proof submitted to the jury does not affect the question of which determinations the jury (or judge) is entitled to make. *Apprendi* and *Ice* indicate that only certain types of factual determinations fall absolutely within the jury province, but the standard of proof does not influence that assignment of fact-finding responsibility under the Sixth Amendment. Choice **C** is incorrect because it states the general rule with respect to facts used to increase the length of sentences and not the rule with respect to the order in which the sentences are served.

14. C An attorney who fails to inform their client of the immigration consequences of a plea agreement, and presumably of a conviction, has not met the minimum constitutional standard of professionalism inherent in the Sixth Amendment Right to Counsel. While the "reasonable professional assistance" standard of *Strickland v. Washington* is meant to be flexible, failure to advise a client regarding the potential for post-plea or post-conviction immigration action falls below that standard as a matter of law. *Padilla v. Kentucky*. Choice **A** is incorrect because it is not the best argument – the facts may be insufficient to ground an argument based on lack of diligence, and the right to receive counsel on the immigration matters is clearly established. Choice **B** is incorrect for similar reasons – the facts do not provide a basis for this argument, so any failure to submit mitigation evidence may be a result of appropriate strategic decisions by defense counsel. Choice **D** is incorrect because the 911 call will almost undoubtedly fall under the "emergency services" exception to the Confrontation Clause and is therefore not properly subject to suppression. Remember, when looking for the **best** answer, you must choose the argument that offers the highest chances of success.

15. **A** Supreme Court decisions pertaining to constitutional aspects of criminal procedure must be given retroactive effect to cases pending on **direct** appeal. *Griffith v. Kentucky.* Choice **B** is incorrect because not *all* errors in the formation of a jury constitute grounds for automatic reversal (e.g., some errors [not including the exclusion of jurors of a particular race or ethnic group] are tested by the "harmless error" standard). Choice **C** is incorrect because use of the "clear break" test for determining when a Supreme Court decision should be given retroactive effect to a case on direct appeal was overruled in the *Griffith* case. Finally, choice **D** is incorrect because, under *Griffith*, an adverse impact upon the administration of criminal justice is **not** a factor to be considered in determining whether a Supreme Court decision should be given retroactive effect.

16. **D** New constitutional decisions of the Court generally will not be applied on collateral appeals, unless (1) the new decision decriminalizes previously criminal conduct, *or* (2) the new decision expands the truth-finding functions at trial and enhances the fundamental fairness of the trial. *See Sawyer v. Smith; Teague v. Lane.* Choices **A** and **B** are incorrect because the "clear break" test was overruled by *Griffith*. To have retroactive effect, it is no longer necessary that the Supreme Court decision represent a clear break with the past. Finally, choice **C** is incorrect because the retroactivity of constitutional decisions is a matter of federal, not state, law.

17. **A** There is ordinarily no right to counsel with respect to photo identifications made outside the defendant's presence. *United States v. Ash.* Choice **B** is incorrect because Dexter's counsel had no legal right to be present at the photo displays. Choice **C** is incorrect because although Dexter's Sixth Amendment right to counsel was effectuated by his arrest, it was not violated in this instance (because photo displays are not a "critical" stage of a criminal proceeding). Finally, choice **D** is incorrect because the facts indicate that several photographs of other persons with similar features were shown to the victim.

18. D A student's personal effects may be searched by school personnel when they have a reasonable basis for suspecting criminal conduct or a violation of school rules. *New Jersey v. T.L.O.* (Note that the Court in *T.L.O.* did not specifically address the issue of whether students have a "legitimate expectation of privacy in lockers, desks, or other school property provided for the storage of school supplies.") Therefore, choice **D** is the *best* answer here. Because the principal had been informed by an eyewitness that Trish was engaging in illegal conduct on school grounds, the principal had a reasonable suspicion that Trish was engaged in criminal activity. An argument can also be made that since Trish had no lock on the locker, she did not have an expectation of privacy as to the locker. Choice **A** is incorrect because minors do have constitutional rights. While probable cause is ***not*** required, school officials cannot act unless they have a reasonable suspicion that criminal conduct or a violation of school rules has occurred. Choice **B** is incorrect because no right to search Trish's locker arose simply because she was not in the appropriate classroom when summoned by the principal. The search was not reasonably related to any school rule that may have been violated by her being in another room. Finally, choice **C** is incorrect because the contents of Trish's locker were not in plain view (i.e., seen from a vantage point that the principal had a right to be in).

19. D Probable cause is determined from the totality of the circumstances. *Illinois v. Gates.* A specific statement by a reliable informant who was an eyewitness to the event described in the affidavit probably would constitute the probable cause necessary to issue a search warrant. Additionally, there is corroborating evidence in that Detective knew that Harry, Bill, and Informant were friends. Choice **A** is legally incorrect (a search warrant may be validly issued on the basis of information received from an informant). Choice **B** is incorrect because the information probably was ***not*** too remote in time (Informant saw Harry sell narcotics to Bill just two days earlier). Finally, choice **C** is incorrect because (1) search warrants must be based on probable (rather than "reasonable") cause; and (2) the mere fact that a crime was committed at the location would not necessarily be sufficient to support a search warrant (rather, there must be probable cause that incriminating evidence will be found when the search is made).

20. A Provided that probable cause exists, arrests by the police without a warrant are valid under the Fourth Amendment unless made within the suspect's home. Because the police merely "believed" (i.e., did not have probable cause) that the Jones sisters were involved in a robbery, the arrest of the group was unlawful. Thus, the fingerprinting procedure was unlawful. Choice **B** is incorrect because there is no right to counsel prior to the time a suspect has been formally charged. Choice **C** is incorrect because while fingerprint evidence is nontestimonial in nature, it cannot lawfully be obtained through an unlawful seizure. Finally, choice **D** is legally incorrect (an individual does have a reasonable expectation of privacy in his or her fingerprints).

21. **C** Pursuant to standardized police procedures, the police may impound a vehicle whose driver has been lawfully arrested. Because Willy was validly arrested under a charge of drunk driving, the police (if acting pursuant to standardized procedures) would be permitted to impound his car so as to prevent theft or vandalism. The impoundment would fall under the "inventory" exception to the search-warrant requirement. *See Florida v. Wells.* Choice **A** is incorrect because the fact that Willy was lawfully arrested would not constitute, in itself, a constitutional basis for the police to ***impound*** his car. Choice **B** is incorrect because there is no indication in these facts that Willy either explicitly or impliedly consented to impoundment of his vehicle. Finally, choice **D** is incorrect because choice **C** is the only right answer.

22. **B** The police may "inventory" (i.e., inspect) items that come lawfully into their possession. Because Willy's arrest and impoundment of the car were, by hypothesis, lawful, the inventory was too if done pursuant to standardized procedures. Choice **A** is incorrect because a proper inventory search need not be done at the time of arrest. Choice **C** is incorrect because probable cause is not required to conduct a valid inventory search. Finally, choice **D** is incorrect because there is nothing to indicate that the police had probable cause, and no warrant is needed for a proper inventory search.

23. **A** Pursuant to standardized police procedures, a valid inventory search may include closed containers like the one in which the guns were found. *See Florida v. Wells.* Choice **B** is factually incorrect (there is nothing to indicate that the police had probable cause to believe the vehicle contained indicia of criminal activity when they stopped Willy). Choice **C** is incorrect because probable cause was not required to search the passenger compartments of Willy's car. Finally, choice **D** is incorrect because while the contents of the

suitcase were not in plain view, the police were entitled to search closed containers in Willy's car.

24. **B** The police are permitted to inventory effects lawfully within their possession if they act pursuant to standard operating procedures. *See Florida v. Wells.* This rule is known as the "inventory" exception. Choice **A** is incorrect because the body is admissible, provided this police department routinely conducted inventory searches of trunks at impoundment lots. Choice **C** is incorrect because there is no "homicide scene" exception to the warrant requirement. *See Mincey v. Arizona.* Finally, choice **D** is incorrect because the victim's body was in the trunk. Incident to the arrest of the occupant of an automobile, police may search the car's passenger compartment and the contents of any container found in the compartment, but not the trunk. *New York v. Belton.*

25. **D** In every capital punishment scheme the Supreme Court has approved, the guilt and penalty phases are conducted in separate, bifurcated proceedings. *See, e.g., Gregg v. Georgia.* Although it is possible to argue that this is not actually required by the Constitution, some lower courts have presumed that it is. The absence of these bifurcated proceedings would certainly cast a capital punishment scheme into constitutional question. Choice **A** is legally incorrect (the murder charge did not have to be tried separately from the other offenses for which Willy was indicted). Choice **B** is also legally incorrect (capital punishment is not, *per se*, cruel and unusual punishment). Finally, choice **C** is incorrect because the principle of proportionality (i.e., a sentence should be reversed when it is too severe under the circumstances) is inapplicable. The jury's verdict establishes that it had found the required elements supporting the death penalty.

26. **C** Under the Double Jeopardy Clause, a person cannot be prosecuted for a crime that arises from the same event or set of facts as another crime for which that person has already been acquitted or convicted. The rule is a narrow one that requires that the facts relating to both crimes be the same. The clause does not apply if the facts relating to the second crime are essentially different or if the prosecution is unable to try both crimes together for reasons that are not the prosecution's fault. Here, Bill was still alive at the time of John's trial and conviction for robbery. The prosecution could not indict John for felony murder until *after* Bill had died. *See Diaz v. United States.* Therefore, the Double Jeopardy Clause does not prohibit John's later

conviction for felony murder. (Note: It's important to this answer that the second crime is a greater crime than the first. If the first crime tried had been the greater one, the second would have been barred on double jeopardy grounds despite the subsequent development of new facts.) Choice **A** is not correct because the elements of the crime of murder were not considered or tried during the trial for robbery. There was no felony murder issue until Bill's death. Choice **B** is incorrect because the Double Jeopardy Clause did not bar the later trial for murder for the reasons cited above. The prosecution could not bring the charges until Bill's death. Finally, choice **D** is incorrect because robbery and felony murder are two distinct crimes even though they may grow out of the same event or the same set of facts. An indictment or conviction for one does not preclude an indictment or conviction for the other. If this were not the case, the entire concept of felony murder would collapse. By definition, felony murder is a crime that arises from the commission of another crime. Strict application of the double jeopardy rule in a trial for felony murder would preclude the trial itself.

27. **A** Police may not conduct a search or seizure in a manner that shocks the conscience. *Rochin v. California*. In *Rochin*, the Supreme Court held that "stomach pumping" a suspect to obtain evidence of a crime violated the Due Process Clause. Moreover, certain highly invasive body intrusions, even if supported by probable cause, are "unreasonable" under the Fourth Amendment. *Winston v. Lee*. Choice **B** is incorrect because even if the heroin would dissipate within Buyer's system (and thereby be lost), the loss of evidence is outweighed by the severe trauma caused to Buyer by injection of the solution into him. Choice **C** is incorrect because although the police had a warrant, it would not be sufficient under these circumstances. Finally, choice **D** is incorrect because choices **B** and **C** are wrong.

28. **A** A grand jury may consider evidence that would be inadmissible at trial. *Costello v. United States*. Even though Paul's confession would be inadmissible at a criminal trial (i.e., besides the lack of *Miranda* warnings, the detention and arrest of Paul were not based on probable cause), it can still be introduced at the grand jury proceeding. Most procedural protections are relaxed in grand jury proceedings, in part because the purpose of the grand jury is not to convict. Choices **B**, **C**, and **D** are incorrect because although supported by the facts (and although Paul's confession would be inadmissible in a

criminal case), the evidence in question is admissible in grand jury proceedings.

29. **C** An individual (even one who may be a suspect) who is subpoenaed to appear before a grand jury must comply with the subpoena. Despite the fact that Paul was improperly arrested and not given *Miranda* warnings, he would be obliged to honor the grand jury's subpoena. Of course, depending on the questions asked, he may invoke his Fifth Amendment right against self-incrimination and refuse to testify. Choices **A** and **B** are incorrect. Though both would be applicable to prevent Paul's confession from being admitted in a criminal trial, neither argument is available in a grand jury proceeding. Finally, choice **D** is incorrect because a grand jury's subpoena must be honored, even if the grand jury has no reason to believe that the witness was involved in criminal activities.

30. **B** There is no right to have counsel present at grand jury proceedings (i.e., actually in the grand jury room). Choice **A** is legally incorrect (there is no right to counsel at grand jury proceedings). Choice **C** is incorrect because even if the evidence obtained from Paul was not admissible in a criminal case, he would still have no right to have counsel present. Finally, choice **D** is incorrect (the mere fact that Paul was arrested prior to the grand jury proceedings would not entitle him to have legal counsel present).

31. **B** A contempt citation may be issued for refusal to comply with a grand jury subpoena. Paul's refusal to remain at the grand jury proceedings despite the warning that he could be cited for contempt can result in a conviction for contempt. Choice **A** is incorrect because Paul had not answered any questions (and therefore could not be accused of lying under oath). Choice **C** is incorrect. Paul may be convicted of contempt even though the evidence in question might be inadmissible in a criminal case. Finally, choice **D** is incorrect because it is factually untrue. (A witness at a grand jury proceeding must affirmatively assert the Fifth Amendment privilege against self-incrimination to enjoy its protections.)

32. **D** Evidence derived from an unlawful detention or arrest is inadmissible in the prosecution's case-in-chief. Because the informant was not known to be reliable and did not state the basis of his knowledge about Paul's gambling, the "totality of the circumstances" test of *Illinois v. Gates* is not met, and the police did not have probable cause to arrest Paul. Because Paul's confession, as well as the notebooks,

was derived from that illegal arrest, *none* of the evidence would be admissible. Choices **A, B,** and **C** are, therefore, incorrect.

33. **C** The Fourth Amendment (applicable to the states via the Fourteenth Amendment) applies only to governmental conduct. Because the evidence was obtained by Jay, who was independent of any governmental influence or supervision, it would be admissible against John. From Jay's testimony and the marijuana itself, a jury could conclude beyond a reasonable doubt that John knowingly had an illegal substance in his possession. Choice **A** is incorrect because although Jay did gain entrance into John's home through a ruse, the evidence that he obtained is nevertheless admissible (because Jay was not a governmental officer). Choice **B** is incorrect because Jay was not a governmental officer. Therefore, the Due Process Clause (which is violated by governmental conduct that "shocks the conscience") would *not* be applicable. Finally, choice **D** is incorrect because there is sufficient evidence on these facts to enable a jury to determine that John knowingly possessed marijuana.

34. **D** Pursuant to a valid search warrant, police have the right to detain the person who has lawful possession of the premises while the search is being conducted (even though neither probable cause nor articulable basis to detain exists). *Michigan v. Summers.* Because the detention of Vic was legal, his "blurt out" is admissible. There is no *Miranda* problem in this instance because Vic's statement was not made pursuant to an interrogation (i.e., Officer Donald had not questioned Vic about his criminal activities). Rather, Vic simply "blurted out" his confession when he saw that Officer Donald had discovered the television set. Choice **A** is incorrect because the fact that Vic asked to leave the area does not detract from Officer Donald's right to detain Vic while the search was being conducted. Choice **B** is incorrect because an arrest warrant is not necessary to detain the person in lawful possession of the premises covered by a valid search warrant. Finally, choice **C** is incorrect because Officer Donald was permitted to detain Vic whether or not he suspected Vic of any wrongdoing.

35. **B** Federal wiretaps are valid for only 30 days. The wiretap must be renewed to be valid. (Title III of the Omnibus Crime Control and Safe Streets Act of 1968.) Because the facts indicate that the court order authorizing the wiretap extended for a period of four months, any information gained after the initial 30 days probably would be inadmissible. Choice **A** is incorrect because electronic surveillance

that is based on a proper court order does not violate the Fourth Amendment. Choice **C** is incorrect because although the wiretap did not exceed the period authorized by the order, the period authorized was longer than permitted under Title III. Finally, choice **D** is incorrect because the basis for a federal wiretap must be reviewed after 30 days.

36. **A** Incriminating statements made in response to police questioning (or to someone acting under police supervision or influence) are admissible, unless (1) the defendant has already been indicted (in which event his Sixth Amendment right to counsel will apply), or (2) the statements result from a custodial interrogation that is not preceded by adequate *Miranda* warnings. In the typical "misplaced trust" case in which an unindicted suspect makes incriminating statements to an undercover operative, the statements are admissible. Because Huffer voluntarily made his statements to Insider and had not previously been formally charged, Insider (even though acting under government supervision) could testify about Huffer's comments. Choice **B** is incorrect because although Insider was a private party, in this instance she would be viewed as a governmental agent (i.e., she acted pursuant to the FBI's guidance). Choice **C** is incorrect because no court order was required in this instance. Finally, choice **D** is incorrect because Huffer's Sixth Amendment rights did not mature in this instance (because he had not been formally charged with a crime prior to the incriminating conversations).

37. **D** The Fourth Amendment (applicable to the states via the Fourteenth Amendment) applies only to governmental searches and seizures. Because Dr. Carla was a private party, Jones could not effectively raise a Fourth Amendment objection to her recovery of the vial of heroin and its delivery to the police. Choice **A** is incorrect because despite Dr. Carla's unlawful conduct, the police had probable cause to arrest Jones. Choice **B** is incorrect because although it is literally true (i.e., Dr. Carla had no right to restrain Jones under these circumstances), the Constitution does not extend to evidence obtained by or derived from private parties. Thus, the fact that Dr. Carla acted unlawfully does not preclude the police from using the fruits of her conduct. Finally, choice **C** is incorrect because Jones's intention to burglarize Dr. Carla's home is irrelevant to the question of whether the heroin would be admissible in a trial against Jones for possession of heroin.

38. C When an individual who has been validly arrested is booked, or within a reasonable time thereafter (provided there is a legitimate reason for the delay), the police may make a full inventory search of his person and clothes (including the contents of any unlocked containers). *Illinois v. Lafayette.* Because Dr. Carla told the police that Jones had attempted to rob her, the police had probable cause to arrest Jones (even though the statement made to the police by Dr. Carla was not supported by the facts). In ascertaining whether probable cause existed, the issue is whether a reasonable officer in Officer Brown's position would conclude that it was more likely than not that Jones had committed robbery. The fact that, unbeknownst to Officer Brown, Dr. Carla was mistaken in her statement is irrelevant. Thus, the vial of heroin was obtained pursuant to a valid inventory search. Choice **A** is incorrect because the police had probable cause to arrest Jones, given Dr. Carla's statement that Jones had attempted to rob her. Choice **B** is incorrect because the police are entitled to conduct a valid inventory search of the belongings of an individual who has been properly arrested. Choice **D** is incorrect because choice **C** is correct.

39. B The "automobile exception" to the search warrant requirement has been extended to mobile homes, at least when the home is being used as a "mobile" device (e.g., in a parking lot rather than permanently anchored in a residential development). *California v. Carney.* Because Bill (1) had heard from several persons at the campsite that Reggie was selling illegal drugs from his mobile home and (2) actually had seen the results of one purchase, he had probable cause to believe that Reggie's mobile home contained contraband. Therefore, under the "automobile exception" to the search warrant requirement, Bill's search of Reggie's mobile home was valid. Choice **A** is incorrect because Bill was acting in his capacity as a law enforcement officer (as evidenced by the fact that he took his badge and gun prior to invading Reggie's vehicle). Choice **C** is incorrect because although Reggie had an expectation of privacy in his mobile home, this situation constitutes an exception to the normal rule requiring a search warrant to be obtained before a search or seizure of personal property occurs. Finally, choice **D** is incorrect because the police could have obtained a warrant authorizing a search of the entire vehicle, including the contents of the sealed container.

40. A Pursuant to a valid, full custodial arrest, the police may make an inventory search of the suspect's person and clothes. *Illinois v.*

Lafayette. Because Reggie was validly arrested for a serious drug crime (i.e., Bill had probable cause to believe that Reggie had been engaged in criminal activity relating to drugs), a strip search prior to (or soon after) his incarceration is likely to be deemed reasonable and valid. A search under these conditions diminishes the risk to guards and other inmates that the suspect may have hidden weapons or will introduce easily concealable narcotics contraband like amphetamines into the jail. Choice **B** is factually incorrect (there is no indication the police perceived an immediate danger to themselves or that evidence might be lost if the strip search did not occur immediately). Choice **C** is incorrect because the fact that a search was unsuccessful would not make it invalid when started. Finally, choice **D** is incorrect because, as discussed in the answer to the preceding question, Reggie's arrest probably was valid.

41. **A** In the absence of consent or exigent circumstances, a search warrant is required before police may enter someone's home to execute an arrest warrant for another individual. *Steagald v. United States.* Because Officer Jane's arrest warrant applied only to Defendant, she had no right to make a nonconsensual entry into Friend's home. Because Officer Jane improperly threatened to use force to secure entry (i.e., break down Friend's door), her entrance into Friend's home was not consensual. Thus, the heroin (which would not have been discovered except for Officer Jane's unlawful entry) is inadmissible in a criminal trial against Friend. Choice **B** is incorrect because it's irrelevant how the heroin was discovered. Officer Jane had no right to be in the house. Choice **C** is factually incorrect (Friend cannot be said to have consented to Officer Jane's entry). Finally, choice **D** is also factually incorrect (the heroin was not found incident to a valid arrest). Because exigent circumstances did not exist, Officer Jane had no right to enter Friend's home to arrest Defendant.

42. **C** A police officer may not use deadly force to effectuate an arrest and/ or prevent escape, unless the police officer has probable cause to believe that the suspect poses a significant threat of death or serious physical injury to the arresting officer or others. *Tennessee v. Garner.* Because Officer Joe had no reason to believe that Billy was armed or constituted a present public danger, the use of deadly force was unreasonable. Choice **A**, although factually true (Officer Joe did have probable cause to arrest Billy), is incorrect because it was improper for Joe to use deadly force in effectuating Billy's arrest under these circumstances. Choice **B** is incorrect because use of deadly force in

effectuating an arrest is proper only when the person seized posed a significant danger to the arresting officer or the public. Whether Billy's conduct constituted a felony under applicable local law is irrelevant. Finally, choice **D** is incorrect because the Eighth Amendment's prohibition against cruel and unusual punishment (applicable to the states via the Fourteenth Amendment) applies to legislative or judicial conduct (not the actions of police officers).

43. **A** Interrogation with respect to a crime unrelated to the arrest does not invalidate an adequate *Miranda* waiver. *Colorado v. Spring.* Assuming the police had probable cause to arrest Defendant for the Main Street fire (the facts are silent on this point), Defendant's confession would be admissible (even though unrelated to the crime for which she was arrested). If the police lacked probable cause to arrest Defendant, her confession would be inadmissible (even though she voluntarily waived her *Miranda* rights) because it would have been derived from an unlawful arrest. Choice **B** is incorrect because the police are under no obligation to inform a suspect of the implications of her confession. Choice **C** is factually incorrect (Defendant had waived her *Miranda* rights by her statement that she would answer questions, unless the police officers began "hasslin"' her). Finally, choice **D** is incorrect because the fact that Defendant was arrested for one crime does not preclude questioning her with respect to a different crime.

44. **A** A voluntary waiver of *Miranda* rights is not invalidated by the disability of the accused. *Colorado v. Connelly.* Because Defendant voluntarily waived her *Miranda* rights (i.e., there was no overreaching by the police), her confession is admissible. Choice **B** is incorrect because the fact that Defendant was a minor does not, *per se,* invalidate her *Miranda* waiver. However, the court will review the waiver more closely and more critically to determine whether the suspect really understood what she was doing. Choice **C** is incorrect because Defendant's confession was not coerced by police conduct. Defendant's erroneous perception of the situation would ***not*** make her statement legally involuntary for *Miranda* purposes. Finally, choice **D** is incorrect because the fact that Defendant was validly arrested for one crime would not preclude the police from questioning her with respect to another offense (after, of course, proper *Miranda* warnings were given and waived).

45. **B** Evidence derived from a custodial interrogation is admissible, even in the absence of prior *Miranda* warnings, if the statements were

voluntary and the questions were reasonably prompted by a concern for the public safety. *New York v. Quarles*. Jack had just emerged from the movie house. It was reasonable for Officer John to suspect that the gun might have been hidden in the movie house by Jack and that it would be found by a child. Officer John could reasonably conclude that a threat to public safety existed. Thus, the questioning (as well as its fruits) was proper. Jack may argue that his statement was not voluntary because Officer John had pointed a gun at him, but Jack was not compelled to answer. Choice **A** is incorrect because, in the absence of exigent circumstances, the lack of proper *Miranda* warnings would prevent the evidence from being admitted (whether or not Jack's crime was a felony). Choice **C** is factually incorrect (because Officer John approached Jack with his gun drawn, Jack probably would be deemed to be in "custody" for *Miranda* purposes). Finally, choice **D** is incorrect. When a threat to public safety is present, the fruits of the interrogation are admissible, even in the absence of *Miranda* warnings.

46. C Evidence derived from an illegal arrest is ordinarily inadmissible. If the police lacked probable cause to arrest Pat, any information derived from her arrest would ordinarily be inadmissible as the fruits of an illegal arrest (regardless of whether *Miranda* rights had been effectively waived). Choice **A** is factually incorrect (Pat's waiver of her *Miranda* rights appears to have been made voluntarily). The fact that her request for a drink of water was honored and that she was spoken to in soft tones does not make her *Miranda* waiver involuntary. Choice **B** is incorrect because although the *Miranda* warnings were not absolutely complete (i.e., Pat was not told that she had a right to appointed counsel if she was indigent), the court probably will conclude that there was substantial compliance with the necessary requisites. Any confusion or inadequacy probably was resolved when Pat acknowledged her entitlement to a free attorney. Finally, choice **D** is incorrect because if there was no probable cause to arrest Pat, her subsequent confession would be inadmissible (regardless of any *Miranda* waiver).

47. C A defendant in a state criminal case may not obtain release through a federal *habeas corpus* proceeding on the ground that evidence used to convict him was obtained in violation of his Fourth Amendment rights, unless he was not given a full and fair opportunity to raise those issues in state court. *Stone v. Powell*. Here, it was Locust's counsel's incompetence, not the state's procedures, that prevented Locust from getting a state court hearing on his Fourth Amendment claim. (This incompetence may raise a Sixth Amendment claim, but that does not preserve the Fourth Amendment claim Locust pursued.) Choices **A** and **B** are incorrect for the reasons just stated. Choice **D** is incorrect because the facts stipulate that Locust was relying only on a violation of his *Fourth* Amendment rights. If Locust had raised a *Sixth* Amendment violation (i.e., he was deprived of effective counsel by reason of the latter's failure to object to particular evidence), a federal *habeas corpus* proceeding might have been appropriate. *Cf. Withrow v. Williams.*

48. **A** Illegally seized evidence can be used *to impeach* a defendant who voluntarily takes the witness stand. *United States v. Havens.* Because Defendant took the stand to deny the allegations against him, the evidence seized illegally at his summer home could be used for the purposes of impeachment. Choice **B** is incorrect because the prosecution can use illegally seized evidence to impeach a defendant's testimony under any circumstances, not just when the defendant improperly refuses to answer cross-examination questions. Choice **C** is incorrect because although factually true (the evidence had been suppressed and, therefore, could not be used in the prosecution's case-in-chief), illegally seized evidence may be used to impeach the credibility of an accused. Finally, choice **D** is incorrect because the fact that an accused asserts the Fifth Amendment upon advice of counsel does not preclude the prosecution from impeaching him with illegally seized evidence.

49. **C** An individual has no reasonable expectation of privacy with respect to objects, items, or information held out to the public. *Smith v. Maryland.* The numbers one dials on his telephone are deemed to be "held out to the public," so police use of a pen register does not violate the caller's Fourth Amendment rights. Choice **A** is incorrect. Although privately owned, the telephone company was acting at the request of the police. It indeed was acting as a governmental entity for Fourth Amendment purposes. But this fact did not make its actions illegal. On the contrary, it was acting with the same authority as the police would have under the same circumstances. Choice **B** is incorrect because, having no legitimate expectation of privacy with respect to the search (i.e., the installation of the pen register), Darlene could ***not*** successfully complain about the absence of a valid warrant. Finally, choice **D** is incorrect because the actions of the police are not measured by their "good faith." The police are

required to comply with all the constitutional safeguards that the courts have confirmed over many years. In the absence of compliance, any evidence obtained will not be admitted.

50. **C** A state may give its citizens greater protection than that afforded to them by the U.S. Constitution. U.S. Const. amend. X. Under the U.S. Constitution, Bob had no expectation of privacy with respect to items within a detached fenced-in area (even if there was a "No Trespassing" sign on the enclosure and even if the fenced-in area was only 50 feet from his house). *Oliver v. United States.* However, the state of Midwest (via its Constitution) affords its citizens greater protection than that provided by the U.S. Constitution, and the federal courts must respect that greater protection. Thus, the state's appeal will be unsuccessful. Choice **A** is incorrect because, if anything, the fact that there was a "No Trespassing" sign on the enclosure would argue for a greater expectation of privacy in the area searched. Therefore, it would *not* constitute a reason why the state should succeed on its appeal. Choice **B** is incorrect because although Bob had no expectation of privacy with respect to the area searched under the U.S. Constitution, the state of Midwest affords protection to its citizens under these circumstances. Finally, choice **D** is incorrect because the fact that the area involved was fenced and locked would arguably create a greater expectation of privacy with respect to the enclosed marijuana. Therefore, it would *not* constitute a reason for granting the state's appeal.

51. **D** The Double Jeopardy Clause does not preclude prosecution for the same offense by a different sovereign. Although Bob initially was tried by state of Midwest authorities, the federal government could prosecute him for exactly the same offense. Choice **A** is incorrect because there is no case law supporting the proposition that the Due Process Clause precludes multiple prosecutions for the same offense by different sovereigns. Choice **B** is incorrect because the double jeopardy doctrine applies only to prosecutions by the *same sovereign* for a second offense based on the same elements as the first. Finally, choice **C** is incorrect because the defense of collateral estoppel in a criminal case (an element of the Fifth Amendment's guarantee against double jeopardy) applies only to *issues of fact* that were necessarily decided in the accused's favor in the first proceeding; the issue here is a legal issue not affected by collateral estoppel.

52. **A** Once a defendant asserts the right to consult a lawyer, he may then waive his *Miranda* rights only when (1) he initiates subsequent

discussion with the police, (2) proper *Miranda* warnings are reiterated before any statement, **and** (3) there has been no intervening interrogation by the police. *Oregon v. Bradshaw*. Here, Defendant asserted his *Miranda* rights, but the three-part test necessary to invoke a *Miranda* waiver was also satisfied when Officer Judy restated the warning. Choice **B** is incorrect because *Miranda* rights must be given even when a minor offense is involved. *Berkemer v. McCarty*. Choice **C** is factually true (Defendant had requested to speak with his attorney), but the request for an attorney does not preclude a subsequent waiver by the accused. Finally, choice **D** is legally incorrect (the police are not legally obliged to provide an accused with a substitute lawyer when the lawyer of his choice is delayed).

53. **C** If an officer reasonably suspects that a person who has been detained for questioning may be armed, he may conduct a limited pat-down of the suspect's outer clothing. *Terry v. Ohio*. Although Informant was known to be reliable, he did not actually see a gun in Suspect's pocket. Officer Joe can be said to have had only a reasonable suspicion (rather than probable cause) to believe that criminal activity was afoot. When Suspect made a move toward her pocket, Officer Joe was entitled to protect himself by restraining her until he could evaluate the danger to him. He would not have been justified, however, in reaching directly into Suspect's pocket. That action would have gone beyond a simple pat-down or frisk, which must be limited to the detainee's *outer* clothing. *Cf. Minnesota v. Dickerson*. But Officer Joe was justified in conducting the pat-down of Suspect's outer clothing; and once he felt what he reasonably believed to be a weapon, he was justified in taking the further step of reaching into the pocket to retrieve the weapon in order to prevent possible harm to himself. Thus, the weapon was seized in a constitutional manner. Choice **A** is incorrect because the weapon was **not** the product of an unlawful detention. Officer Joe did have a reasonable suspicion that Suspect might be engaged in criminal activity. It is even arguable that Suspect voluntarily consented to remain parked and speak with Officer Joe. Choice **B** is incorrect because evidence can be obtained without a warrant under circumstances like those described here. Finally, choice **D** is incorrect because Officer Joe did **not** have probable cause to believe Suspect was engaged in criminal activity—when Officer Joe approached Suspect, he merely had a reasonable suspicion that she might be involved in criminal conduct.

54. B The right to a jury trial exists only with respect to those crimes punishable by imprisonment for over six months. *Baldwin v. New York.* Because the offense involved carried a maximum prison term of three months, Suspect had no right to a jury trial. Choice **A** is legally incorrect (there is a constitutional right to a jury trial in all criminal cases in which a defendant may be imprisoned for a term longer than six months). Choice **C** is legally incorrect (there is no absolute right to a jury trial in *all* criminal cases). Finally, choice **D** is legally incorrect: There is no right to a jury trial simply because an accused affirmatively requests it (e.g., the request will be rejected when the charge carries a maximum prison term of under six months).

55. C Under the Sixth Amendment, an absolute right to counsel exists in situations in which imprisonment, however short, is **actually imposed** upon the defendant. *Scott v. Illinois.* If Suspect was actually imprisoned (even for one day), her Sixth Amendment right to counsel was violated by the refusal to provide her with an attorney. Choice **A** is legally incorrect (there is no right to counsel in *all* criminal cases). Choice **B** is incorrect because the fact that a crime is potentially punishable by imprisonment does not, *per se*, result in a right to counsel. Imprisonment must be imposed before the right to counsel can be used as the basis for appeal. Finally, choice **D** is legally incorrect (the right to counsel is violated in the case of a prisoner who is incarcerated even if the crime charged is punishable by imprisonment for less than six months).

56. A A prisoner in a state court proceeding generally must exhaust all available state court remedies before seeking *habeas corpus* in a federal court. *Cf. Delo v. Stokes.* If Suspect has not exhausted her state court remedies, a writ of *habeas corpus* made to a federal court usually will be denied. Choice **B** states a correct legal conclusion, but is incorrect on the facts; the term "custody" for purposes of federal *habeas corpus* includes parole supervision. *Fay v. Noia.* Choice **C** is legally incorrect (there is a right of *habeas corpus* from state court to federal court in many instances). Finally, choice **D** is incorrect because there is no constitutional right of review by a federal court through a writ of *habeas corpus* in *all* instances. For instance, where a state defendant contends that evidence was used to convict her in violation of the Fourth Amendment, *habeas corpus* ordinarily will be denied (unless the defendant can show that she was not given a full and fair opportunity to raise the Fourth Amendment issues in state court). *Stone v. Powell.*

57. **A** In light of the important government interests in maintaining safety and order in the public educational environment, administrative searches of public school students involved extra-curricular activities will be governed by the standard of reasonable suspicion rather than probable cause. *New Jersey v. TLO.* Reasonable suspicion exists where specific and articulable facts known to the government actor would support the belief that the suspect (or, in this case, student) may be involved in illegal activity. Here, the Vice Principal was aware of Susan's of positive drug test results, and had additionally become aware of the detailed allegations contained in the anonymous letter. These independent factors provide the reasonable suspicion, particularized to Susan, necessary to justify Mr. Brown's decision. Choice **B** is incorrect because, while the conclusion may be accurate, the reasoning is not. Schoolchildren do not altogether lack privacy protection at school, but rather are subject to diminished protections deemed necessary in light of the individual and collective interests involved. Choice **C** is incorrect because, while the characterization may be true, the two prongs referenced in the answer are not dispositive of this question. An anonymous tipster's veracity and basis of knowledge may be relevant to the weight that should be given to the letter, but they are not absolute requirements for probable cause and are even less elemental in the reasonable suspicion inquiry. D is incorrect for two reasons. First, the search at issue in this case will be governed by reasonable suspicion analysis, and not the higher probable cause standard. Second, the Supreme Court has determined that, in the school setting relevant here, even random and suspicionless drug tests may be reasonable if justified by sufficiently strong administrative needs. *Vernonia v. Acton.*

58. **D** Despite having substantially diminished expectations of privacy in the school context, public school students are not completely without constitutional protection, and any otherwise justified instruction into that remaining right to privacy must still be reasonable. Mr. Brown will most likely be found to have developed sufficient suspicion to investigate Susan (see above), but a court would have difficulty with the decision to strip search when he called her into his office. In *Safford v. Redding*, the Supreme Court confronted substantially similar circumstances, and held that a strip search of a young female student was an inherently unreasonable way to investigate a minor drug crime. This was true even though the search was conducted by a female administrator, and even though the

administrators took care to be no more invasive than necessary to accomplish the search. Choice **A** is incorrect because such caution does not make what is otherwise unreasonable behavior less so. Choice **B** is incorrect because the reasonableness of the suspicion cannot justify an unreasonable execution of the search based on such reasonable suspicion. Finally, choice **C** is incorrect because the presence or absence of Susan's parents is not relevant to the question regarding her right to be free from the search that uncovered the capsules. Whether Susan's parents were present is a matter that might arise in connection with any official interrogation, but not in connection with Mrs. Green's search.

59. B In general, questions regarding the application of the *Miranda* doctrine, such as custody, interrogation, and waiver, will be resolved using objective standards that do not turn on the subjective characteristics of the actual suspect in the case. However, the doctrine has evolved such that officers who know or should know that they are dealing with a youthful offender must take age into account when considering the individual's actions and choices, and that age may be relevant to whether a suspect is in custody for *Miranda* purposes. *JDB v. North Carolina.* In this case, Susan unquestionably faces direct interrogation without proper warnings, so the primary admissibility question will be whether her interrogation took place in a custodial setting. Custody will be determined by asking whether, under the circumstances, a reasonable person in the suspect's position would have felt free to leave. Given that the officers knew or should have known that they were dealing with a 13-year-old child, the determination with respect to her custodial status will be made in light of her age and the implications that age has regarding her awareness of her right to terminate the interview. Choice **A** represents the formal, objective approach that has been modified for factors relating to youth, and is incorrect for the reasons discussed with respect to choice **B**. Choice **C** is incorrect because the strip search and the interrogation are separate and distinct events. There is of course a question as to the constitutionality of the strip search, and if Susan had been strip searched in conjunction with her interrogation that fact might be relevant to the voluntariness of her waiver, but the facts do not support any analytical connection. Choice **D** is incorrect because both choices **A** and **C** are incorrect.

60. D An accused has no constitutional right to be represented by out-of-state counsel. While an accused who is being prosecuted for a serious felony is entitled to counsel, she has no right to insist upon being represented by an attorney who is not licensed to practice law in the jurisdiction in which she's being tried. Choice **A** is incorrect because a defendant's Sixth Amendment right to effective counsel is not violated unless the attorney's performance (1) falls below an objective standard (i.e., he performs below the level of competence reasonably expected of lawyers handling the same or similar matters); and (2) "but for" the lawyer's incompetence, there is a reasonable probability that the result of the case would have been different (i.e., the attorney's errors were of such magnitude as to undermine confidence in the outcome of the case). *Strickland v. Washington.* Finally, choices **B** and **C** are incorrect because there is no case law supporting the proposition that a criminal defendant's rights to due process and a fair trial are violated by her inability to obtain representation by an attorney who is not licensed to practice law in the jurisdiction.

61. **D** Although *federal* criminal trials require a 12-person jury and a unanimous verdict, the U.S. Supreme Court has declined to impose either of these requirements for state court trials. (But there must be a "substantive" majority; a bare majority—e.g., a 5-to-4 verdict—would not suffice.) The Court has upheld a 9-to-3 verdict. *Johnson v. Louisiana.* On that reasoning, a 9-to-1 verdict presumably would be valid. Choice **A** is incorrect because a 12-person jury is not required in *state* court criminal proceedings. Choice **B** is incorrect because unanimity is not always required in *state* court criminal proceedings. Finally, choice **C** is incorrect because there is no established case law supporting the proposition that an accused may insist on being represented by a lawyer who is not licensed to practice law in that state.

62. **D** The Sixth Amendment right to counsel for indigent criminal defendants does not extend to discretionary appeals. *Ross v. Moffitt.* Linda was **not** denied her right to effective counsel because her appeal to the state X Supreme Court was discretionary with the court. Choice **A** is incorrect because an indigent criminal defendant has no right to appointed counsel with respect to a discretionary appeal. Choice **B** is incorrect because, as discussed above, Linda had no right to appointed counsel in this instance. Finally, choice **C** is incorrect because, even if Linda could show that her chances of being successful on appeal would be greatly enhanced by the assistance of coun-

sel, she has no right to appointed counsel in this instance (her appeal being discretionary in nature).

63. D The right to counsel is deemed to exist in criminal prosecutions if imprisonment, however short, is actually imposed. *Scott v. Illinois.* Because Wanda was not imprisoned, the denial of her request for counsel did not violate her Sixth Amendment rights (applicable to the states via the Fourteenth Amendment). Choice **A** is legally incorrect (there was no constitutional error). Choice **B** is incorrect because there was no error and the "harmless error" standard does not arise (Wanda had no right to be represented by counsel at the initial trial). Finally, choice **C** is incorrect because there was no error because Wanda was not imprisoned, not because she was charged with a misdemeanor.

64. D A defendant has an absolute right to waive counsel, as long as this is done knowingly and intelligently. *Faretta v. California.* Notwithstanding the waiver, the court may appoint a backup attorney who will intervene on her client's behalf as long as the defendant's basic right of self-representation is not undermined. That is, the defendant must both appear to be in control and be in actual control. *McKaskle v. Wiggins.* Choice **A** is incorrect because Wanda is still primarily responsible for her own defense. Choice **B** is incorrect because there is no case law supporting the proposition that a criminal defendant's due process rights are violated by the appointment of standby counsel. Finally, choice **C** is incorrect because (1) Wanda chose to represent herself, and (2) standby counsel would promote (rather than impair) Wanda's right to effective representation.

65. D An earlier conviction of an indigent defendant, even though she was constitutionally denied counsel because no imprisonment was imposed, can be used under an enhancement statute to increase the sentence for a subsequent conviction. *Nichols v. United States.* Choice **A** is incorrect because a five-year sentence for a conviction for grand theft probably would ***not*** be deemed disproportionate. Choice **B** is legally incorrect (a recidivist sentencing statute does not, *per se*, violate the Double Jeopardy Clause). Finally, choice **C** is legally incorrect (the enhanced sentence imposed upon Wanda because of her previous conviction does not violate her Sixth Amendment rights) because she was not imprisoned after the first conviction.

66. C When a first trial of a suspect ends in a hung jury after the prosecution has introduced all its proof of guilt, the Double Jeopardy Clause of the Fifth Amendment (applicable to the states via the Fourteenth Amendment) does not prevent retrial of the suspect on the same charge. *Richardson v. United States.* Choice **A**, although legally true (i.e., jeopardy had attached because the jury had been impaneled and sworn), is incorrect because the Double Jeopardy Clause does not prevent retrial when (1) the initial proceeding resulted in a hung jury, and (2) the prosecution introduced sufficient evidence to support a guilty verdict. Choice **B**, although factually true (the jury had been impaneled and sworn), is incorrect because the Double Jeopardy Clause does not prevent retrial when the original proceeding ends in a hung jury after the prosecution has introduced the evidence necessary to support a finding of guilt. Finally, choice **D** is factually incorrect (no verdict was returned in the first trial).

67. **C** A criminal defendant may be retried when reversal on appeal is based on the **weight**, rather than sufficiency, of the evidence. *Tibbs v. Florida.* Because the court decided that the verdict was against the weight of the evidence (rather than that the prosecution had failed to introduce sufficient evidence to support the verdict), Bill may be retried a third time. Choice **A** is incorrect because retrial after a hung jury is not precluded by the Double Jeopardy Clause, unless the prosecution has failed to introduce sufficient evidence to meet its burden of proof. *Burks v. United States.* Although choice **B** states the law correctly (double jeopardy would bar retrial if the earlier proceeding had been reversed due to the prosecution's failure to produce sufficient evidence), the facts establish that reversal in the second case was based on the *weight* (rather than sufficiency) of the evidence. Finally, choice **D** is legally incorrect (there is no rule permitting only a single retrial).

68. **B** Under the Double Jeopardy Clause, a defendant may not be tried for a crime when the jury in a previous trial has found for the defendant on a fact essential to the prosecution of the crime. *Ashe v. Swenson.* Because in the first trial Jim persuaded the jury that he had a valid alibi, an issue essential to the prosecution has been resolved in the defendant's favor and may not be relitigated. (This was the only issue Jim raised in his defense.) State X may not retry Jim for robbery of any of the other workers. Choice **A** is legally incorrect (the prosecution ordinarily is **not** obliged to bring all criminal charges arising from a single incident or occurrence in one case). Unless double jeopardy has attached, a sovereign may bring several different prosecutions against an individual as a consequence of a single

occurrence or incident (provided each subsequent charge requires proof of at least one element that was not resolved in the earlier trial). Choice **C** is incorrect because although factually accurate (the charge against Jim for the robbery of Allan does constitute a different case), Jim cannot be prosecuted because the alibi issue has been litigated and resolved in Jim's favor. Finally, choice **D** is incorrect because although there may be different issues in the case against Jim for the robbery of Allan, resolution of the alibi issue in Jim's favor precludes his prosecution for the offense in question.

69. B An identification procedure that is so suggestive as to create a substantial likelihood of misidentification at trial violates due process. Under this principle, an in-court identification that is predicated upon an unlawful out-of-court identification is not admissible. *Stovall v. Denno*. Although Jones was taller than each of the other participants in the lineup (they were between 5´ 9″ and 6´ 2″), this disparity probably would not by itself be deemed so unnecessarily suggestive as to create a substantial likelihood of misidentification. However, Green's question to Witness, "What about the guy standing to his right?" is very suggestive and undermines the purpose of a lineup. The height disparity and Green's question, taken together, probably would lead a court to conclude that the whole procedure was unduly suggestive, in which case the identification of Jones by Witness would be excluded at trial. Choice **A** is incorrect because Jones did not have a right to counsel at that time because he had not been formally charged with a crime. Choice **C** is incorrect because the undue suggestiveness was a constitutional violation. Finally, choice **D** is incorrect. If the police lacked probable cause to arrest Jones, his objection to this evidence would be sustained (i.e., the identification at the lineup would have been derived from an illegal arrest).

70. A Pursuant to a valid arrest, police may search the area within the suspect's immediate control. *Chimel v. California*. Because (1) Witness identified Bad Lad as the person who had robbed him that morning, and (2) Bad Lad immediately attempted to flee, Officer Green had probable cause to arrest Bad Lad. As a result, items found in Bad Lad's outer garments would be admissible against him. Choice **B** is incorrect because an arrest that is based on probable cause ordinarily requires no warrant under the Fourth Amendment (unless effectuated in the suspect's home). Choice **C** is incorrect because *Miranda* warnings need not be given prior to the search of an individual pursuant to a valid arrest. Finally, choice **D** is incorrect. The fact that

Green had taunted Bad Lad into discharging his civic duties and cooperating in a legitimate police activity could not reasonably be construed as inducing an unlawful detention.

71. **B** Evidence derived from a custodial interrogation is inadmissible in the prosecution's case-in-chief, unless voluntarily obtained and preceded by adequate *Miranda* warnings. But no interrogation had taken place here; Bad Lad simply blurted out the statement, "I might as well confess." The fact that *Miranda* warnings had not yet been given does not preclude Bad Lad's statement from being admitted into evidence. Choice **A** is incorrect because no interrogation had occurred and *Miranda* warnings were not necessary. Choice **C** is incorrect because, as we've discussed, no illegal detention had occurred. Finally, choice **D** is incorrect because Bad Lad (even if indigent) was not entitled to the appointment of counsel until he was formally charged, an event that had not yet occurred.

72. **A** Police may **not** make a warrantless arrest of an individual in her home, unless exigent circumstances exist. *Welsh v. Wisconsin.* Since exigent circumstances were not present, Mel was obliged to obtain an arrest warrant before arresting Ann in her home. Choice **B** is incorrect because approval by a law officer, even a U.S. attorney, does not negate the necessity for following the procedures necessary for a valid arrest warrant. Choice **C** is incorrect. Probable cause alone is not sufficient to justify arrest of a suspect in her own home; exigent circumstances must exist. Finally, choice **D** is incorrect because, even if Ann's conduct constituted a felony, a warrant was necessary to effectuate the arrest in her home.

73. **D** Mel unlawfully forced his way into Ann's house. Suzy did **not** consent to Mel's entry into the house (she tried to slam the door on him). Choice **A** is incorrect because, in the absence of consent, Mel needed a warrant to enter Ann's home to arrest her (even if probable cause existed). Choice **B** is factually incorrect since there was no consent, although a 17-year-old likely would be able to grant such consent. Finally, choice **C** is factually incorrect (the facts do not indicate that exigent circumstances existed).

74. **B** Evidence derived from an unlawful search or seizure is ordinarily inadmissible. Because Mel was not lawfully in Ann's house and could not lawfully arrest her, the prosecution cannot use or assert the plain view doctrine. Choice **A** is incorrect because the plain view doctrine is inapplicable. Mel had no right to be in the place that enabled him to see it. Choice **C** is incorrect because Mel could not lawfully seize any evidence, whether or not it was within Ann's immediate control.

Finally, choice **D** is incorrect. Had the arrest been proper, Mel would have been able to seize the evidence (i.e., the machine), which was within Ann's control without a search warrant.

75. **C** Under a valid search warrant, police are permitted to scan the entire premises if they have reasonable suspicion that an armed accomplice is present. *Maryland v. Buie*. Because Mel had a reasonable suspicion that Ann's "violence-prone boyfriend" might be present, he had a right to conduct a "sweep" of the premises to locate the boyfriend, including the closed closet (a good hiding place) where the unlawful gun (i.e., contraband) was found in "plain view." Choice **A** is incorrect because, having obtained a valid search warrant, Mel was entitled to enter the apartment. Choice **B** is incorrect because the fact that the shotgun was not directly connected to the counterfeiting scheme, alone, would not invalidate its seizure (e.g., since it was in "plain view," it could be seized as contraband). Finally, choice **D** is incorrect for the same reasons that choice **C** is correct.

76. **C** When a search warrant specifies the items to be found, police officers may not search into areas in which the items cannot possibly be located. Because the machine could not possibly have been enclosed within the jewelry box, Mel had no authority to open the box (even though it was in Ann's bedroom). Choice **A** is incorrect because it is overly broad. Officers executing a search warrant may seize items not described in the warrant if they are related to criminal activity and in plain view. Choice **B** is incorrect. Although the jewelry box was in plain view, Mel had no right to open it because the warrant was limited to the machine and the box could not reasonably be related to the crime of counterfeiting. Choice **D** is incorrect because, in addition to the machine, Mel was entitled to seize any contraband or potential evidence that was in plain view, but not to open closed containers that could not have contained any item listed on the warrant or been related to criminal activity.

77. **D** Evidence seized pursuant to a valid search warrant is admissible. Because the warrant permitted Mel to search Ann's bedroom, Mel could lawfully search the entire room until (1) the item was located, or (2) the entire area had been investigated. Choice **A** is incorrect because the warrant entitled Mel to search Ann's entire bedroom, including closets, if necessary, to locate the machine. Choice **B** is incorrect because the fact that the item wasn't where Mel had previously seen it did not affect his authority to search the entire bedroom. Finally, choice **C** is incorrect because Suzy's consent was not

material or necessary to the search. Mel was proceeding under the authority of a valid search warrant.

78. **B** Under the plain view doctrine, when a lawfully positioned police officer sees (hears or smells) an item that (relying on his knowledge or experience) he has probable cause to believe is (1) contraband or (2) the proceeds or instrumentalities of a crime, he may seize the item. *Texas v. Brown*. Because Mel had the right to search Ann's entire bedroom (including the closet), he was able to observe the counterfeit bills from a vantage point that he had a right to be in. Mel had probable cause to believe that the bills were counterfeit (i.e., they were near the machine and people do not normally throw real currency onto a closet floor). Choice **A** is factually incorrect. As discussed above, Mel had probable cause to believe that the bills were counterfeit and, thus, contraband. After all, Mel's concern was to obtain proof of the crime of counterfeiting. Choice **C** is incorrect because although factually true (an assistant U.S. attorney cannot expand the scope of a search warrant), the counterfeit bills were in plain view. Finally, choice **D** is factually incorrect (Mel's warrant covered the machine, not the counterfeit bills).

79. **D** The Fourth Amendment prohibits unreasonable searches and seizures by federal officers. Because Mel is a federal governmental official, Ann's objection would be asserted under the Fourth Amendment. Choice **A** is incorrect because the Fifth Amendment protects individuals only from compelled disclosures of a testimonial nature. Choice **B** is incorrect because the police may obtain a warrant to search for additional evidence even after a person is indicted. (In any event, it's not clear from the facts whether Ann had yet been formally charged.) Finally, choice **C** is incorrect because the Fourteenth Amendment applies to actions by the state.

80. **C** Police ordinarily may not detain someone without a warrant for the purpose of questioning him unless they have an articulable, objective basis for believing that criminal activity may be under way. *Terry v. Ohio*. This exception to the requirement of probable cause has been extended to investigations of **completed crimes** when the police have a "**reasonable suspicion**, grounded in specific and articulable facts," that a person was involved in the previous crime. *United States v. Hensley*. Because Hoover had heard a rumor that Doyle had knowingly received stolen money, he arguably had a reasonable suspicion of Doyle and, therefore, was permitted to detain him in a "stop and frisk," even though Hoover lacked probable cause (a rumor would

not constitute substantial reason to believe that Doyle had received stolen money). Choice **A** is incorrect because Hoover had not arrested Doyle at the time of the search, but had merely detained him as part of a "stop and frisk." Therefore, the search was not incident to arrest. Choice **B** is incorrect because Hoover told Doyle that he was a suspect and instructed him to raise his hands; Doyle was not asked whether he consented to the search. Choice **D** is incorrect because, as stated above, the detention was valid and reasonable, based on Hoover's reasonable suspicion.

81. **D** When a vehicle is at rest on a public street and the police have probable cause to believe that it contains contraband or evidence of a crime, a warrantless search of the vehicle and its contents may be made, limited in scope, however, to the search that would be authorized by a judicial officer. Hoover saw the contents of Doyle's car as he was leading him away after Doyle's arrest. He was also able to see that the car matched the description of the getaway car and had the same license plate. Hoover had probable cause to believe the car would yield evidence of the robbery and was justified in searching it. *United States v. Ross.* Choice **B** is factually incorrect (Doyle had been arrested and, therefore, was not "at large"). If the suspect referred to was not Doyle but Fingers, the fact that Fingers might have a key to the ignition would not justify a warrantless search of Doyle's car. Choice **C** is incorrect because the circumstances constitute an exception to the rule requiring a warrant to search and seize personal property. Choice **A** is incorrect because it's not as good an answer as choice **D**. Although the search of the car followed almost immediately on the heels of Doyle's arrest, Doyle was not in control of the car at the moment of the arrest. For this reason, it cannot be said that the search was incident to the arrest.

82. **A** Law enforcement officers generally need an arrest warrant (in addition to probable cause) to arrest a person in his home. *Payton v. New York.* However, if an officer is lawfully present in a person's home pursuant to a valid search warrant (the answer assumed Hoover's search warrant was valid), there is no need to also obtain an arrest warrant for the individual (of course, probable cause to make the arrest is still required before the arrest is permissible). Obtaining a judicially authorized search warrant protects the privacy interests that led to the arrest warrant requirement in *Payton*. *United States v. Winchenbach.* Choice **B** is incorrect because there is no need to obtain an arrest warrant under these circumstances (as noted above).

Choice **C** is incorrect because there is no right to arrest a person in his home simply because there is probable cause (as noted above). Finally, choice **D** is incorrect because the type of the crime an individual is suspected of committing does not alter the requirements discussed.

83. **B** Searches of areas that were intended to be covered by a search warrant (but that, because of an error in transcription, are not accurately described in the warrant) are ordinarily valid under the good faith exception. *United States v. Leon.* Hoover's entry into Fingers's home was valid because the home was the target of the search and the location that the warrant was meant to describe. Choice **A** is factually incorrect. Hoover did *not* gain entry by a ruse. Although Hoover misrepresented his identity when he announced his presence at Fingers's home, he described his authority and purpose accurately before entering the premises. Choice **C** is incorrect because the fact that there may be a firearm on the premises does not constitute, in itself, "exigent circumstances" entitling a police officer to enter a dwelling without a warrant. Finally, choice **D** is incorrect because the error in transcription probably would not make the search invalid (as noted above).

84. **D** Under the plain view doctrine, when a lawfully positioned police officer sees (hears or smells) an object that he has probable cause to believe is (1) contraband or (2) the proceeds or instrumentalities of a crime, he may seize the item. Because Hoover had no reason to believe that the envelope contained evidence of a crime, his seizure of that item was invalid. Choice **A** is incorrect because under a valid search warrant, police may seize, in addition to the items described in the warrant, all contraband or instrumentalities of crime that are in plain view. Choice **B** is incorrect because although the envelope was in plain view from a position that Hoover had a right to occupy, Hoover had no reason to suspect that it was related to the bank robbery. Finally, choice **C** is incorrect because the facts fail to indicate that the envelope was within Fingers's control at the time of his arrest.

85. **A** Assuming that Hoover lawfully arrested Fingers (see earlier answer), Hoover properly accompanied Fingers (at his request) to his bedroom (a police officer has a right to accompany the prisoner after a valid arrest). While lawfully in Fingers's bedroom, Hoover then saw the wig in "plain view." Because the wig matched the description of

a wig worn by one of the robbers and was in plain view, Hoover was authorized to seize it. Choice **B** is incorrect. Instrumentalities of a crime (such as the wig) may be seized (even though they are not specifically described in the warrant) if they satisfy the plain view test (as noted above). Choice **C** is incorrect because a typographical error does not render a search warrant constitutionally defective (see the answer to question 83). Finally, choice **D** is incorrect. The rule is that items within the suspect's control may be seized incident to a valid arrest. However, the wig was not within Fingers's control at the time of his arrest (which took place in another part of the house), and Fingers was handcuffed while in his bedroom.

86. **A** Any individual who makes statements to another individual is deemed to assume the risk that his trust may be "misplaced" (i.e., that the individual will disclose his statements and even testify against him as to their content). Because Brawler's statements to Smitch were made voluntarily, they can be used against him, even though they were recorded without his consent or knowledge. *United States v. White.* Choices **B**, **C**, and **D** are incorrect because no violation of Brawler's constitutional rights occurred. Choice **B** is incorrect because, even though Smitch would be deemed to be a governmental agent (he was acting under the police's supervision), no Fourth Amendment right ordinarily exists (as noted above). Choice **C** is incorrect because Brawler's statements were not obtained by the FBI in a compulsory or involuntary manner. Therefore, no Fifth Amendment due process rights were implicated. Also, no *Miranda* violation occurred. Although statements made in response to police questioning are inadmissible at trial if the statements resulted from a custodial interrogation that was not preceded by adequate *Miranda* warnings, here, *Miranda* warnings were not required. Brawler was not in custody. Finally, choice **D** is incorrect. Brawler's Sixth Amendment rights had not matured because Brawler had not yet been formally charged with a crime.

87. **D** In order to resolve the evidentiary question in this case, the court will have to balance the defendants' interest in preserving their privacy with the government's right to collect publicly available information. To the extent that the beeper transmitted information such as the location of defendants' car as they traveled the roads from store to store, and then to the motel, police officers could have collected the same information simply by following the car and observing the defendants' route with the naked eye. Using an electronic

beeper to capture and transmit information that is readily available to any member of the public does not convert the activity into a Fourth Amendment event. *United States v. Knotts*. However, to the extent that the beeper provided officers with information regarding the unloading of the chemicals or their movement into or within the motel, they could only otherwise get this information by intruding on defendants' reasonable expectation of privacy and the collection of that evidence is subject to constitutional protection. *United States v. Karo*. The admissibility of evidence will be determined through application of these complimentary principles. Choices **A** and **B** are incorrect because Fourth Amendment rights are no longer determined solely by reference to the property interests possessed by the owner. Choice **C** is incorrect because it fails to differentiate between the various types of information collected and fails to contend with the range of privacy interests that might be implicated.

88. **D** This is the general rule for all statements voluntarily made to a third party: even if the third party is wearing a recording or transmitting device, the defendant will be held to have assumed the risk of disclosure by voluntarily communicating with the "false friend." *Lopez v. United States*; *United States v. White*. Choice **A** is incorrect both factually and most likely as a matter of evidence law and is otherwise unrelated to a criminal procedure issue. Choice **B** is incorrect because the voluntary disclosure of the statement placed it categorically beyond the reach of the warrant requirement. Choice **C** is incorrect because it mistakenly relies on the confrontation clause doctrine that testimonial evidence cannot be admitted unless the testifying witness can be presented at trial. While that basic rule is observed, the confrontation clause applies to statements made by non-testifying witnesses and does not apply to recorded statements made by the defendant himself.

89. **D** Relying on the Eighth Amendment's Cruel and Unusual Punishment Clause, the Supreme Court decided in 1986 that it was categorically unconstitutional to execute a prisoner who is "insane" (or mentally ill), even if they had been properly convicted of the underlying crime. Positing the that death penalty is only justifiable where it serves legitimate penological purposes, the Court concluded that no such purpose is served where mental illness prevents an offender from appreciating the nature of the penalty and the basis of its imposition. *Ford v. Wainwright*. It has since expanded the reach of the Eighth Amendment to prohibit the execution of those offenders

who are "mentally retarded." *Atkins v. Virginia.* Choice **A** is incorrect because competence to stand trial is a question wholly separate from the issue of whether a capital sentence may be imposed upon an individual notwithstanding the legitimacy of their conviction. Choice **B** is incorrect because the understanding of right and wrong at the time of commission is similarly relevant to the underlying question of guilt, and not directly relevant to the proper analysis of whether the death penalty can subsequently be imposed. Choice **C** is incorrect because it misapprehends the significance of Percy's mental illness. Percy's post-trial loss of normal functioning cannot be used to retroactively raise an insanity defense.

90. **C** Executing an individual who was under 18 at the time of their crime constitutes cruel and unusual punishment and is impermissible as a matter of law. *Roper v. Simmons.* Owing to their impressionable nature, and given that juveniles typically enjoy some prospects for rehabilitation, there is no penological justification for the death penalty in such cases. Choice **A** is incorrect because the degree of Maynard's involvement was not at issue in the case. Choice **B** is incorrect because, while we most likely was an active participant in the crime, this does not in any way establish the constitutionality of the penalty itself. Choice **D** is incorrect because it mistakenly suggests that age at the time of execution, rather than age at the time of offense, is the factor that determines the constitutionality of Maynard's sentence.

91. **A** After a person has been validly arrested and booked, the police may make an inventory search of his person and his clothes and of any items he may be carrying. The purpose of an inventory search is to avoid a claim that the accused's property is later mislaid or appropriated by the police and to confiscate dangerous weapons or contraband. The search does not require a warrant; the need to obtain an inventory of a prisoner's personal effects provides its own rationale for seizing and searching those effects. *Illinois v. Lafayette.* Because Mark's arrest was valid, his personal effects were properly inventoried and are admissible at trial. Choice **B** is incorrect because an inventory search may be made whether or not *Miranda* rights have been waived. Choice **C** is incorrect because no search warrant is necessary for an inventory search. Finally, choice **D** is incorrect. The suspect's consent to an inventory search is not necessary.

92. **B** Incident to a valid arrest, the police may make a full search of the area within the suspect's immediate control in order to prevent him

from destroying evidence. It's not necessary to a valid search that the police officer fear for his own safety. *Chimel v. California*. Because Jason "matched" the perpetrator's description and was running in the direction pointed out by the cashier, Officer Johnson had probable cause to arrest him. The search was incident to a valid arrest, and the area within Jason's immediate control, including Jason's person himself, could be searched. Choice **A** is incorrect because "reasonable suspicion" entitles a police officer only to temporarily detain a possible suspect; it does not justify an arrest. Choice **C** is incorrect because no warrant was needed for a search on these facts. Finally, choice **D** is incorrect because a recitation of *Miranda* rights is not necessary for a valid search in these circumstances.

93. **C** Neither the prosecution (nor the judge) may make any adverse comment to the jury about the refusal of a criminal defendant to testify. Upon a defense request, the jury must be advised that no adverse inference may be drawn from an accused's failure to testify. Therefore, the prosecution may not comment upon Jack's failure to testify. Choice **A** is incorrect because no comment may be made about an accused's failure to testify. Choice **B** is incorrect for the same reason. Finally, choice **D** is incorrect. The jury must be advised, if the defense requests the instruction, that no adverse inference may be drawn from a criminal defendant's failure to testify.

94. **B** Police comments that are reasonably calculated to elicit an incriminating response by a suspect constitute interrogation for purposes of interpreting and applying the *Miranda* rule. *Rhode Island v. Innis*. If the police officer's comment about Cynthia was designed to elicit an incriminating response from Phyllis (Phyllis was in custody and the *Miranda* warnings had not been given and waived), Phyllis's statement will be inadmissible. Choice **A** is incorrect because police officers are permitted to talk with a suspect prior to giving her *Miranda* warnings. The prosecution, however, is precluded from using any response to the questions (other than routine booking questions) by the defendant (except for impeachment purposes). Choice **C** is incorrect because Phyllis did not waive her *Miranda* rights. She was never given *Miranda* warnings. Finally, choice **D** is incorrect because Phyllis's response to the comment is not a so-called blurt-out. A blurt-out occurs where a suspect makes a comment without being subjected to a police interrogation.

95. **D** To constitute an interrogation within the *Miranda* rule, the defendant must be not only in custody but also the object of questioning

by a police officer. Interrogation by private citizens does not invoke the rule. Some courts have included probation officers and IRS agents in the category of police officers, but it seems unlikely that the category would include rank-and-file firefighters (unlike, say, fire department arson investigators). More importantly, the remark by the firefighter did not constitute an interrogation since it was not designed to elicit incriminating information. Furthermore, the facts show that Gina was not asked a question by any police officer. Choice **A** is wrong because it's immaterial to *Miranda* issues whether the arrest was under a warrant. So long as the defendant is in custody, *Miranda* applies. Choice **B** is wrong because it's inconsistent with the facts. There is nothing to indicate that the firefighter's remark was part of a calculated police plan to draw a confession from Gina. The firefighter was acting on his own and did not even know that anyone had been arrested. Finally, choice **C** fails to recognize that, as noted above, this would not have constituted an interrogation, so her *Miranda* warning status is immaterial.

96. A Evidence derived from a custodial interrogation is admissible, even in the absence of prior *Miranda* warnings, if there is a risk to the public safety at the time of questioning (and especially if the questioning helps to eliminate the risk). *New York v. Quarles.* Because the police knew that Madolyn had used a gun and had reason to believe that the gun was hidden either on her person or somewhere in the premises, the police officer's questioning was proper, and the gun is probably admissible. Choice **B** is incorrect because *Miranda* warnings are not necessary under these circumstances. Choice **C** is incorrect because the police had probable cause to arrest Madolyn because she and her Rolls fit the description given by the store manager and because she attempted to flee. Finally, choice **D** is incorrect because questioning someone "sternly" about a public safety hazard does not constitute obtaining information in a coercive manner.

97. B The question assumes that Marcus was not given his *Miranda* rights at any stage prior to the conversation with Tony. Tony was acting as a police agent, and his questions must be construed as interrogation by a police officer. Once a person has been formally charged with a crime, he is entitled to have an attorney present at every critical stage of the case thereafter. *See, e.g., Fellers v. United States; Massiah v. United States.* Because Marcus had been charged and was out on bail, he was entitled to have an attorney present at every stage of police questioning. Choice **A** is incorrect because evidence is not necessarily inadmissible because it's been obtained by tricking the defendant. (If Marcus had not previously been charged, his statement to Tony would be admissible.) Choice **C** is incorrect because Tony was acting as agent for the police. Finally, choice **D** is incorrect because although no longer in custody, Marcus had been charged with a crime and was entitled to legal representation prior to police questioning.

98. **B** The Double Jeopardy Clause of the Fifth Amendment (applicable to the states via the Fourteenth Amendment) precludes prosecution by any sovereign for a crime previously charged and tried by that sovereign. For purposes of this definition, each state is a separate sovereign from every other state, and the federal government is a separate sovereign from each state. In this case, because the former prosecution was conducted in a state court, double jeopardy does not bar retrial of Baldonado for similar federal crimes in a federal court, even though the facts giving rise to each set of crimes may be similar. (Note, however, that federal prosecutors will not always prosecute when there has already been a state prosecution for substantially the same act or acts. In this case, a RICO prosecution is really different in nature from the specific crime of extortion and, under the circumstances, the prosecutor might not be reluctant to prosecute.) Choice **A** is incorrect because there is no necessity under double jeopardy rules that the federal crimes contain an additional legal element to the state court offense. Choice **C** is incorrect because, as explained above, double jeopardy does not bar Baldonado's federal prosecution. Finally, choice **D** is incorrect because prosecution is not barred even if there is a common element in the crimes charged in the state and federal courts.

99. **C** The double jeopardy doctrine also encompasses the doctrine of collateral estoppel. When an issue of ultimate fact—in this case, that Madison was not at the scene of the crime—has been determined by the jury in one criminal trial, that issue cannot again be litigated in any future trial by the same sovereign. *Ashe v. Swenson.* The issue whether Madison had an alibi was resolved in his favor by the jury at the initial trial. It was established that Madison was two hours away at the time of the crime. He may not be prosecuted for the murder of the other two coeds, even if the prosecution is later able to prove that Sheila committed perjury. Choice **A** is incorrect because double jeopardy does preclude a second prosecution (even involving different victims) after a jury verdict of acquittal on the same facts. Choice **B**

is incorrect because the double jeopardy principle (which encompasses *resjudicata* and collateral estoppel) are applicable even as to different victims if the jury has already accepted as fact an element that results in acquittal. Finally, choice **D** is incorrect because the prosecution is not permitted to challenge a jury's verdict after acquittal, even if the essential testimony was perjured.

100. A Under the Sixth Amendment, the right to counsel for a criminally accused indigent exists for both felonies and misdemeanors, but only when imprisonment, however short, is actually imposed. *Scott v. Illinois.* Because Margot was not actually imprisoned, she had no constitutional right to appointed counsel. Choice **B** is incorrect because an indigent accused is entitled to appointed counsel, even when a misdemeanor is involved, if the charge results in imprisonment. The right to appointed counsel exists as long as imprisonment occurs. Choice **C** is incorrect because Margot was not imprisoned. Finally, choice **D** is incorrect. The fact of conviction is immaterial. What matters is whether the defendant is imprisoned.

101. A In the absence of exigent circumstances, such as the imminent destruction of evidence, the threat of harm to persons, or "hot pursuit" of a suspect, an arrest warrant is constitutionally required before the police may enter a suspect's home to effectuate an arrest. *See, e.g., Payton v. New York.* Yet even exigent circumstances may not authorize the warrantless entry into a home in order to make an arrest for a minor offense. Arguably, Carla was in "hot pursuit" of Douglas. *See, e.g., United States v. Santana.* (Even this conclusion is uncertain since some courts limit the "hot pursuit" concept to fleeing felons, and Douglas did not commit any felonies.) However, Carla had observed Douglas committing only several minor traffic offenses, for which imprisonment is not authorized. It is unlikely that courts would allow for a "hot pursuit" warrantless entry to make an arrest for these minor offenses. *Cf. Welsh v. Wisconsin* ("we note that it is difficult to conceive of a warrantless home arrest that would not be unreasonable under the Fourth Amendment when the underlying offense is extremely minor"). Once Douglas had entered his home, Carla was likely obliged to obtain an arrest warrant. Because Carla had not obtained a warrant, the arrest was invalid, and Douglas's subsequent confession was inadmissible. Choice **B** is incorrect because the fact that a suspect appears distraught does not prevent the police from questioning him. Choice **C** is incorrect because Douglas could not validly waive his *Miranda* rights under the circumstances of an illegal arrest. Finally, choice **D** is incorrect because, even though she had seen him commit several minor traffic offenses, Carla was constitutionally obliged to obtain an arrest warrant prior to entering Douglas's home.

102. **D** A defendant may assert the exclusionary rule only to bar evidence obtained through a violation of his own constitutional rights. And, in search and seizure cases, a defendant may seek to exclude evidence derived from an illegal search or seizure only if his "legitimate expectation of privacy" was violated. *Rakas v. Illinois.* Because Stan gave the duffle bag to Marcia, he had no right to prevent Marcia or anyone else from looking through the bag, and he may not claim that his legitimate expectation of privacy was violated when the police searched the bag. Therefore, even if the police had no right to search Marcia, Stan lacks standing to object because his constitutional rights were not violated. The cocaine is admissible. Choices **A**, **B**, and **C** are incorrect for the reasons in choice **D**.

103. **C** Having seen her violate the seatbelt law, Officer Johnson was authorized to stop Anita. The question is whether Officer Johnson may, consistent with the U.S. Constitution, arrest Anita for this very minor violation. The Supreme Court faced precisely this question in *Atwater v. City of Lago Vista* and found the arrest constitutional. The Supreme Court concluded that this custodial arrest (which was permitted by state law) for a minor offense that was not a "breach of the peace" did not offend the Fourth Amendment's prohibition against unreasonable seizures. Choice **A** is incorrect because Officer Johnson's level of concern about seatbelt violations is irrelevant to the constitutionality of the arrest. Choice **B** is incorrect because the existence of discretion to arrest in this circumstance does not impact the constitutional analysis. In fact, the officer in *Atwater* also could have issued a citation (the usual procedure) instead making an arrest. Choice **D** is incorrect for the reasons in choice **A**.

104. **B** As part of the exigent circumstances doctrine, the Court has recognized an "emergency assistance" exception to the general rule against warrantless intrusions into the home. So long as police enter in order to render aid to or prevent an immediate threat of personal injury or harm to the public, they will be excused

for failing to secure a warrant in advance. *Brigham City v. Stuart.* The two-on-one fistfight Officer Alvin observed from the back door would likely represent such an immediate threat. Choice **A** is incorrect because, although the complaint may have furnished suspicion with regard to violation of a noise ordinance, that suspicion has no bearing on the authority to enter. Choice **C** is incorrect because there is only a presumption, not a *per se* rule, against warrantless intrusions. Choice **D** is incorrect for the same reason choice **A** is incorrect.

105. **D** *Miranda* warnings are required prior to police interrogation but only if questioning of the suspect takes place in a custodial setting. Here, Donna faced direct questioning, but she made her statements before being taken into custody such that *Miranda*'s protections were not triggered. Choice **A** is incorrect for this reason. Choice **B** is incorrect because there is no indication in the hypothetical that Donna had consumed LSD and no indication that such consumption was known to or exploited by Officer Alvin. Choice **C** is incorrect because, although factually true, it assumes a false premise about the relationship between admissibility and suspicion.

106. **D** Officer Alvin may have been permitted to conduct a brief pat-down of other party guests to ensure his safety but only if he had reasonable suspicion as to their criminal activity and possession of a weapon. *Ybarra v. Illinois.* Moreover, Officer Alvin would not be permitted to seize any contraband discovered during the pat-down unless he could establish probable cause as to its illegal nature through "plain feel," without additional inspection or manipulation. *Minnesota v. Dickerson.* Choice **A** is factually true and may be an issue in Donna's trial if the entry is not found to be subject to an exception, but Ray lacks standing to challenge the entry because, as a guest, as he had no expectation of privacy in the premises. Choice **B** is not the strongest argument because the officer may reasonably have suspected that Ray and the other attendees were the "friends" to whom Donna gave her narcotics. Relatedly, choice **C** is incorrect because, even assuming the order not to move resulted in their detention, the officer had arguably been furnished reasonable suspicion to believe a crime had occurred, or was occurring, and had the authority to investigate further.

107. **B** In contrast to an ongoing physical altercation, and in spite of serious health effects, underage drinking is most likely not a sufficient threat of immediate personal injury or harm to the public that

would qualify as an exigency excusing compliance with the warrant presumption. *Cf. Brigham City v. Stuart.* Choice **A** is incorrect because, even if true, it is the threat of harm and not a measure of social importance that is relevant to the exigency inquiry. Choice **C** is incorrect because, even if true, the plain view doctrine justifies warrantless *seizures* only and does not permit additional searches or intrusions upon protected areas. Choice **D** is incorrect because, even if true, the statement is not relevant to the authority to enter the home and only operates to explain why Officer Alvin was at the home to begin with.

108. **B** In *Hudson v. Michigan*, the Court concluded that the interests protected by the "knock-and-announce" rule are sufficiently distinct from the interests served by application of the exclusionary rule that failure to knock and announce should not result in exclusion. Choice **A** is incorrect because the success of the search is a post-hoc justification, which is not, standing alone, a relevant consideration with respect to admissibility. Choice **C** is incorrect because, although the knock-and-announce rule is integral to Fourth Amendment reasonableness, it is no longer automatically linked to the remedy of suppression. Choice **D** is incorrect because the officers did not need an exigency as the basis of their actions.

109. **A** Even though the officers might argue that the laptop fell within the scope of the warrant they were executing, the examination of the computer desktop most likely constituted an additional search that went beyond the location where potentially stolen goods could be found. *See Arizona v. Hicks.* Choice **B** is incorrect because inadvertence is no longer relevant to whether an item is discovered in plain view and therefore may be seized without a warrant. *Horton v. California.* Choice **C** is incorrect because the computer may have been in plain view, but the incriminating nature of its contents was not readily apparent. Choice **D** is incorrect for the reasons stated with respect to choice **A**.

110. **D** In *California v. Hodari D.*, the Court confronted very similar circumstances and concluded that the evidence discarded by the suspect during the foot chase was voluntarily abandoned rather than discovered by virtue of a search or seizure. Choice **A** is incorrect because, while it may be arguably true, the defendant had not been arrested at the time the crack was surrendered. Choice **B** is not correct because the chase was neither a search nor a seizure and therefore need not be justified by probable cause. Choice **C**

is incorrect because, although true, the challenged evidence was discarded prior to the time the arrest was made.

111. **D** Although "mere" flight from the police may not furnish probable cause to believe a crime is taking place, that flight coupled with other attendant circumstances may justify the conclusion with respect to criminal activity. *Illinois v. Wardlow*. Here, defendant's flight coupled with his prior location in a high crime area and actions during the chase most likely furnished probable cause, or at least reasonable suspicion, with respect to illegal activity. Choice **A** is not correct because, although true, it does not answer the question of whether the seizure was lawful and thus would not provide a sufficient argument for suppression. Choice **B** is incorrect because the statement is not germane to the question of whether the arrest was lawful. Choice **C** is incorrect because the Court has not recognized a public safety exception to the traditional requirement that all searches be justified by probable cause, or at least reasonable suspicion.

112. **D** In *Montejo v. Louisiana*, the Court concluded that an automatic appointment of counsel for a defendant who stands by silently during the appointment, as opposed to an active or express request for the appointment of counsel, does not irretrievably bar subsequent waiver of the Sixth Amendment right (overruling *Michigan v. Jackson*). Choice **A** is incorrect because, although the Sixth Amendment does permit impeachment use of confessions that violate the right, that is not the ***only*** permissible use. Choice **B** is incorrect for the reasons stated with respect to choice **D**, above. Choice **C** is incorrect because voluntariness is relevant to the Fifth and Fourteenth Amendments but not to the Sixth Amendment right to counsel.

113. **A** This is the bright-line rule announced in *Georgia v. Randolph*. The court reasoned that disputed consent must be construed in light of prevailing social conventions and that such norms would lead a reasonable person to defer to the objecting co-occupant. Choice **B** is incorrect because the Court has never recognized length of cohabitation as being relevant to the question of common authority. Choice **C** is incorrect because, assuming joint access to and control over the premises, the dispute must be resolved in favor of the nonconsenting co-occupant. Choice **D** is incorrect because the Court has not recognized the order of the co-occupants' response as being relevant to the question of consent; as long as the objecting

party has joint control and is physically present, he or she need not answer first to have his or her will prevail.

114. **D** This was essentially the Court's conclusion in *United States v. Place*. There, the Court reasoned that officers had sufficient justification to approach the defendant and initiate a *Terry* stop but extended the detention beyond the limited duration permitted by their reasonable suspicion. Choice **A** is incorrect because they arguably had at least reasonable suspicion given Carrie's demeanor at the airport. Choice **B** is incorrect because, although the officers may have lacked probable cause, the Court concluded in *Place* that a dog sniff is not a search that requires justification under the Fourth Amendment. Choice **C** is incorrect because, assuming the dog sniff is permissible, it provided the officers probable cause to believe contraband would be found, and the Court has refused to require officers to use more conservative measures (like obtaining a warrant) simply because it was feasible to do so.

115. **C** Because the Court has excluded dog sniffs from the category of Fourth Amendment searches, there would be no behavior on these facts that could be challenged under the Constitution. *United States v. Place*. Choice **A** is incorrect because officers need not have any level of suspicion to approach and engage a person found in a public place. Choice **B** is incorrect because, as stated above, a dog sniff is no search at all. Choice **D** is incorrect because the Fourth Amendment is not wholly inapplicable at airports, and thus this response overstates the scope of the "special needs" cases.

Table of Cases

Index

References are to the number of the question raising the issue. "E" indicates an Essay Question; "M" indicates a Multiple-Choice Question.